TRADITIONALISM AND **MODERNITY**

ISSUES AND PERSPECTIVES IN SOCIOLOGY AND SOCIAL ANTHROPOLOGY

DR. A.H.M ZEHADUL KARIM
DR. NURAZZURA MOHAMAD DIAH

PARTRIDGE
A Penguin Random House Company

To order additional copies of this book, contact
Toll Free 800 101 2657 (Singapore)
Toll Free 1 800 81 7340 (Malaysia)
orders.singapore@partridgepublishing.com

www.partridgepublishing.com/singapore

Contents

FOREWORD

This book is the result of a solid research on important sociological and anthropological themes. Evidently traditionalism, modernity and indigenization are valuable categories of thought for both understanding and evaluation of human societies. It should be remembered that it is no longer viable to speak about one type of modernity or traditionalism. There are many forms of traditionalism and equally different forms of modernity. Therefore, understanding change necessitates a rigorous analysis of specific cases without a tendency to generalize and superimpose Eurocentric categories on other societies. This new trend in sociological and anthropological studies that calls for indigenization is much less about emphasizing the logic of difference, but rather about knowing what there is in the field. Obviously, the interpretation of the data requires a high sense of informed sensibility that both opens to universal rationality and situated in a particular set of concrete datum. Without this new epistemological development new knowledge about non-European societies will not be possible.

I would like to register my heartfelt gratitude to the editors of this volume, Dr. AHM Zehadul Karim and Dr. Nurazzura Mohamad Diah of the Department of Sociology and Anthropology at the International Islamic University Malaysia. It is indeed a nice gesture to hold this work in honour of Prof. Dr. Mohamed Aris bin Haji Othman. He is certainly a scholar and administrator who served both the Faculty and the Department of Sociology and Anthropology very well. The book has incorporated eleven articles written mainly by focusing on the above-mentioned two broad themes and the editors have taken a painstaking task of preparing the manuscript and organizing them in a book format. These issues included here are diversified, but they contain some valuable and provocative accounts based on each author's expertise. Based on traditionalism, modernity and indigenization, the authors provided us with lucid account of some of the most enchanting current issues having described them from socio-anthropological perspectives.

I am quite sure that this book will be a valuable addition in the field of Sociology and Social Anthropology which deal with diversities in cultures. The academic network that has been assembled in this volume shows a new breed of Sociologists and Anthropologists who are well-informed about the boundaries of science and the ideological supposition behind its claim. Because of this the new knowledge which has been developed in this volume is a step in the right direction which will refreshingly enlighten the students of sociology and anthropology and the community of researchers about this new development.

PROFESSOR DR. IBRAHIM M ZEIN
Dean
Kulliyyah of Islamic Revealed Knowledge and Human Sciences
International Islamic University Malaysia

In Honour of Prof. Dr. Mohamed Aris bin Hj. Othman

Professor Dr. Mohamed Aris bin Hj. Othman occupied an eminent teaching position at the Department of Sociology and Anthropology, International Islamic University Malaysia (IIUM) for about two decades beginning from 1990 until 2012. The present volume and the essays incorporated in this book are dedicated to him to show our honour and gratitude.

Born in Malaysia in 1938, Mohamed Aris Othman had his early schooling in this country. He received his BA (Hons) and MA degrees from the University of Malaya in the years 1968 and 1971 respectively. Prior to starting his postgraduate studies, Mohamed Aris went to England to undertake a certificate course at the Teacher Training College, KIRKBY, UK which he completed in 1959. Having been inspired into teaching from KIRKBY, Mohamed Aris Othman then went to the United States for his PhD in Cultural Anthropology, which he completed in 1977 at the University of Illinois, USA. Dr. Aris Othman's formal career in the field of Sociology and Anthropology started as soon as he returned to Malaysia to accept an offer to work as a lecturer at the University of Malaya.

Prof. Dr. Mohamed Aris Othman has a number of scholarly publications to his credentials which include published articles, books, chapters in books and seminar presentations. Apart from these academic contributions, Prof. Dr. Mohamed Aris Othman also headed a number of administrative positions at this university. He was Head of the Department of Sociology and Anthropology from

1991 until 1999. He was the Deputy Dean of ISTAC between 2002-2003 and prior to that, he held the position of Dean of IRK and Social Science at IIUM during 1999-2002. Additionally, Prof. Dr. Mohamed Aris Othman headed and remained chairman of at least one dozen of academic and professional organizations. He supervised many MA and PhD theses in the department and as such he has a reputation that contributed much to his credentials.

Dr. A.H.M Zehadul Karim
Dr. Nurazzura Mohamad Diah

ACKNOWLEDGEMENT

The idea of editing this book on 'Traditionalism and Modernity' is an initiative from the Department of Sociology and Anthropology at the International Islamic University Malaysia. We have been thinking about having such an academic publication for a few months, but we could not make it materialize due to many factors and constraints. At this juncture, our present Head of Department, Dr. Nurazzura Mohamad Diah delegated the responsibility to us to be the editors of the book. We gratefully acknowledge and appreciate all our colleagues in the department for having confidence in us.

As indicated, the book is designed to show respect to our former colleague, Prof. Dr. Aris Othman who served this department most gloriously for more than twenty years until his retirement last year. The authors wish to acknowledge his past contributions as an esteemed colleague at the department and would like to see him in good health in his future.

This book would not have been published if the writers and authors of this volume had not contributed their articles on various topics covering our thematic title of this book. We have been able to assemble a few potential writers having strong background in social sciences. In compiling this book, we have inevitably benefited through their writings in their respective fields of specialization. The topics included in this volume mostly emphasize the socio-anthropological perspective, reflecting their interest and special research to contextualize them into traditionalism and modernity. We would like to thank all of them for their valuable contributions.

We are also indebted to many persons who remained involved with us in different phases of this work: Ms. Sohela Mustari, a doctoral student assisted us in coordinating the corresponding link-up with the writers to accumulate the manuscript and other requirements from time to time. And Mr. Md. Anisur Rahman, a PhD student from Information and Communication Technology who provided us with the technical support in finalizing the formatting and other required styles.

We are also grateful to our colleagues: Prof. Dr. Jamil Farooqui, Prof. Dr. Fatimah Daud, Assoc. Prof. Dr. Hazizan Md. Noon, Assoc. Prof. Dr. Awang Hasmadi Awang Mois, Dr. Noor Azlan Mohd Noor Dr. Rohaiza binti Abd. Rokis, Dr. Nor Azlin Tajuddin, Norasikin Bt. Basir, Khairulanuar Abd. Rahman and others for their constant inspiration and cordiality. We are especially grateful to our Dean of the Faculty, Prof. Dr. Ibrahim M. Zein for writing a foreword in this book.

We hope our ideas in this book will be a useful source of learning for students seeking knowledge on diversities in the field of Sociology and Social Anthropology.

March, 2014   Dr. A.H.M Zehadul Karim
                                     Dr. Nurazzura Mohamad Diah

PREFACE, INTRODUCTION AND EDITORS' NOTES

This book contains eleven articles contributed by a few renowned sociologists and social anthropologists from a number of countries around the world, focusing on diversified issues on traditionalism and modernity. The papers are written on the basis of each author's expertise in their respective field which are compiled to make them a suitable document in the field of Sociology and Social Anthropology.

Traditionalism and modernity are two dichotomous but coexisting situations and concepts where the former precedes the later. When we talk about traditionalism, we are frequently guided by our glorious past based on the normative values in performing activities because these were done in such manners through generations. Modernity, on the other hand, is the outcome of a total transformation of society resulting from industrialization where the process of social change emerged after the Industrial Revolution through technological transformation. The concepts of traditionalism and modernity are very important and related to issues in Sociology and Social Anthropology that many theoretical discussions have been carried out in these areas and several theoretical paradigms conceptualized on this issue. Although the concept of modernization began in Western Europe in the mid-18th century and later spread over many developing countries, modernization has now become the target of all nations of the world.

Having emerged as a discipline in the post-industrial era, Sociology is dominated by views on modernization and development. There are a number of sociologists and social anthropologists who view modernization as a significant approach to explain social phenomena in terms of social process and change (e.g., Rose, 1960; Moore, 1963; Black, 1967; Smith, 1973, etc.). The dichotomous way of classifying society as being traditional and modern is not a new idea in social sciences; rather it was quite dominant in the writings of the founding fathers of sociology. In this context, a German sociologist named Ferdinand Tonnies provided a significantly lasting account of the theory of Gemeinschaft and Gesellschaft where he mentioned that approaching modernization is the loss of Gemeinschaft or traditionally-based community life. According to him, modernization simply turns community life into a more impersonal status associated with self-interest and mechanized situation which has been regarded by him as Gesellschaft (see Tonnies, 1963; orig. 1887).

Borrowing from Ferdinand Tonnies's (1887) dichotomous paradigm and also later taking the views of sacred-secular continuum of Leopold von Wiese (1932/1974) and Becker (1950/1962) simultaneously, Redfield (1962) conceptualized the term "folk culture", which he later called "the little community" in his writings about the Tepoztlan Mexicans. Robert Redfield was very much overwhelmed by the sacredness of the "folk culture" and thus identified the congeries and unhappiness of metropolitan living. He also applauded the rural people for their simplicity and uniqueness and clearly stood against industrialism and the urban way of life, blaming them for a rapid adoption of urbanism.

Almost following a similar sentiment, Emile Durkheim classified the society according to two opposing concepts of mechanical and organic solidarity. According to Durkheim, organic solidarity or techno-modernization is the outcome of an increased division of labour or specialized economic activity. With modernization, the division of labour becomes more pronounced in the concept of organic solidarity where society moves towards specialization (see Durkheim, 1961; orig. 1893). Max Weber identified modernity as a replacement of the traditional worldview with a more rational thinking. Echoing the same sentiments of Ferdinand Tonnies and Emile Durkheim, Max Weber regarded modern society as a rational full of formal structure which weakens the tradition (Weber, 1978; orig. 1921).

Another interpretation of modernity is derived from the writings of Karl Marx (1967; orig.1867) who formulated the conflict perspective of defining traditionalism and modernity. He was of the view that modern society is expanding with increasing economic differentiation in class-based society and it occurs due to unstable societal situation. Marx argued that accumulation of capital through privatization destroyed the traditional way of life and paved the way for modernity. Karl Marx blamed the capitalistic system which asked people to assemble in the industrial towns and cities, leaving behind their peasant farms and traditional way of life.

In the preceding sections, we have given contrasting explanations of traditionalism and modernity as they were conceptualized by a few renowned classical sociologists; in the proceeding discussion, we will however, make further clarify these two concepts as viewed by a few contemporary social scientists. Traditionalism and modernity as conceived by Ferdinand Tonnies (1887), Emile Durkheim (1893), Karl Marx (1861), Max Weber (1921), Robert Redfield (1962) and others in the past have now reemerged differently with a new concept in recent times.

Traditionalism has now been recapitulated with a new concept of 'indigenization' which is designated as a local situation and behavior prevailing among a group of more traditionally-oriented non-industrial people. They are also often known as local people or/and rural people mostly living in villages and are less affected by the so-called globalization. The developmentalists at present are becoming more concerned about this local knowledge generated by these groups of indigenous people who have their own techniques of dealing with biodiversity and resource management in their surrounding environment and ecology. It is now increasingly accepted that the local knowledge generated by these groups of people is no less significant than those of the modern scientific knowledge of the present world. This book gives us an idea about the traditional way of life with a new direction to show modernity in contrast to that of traditionalism. We have a few articles which have been incorporated here in this book generating discussion to that direction. In the following pages however, we provide a very brief discussion on modernity as viewed by a group of renowned academics in this field.

In the 1960s and 1970s, the concept of modernization was very much influenced by the development approach fully dominated by economists who wanted to make a meaning to it in showing the total transformation of life and living of the people in context to attaining their economic well-being, resulting in technological achievement. This explanation however, deviates slightly from that of sociologists and social anthropologists who place importance on the social structure and social organization to contextually relate them to modernization. In this perspective, G.K. Douglas (1984) mentioned that development that preserves the interrelationships within communities will provide better performances by creating a close sociological bond among the members.

If we look back to see the earliest studies on modernization, we find one important empirical investigation which was conducted by Daniel Lerner under the title, 'The Passing of Traditional Society' which came out in 1958. In focusing on modernization in a few Middle Eastern countries, he gathered information about the villages through his longitudinal data-base. Lerner documented how the villages in Balgat in Turkey had transformed from a traditional way of living to a modern one due to getting exposure to infrastructural development.

ABOUT THIS BOOK

This book has outlined many aspects of traditionalism and modernity, although the topics here are divergent; the consistent part of it is that all of the authors mostly come from the same disciplines of Sociology and Social Anthropology. The authors' concern is to find out the socio-cultural changes that have occurred due to modernization and development. From that perspective, the book is very useful to understand Sociology and Social Anthropology from diversities based on traditionalism and modernity.

A total of eleven articles have been included in this volume. The first is on 'Natural Resource Management: A Synthesis of Traditionalism and Modernity for Future Global Protection' which has been contributed by A.H.M. Zehadul Karim who describes traditionalism in relation to indigenization, simultaneously comparing it with modernization. In this article, the author has borrowed the viewpoint of Warren et al. (1995) and notably has given a clear conceptualization of indigenous knowledge which is a unique episteme to a given culture or society in contrast to modernity. The term 'indigenous knowledge' in this paper more appropriately focuses on natural resource management with regard to protecting the environment. In the conclusive part of the paper, the author has shown how demographic growth has contributed to the decay of natural resource base throughout the world and in this context; the author however, has shown his inclination towards David Pimentel's theoretical bend.

In her paper on biodiversity conservation, Aida Luz Lopez Gomez has written on indigenous traditional knowledge and biodiversity conservation in Mexico which are associated with scientific development and technological innovation which increase economic benefits. Moreover, the paper has demonstrated that Earth's biological diversity is tying together many indigenous people and communities who are also the great protectors of biodiversity. The paper mentions that both the reflections have arguments in regard to environmental education as long as it constitutes an alternative culture proposal to face environmental crisis.

Based on an ethnographic study about Torrens River catchment in South Australia, Nor Azlin Tajuddin explores people's perceptions and responses to river pollution. Drawing from her ethnographic data, Nor Azlin presents three stories of women volunteers in the Torrens River catchment which highlight their unique knowledge and expertise in river restoration works in which they are so passionately engaged.

The urban Malay perspective on menopause is another article which is part of Nurazzura Mohamad Diah's doctoral dissertation conducted in a very stimulating academic environment of University of Western Australia. The paper attempts to bring to the fore the importance of liminality as a concept which has rarely been used to help explain menopausal experiences among women in urban areas. The notion of liminality shows as to how urban working Malay women adapt themselves to an environment which is seen as imposing some threats and/or danger to their well-being compared to that of the rural women.

Based on an empirical research conducted among Malay postgraduate students in Western Australia, the next paper by Rosila Bee Mohd Hussain on Malay Cosmopolitannees and Reciprocity discusses how these postgraduate students prepare themselves to undertake overseas study and the various new challenges they need to deal with upon arrival. What is highlighted throughout the paper is that the students prioritise their religious identity compared to other forms of identity.

Like many other modern people, formal education has also been identified as the most effective mechanism through which *Orang Asli* groups of indigenous people of Peninsular Malaysia can used to change and improve their lives. Ahmed A. Nasr and his associate in their paper titled "The Use of Folk Literature in Aborigine Education: A Review of the UNICEF project in Malaysia" found that schools and education often seem to be very unimportant to them. The paper evaluates the fact that despite such unattractiveness to education, this could be overcome by promoting cultural knowledge to them.

The paper on 'Traditional Monarchy versus Modern Democracy in the Province of Yogyakarta' is a documentation of the traditional power-base in present day Indonesia by Ahmed Nizar Yaakub. This is the last remaining Sultanate in Indonesia where the real political power of Sultan Hamengku Buwono X of Yogyakarta, a unique example of a hereditary monarchy is found. The Sultan automatically holds the post of Governor of Yogyakarta based on Law No 3 of 1950 on the special status of Yogyakarta, which does not go well with Indonesian democratization process as it requires the post of all Governors and Vice Governors in all 35 provinces to be elected through direct election based on Law No 32 of 2004 on Regional Autonomy Law. The paper investigates the polemic of central government planning in conducting democratic elections in Yogyakarta in order to uphold democracy. It also focuses on the reactions of Yogyakartans and the two royal households on the election plan and thus describes the trade-off and concession made by both parties in solving the tension.

The next article written by Siti Zanariah demonstrates how social-trading networks of housewives are particularly important in the context as they provide a means for affording expensive lifestyle goods and create a marketplace for those selling goods bought often in Kuala Lumpur or Sarawak. The moral aspects of mutual obligation, compassion and trust underscore the housewives' economic participation as traders and consumers. Their consumption includes clothing items, jewellery, personal care items, furniture and electronic devices of which some have allowed them to have a good image of television and movie characters from other cultures. Kuala Lumpur, which is seen as a foreign place being fully different from Kuching is regarded as a model for affluent lifestyles that Tabuan housewives aspire to and television has contributed to the construction of cosmopolitan images of Kuala Lumpur. Some Tabuan housewives and men talk about lifestyle commodities from the border towns with Indonesia and Thailand to consume outside goods. The comfortable feeling to have an image association with people from other cultures shows the recognition of cultural diversity beyond the national level.

Yukimi Shimoda in her paper on "The Maintenance and (Co-) Creation of Tradition in Japanese Transnational Corporations/ Organisations in Indonesia" has shown the existence of transnational corporations/organisations that can be considered as those who have been providing 'the essence of modernity' in terms of their participation in global flows of information, goods and people through business activities beyond geographical boundaries. However, observations within modern transnational corporations/ organisations tend to reveal the maintenance and (co-)creation of tradition among employees. By exploring the everyday activities of both Japanese expatriates and Indonesian employees who work for Japanese transnational corporations/organisations, this ethnographic study investigates the extent to which tradition and modernity play their roles in transnational office spaces. In conclusion, this study highlights the ambiguity of the boundary between tradition and modernity.

M. Zulfiquar Ali Islam's paper gives us an idea about the traditional catechu production techniques and survival strategies of producers in Bangladesh with their native mechanisms and strategies for forest resource management confronting economic adversity. The paper details their everyday experiences and traditional knowledge and utilization of this worldview in regard to managing forest resources in a unique way. The productive catechu resource utilization befitting their traditional fashion and sustainable livelihood strategies for its producers are pinpointed in this paper.

The last paper of this volume is a contribution of Habibul Haque Khondker who provides an analytical discussion on globalization to modernization, dealing with it from a critical point of view. In this context, the paper examines the various types of modernization theories starting from the theoretical conceptualization from a Eurocentric point of view to meta-theoretic assumptions. The difference of perspective in the explanation of change is rooted in contextual difference of the disciplines. Accordingly, the paper exemplifies economics as an academic discipline that looks at social change through the lenses of economic development and obviously sociologists have some differential perspective focusing on it from socio-structural explanations.

References

Becker, H. (1962, orig. 1952). Through Values to a Social Interpretation: Essays on Social Contexts, Activity Types and Prospects. New York: Greenwood.

Black, C.E. (1966). "Change as a Condition of Modern Life" in M. Weiner (ed.) Modernization: The Dynamics of Growth. Washington DC: Voice of America, US Information Agency, PP17-127.

Douglas, G.K. (1984). "The Meaning of Agricultural Sustainability Pp 3-29 in G.K Douglas (Ed) Agricultural Sustainability in a Changing World Orlder. Boulder, Ca: Westrierr Press.

Durkheim, Erile (1961, orig.1893). The Division of Labor in Society, New York. Free Press.

Lerner, Daniel (1958). The Passing of Traditional Society: Modernizing the Middle East. New York: Free Press.

Marx, Karl (1967, orig 1867). Capital, New York: International Publishers

Moore, W.E. (1963). Social Charge. Englewood Cliffs, NY: Prentice Hall.

Redfield, Robert (1962). The Folk Society and Civilization" in M.P. Redfield (Ed). The Papers of Robert Redfield: Vol.1 Human Nature and the Study Of Society. Chicago University Press.

Redfield, Robert (1962) A Village That Choose Progress: Chan Kom Revisited. Chicago:Chicago University Press.

Smith, A.D (1973). The Concept of Social Change: A Critique of the Functionalist Theory Of Social Change. London: Routledge and Kegan Paul.

Tonnies, Ferdinand (1963, orig. 1987).Community and Society (Gemeinschaft and Gesellschaft), New York: Harper

Warren, DIM, L.J. Slikkerveer and D. Brokensha (eds). (1995). The Cultural Dimensions of Development: Indigenous Knowledge Systems. London: Intermediate Technology Publications.

Weber, Max (1978, orig 1921). Economy and Society I. Roth and C. Wittresh (eds) Berekley: University of California Press.

Contributors

Dr. A.H.M Zehadul Karim
Department of Sociology and Anthropology, KIRKHS
International Islamic University Malaysia
Malaysia

Dr. Aida Luz López Gómez
Environmental Education Postgraduate Program
Universidad Autonoma de la Ciudad de Mexico
MEXICO

Dr. Ahmad A. Nasr
Department of Sociology and Anthropology, KIRKHS
International Islamic University Malaysia
Malaysia

Dr. See Hoon Peow
KBU International College
Malaysia

Dr. Nor Azlin Tajuddin
Department of Sociology and Anthropology, KIRKHS
International Islamic University Malaysia
Malaysia

Dr. Nurazzura Mohamad Diah
Department of Sociology and Anthropology, KIRKHS
International Islamic University Malaysia
Malaysia

Dr. A.H.M Zehadul Karim

Dr. Ahmad Nizar Yaakub
Department of Politics and International Relations
Faculty of Social Sciences
Universiti Malaysia Sarawak
Sarawak. Malaysia

Dr. Rosila Bee Mohd Hussain
Faculty of Arts and Social Sciences
Department of Anthropology and Sociology
Universiti Malaya
Malaysia

Dr. Yukimi Shimoda
JICA-Research Institute (Tokyo)
Japan

Dr. Siti Zanariah Ahmad Ishak
Department of Communication
Faculty of Social Sciences
Universiti Malaysia Sarawak
94300 Kota Samarahan
Sarawak, Malaysia

Dr. M. Zulfiquar Ali Islam
Department of Sociology
University of Rajshahi
Bangladesh

Dr. Habibul Haque Khondker
Department of Humanities and Social Sciences
Zayed University
Abu Dhabi, UAE

TRADITIONALISM AND MODERNITY: A SYNTHESIS FOR GLOBAL ENVIRONMENTAL PROTECTION

Dr. A.H.M Zehadul Karim

Abstract

Traditionalism in the form of indigenization or local knowledge is a unique episteme to a given culture or society which may also be generated simultaneously with modern knowledge in global situation. Traditionalism in this paper more appropriately focuses on the natural resource management and indicatively relates it contextually to protecting the global environment. Throughout the paper, the author has consistently put arguments identifying demographic growth as an important factor for the decay of traditionalism and indigenous practices throughout the world. In spite of all upheavals and criticality, in the final part of the paper, the author has provided a suggestion for integrating the indigenous traditional practices with that of the newly-evolved development devices for a better synthesis and fruitful outcome for human survival.

Introduction and Background of the Study

Since the very beginning of time, people have long been using their own 'intuitive and sensual' local knowledge which is regarded as 'traditional folk knowledge'; most recently from an epistemological point of view and also in a very formal way, it has been termed as Indigenous Knowledge System or IKS in anthropological literature (see Sillitoe, 1998; Karim, 2010; Vayda, 1996)[1]. Whatever the term we may use, indigenous knowledge system or IKS has now become a very widely accepted paradigm in academic discourse and simultaneously the concept, has now been globalized across disciplines to reinforce the conception of some kind of unique traditional cultural heritage (see Purcell, 1998; Agrawal, 1995; Trutmann et al, 1996). Warren et al., (1995) have given a clear definition of it by saying that indigenous knowledge or local knowledge is a unique episteme to a given culture or society in contrast with modern knowledge which may also be generated through scientific assessment at the global network of universities and research institutes. The term 'indigenous knowledge' in this paper more appropriately focuses on the natural resource management and protection of the environment. Throughout my paper, I have consistently put arguments relating demographic growth as an important factor for the decay of indigenous practices throughout the world.

In contrast to applying indigenous knowledge, the world today is amassed with enormous newly-developed scientific models for generating technological achievements in the global context. A great majority of the people in traditional Third World societies are readily accepting the western models of development in order to overcome starvation, sickness and poverty. From the anthropological point of view, this shift towards development perspective is a major deviation for human beings from a traditionally-oriented 'natural paradigm' to a 'more controlled and artificial way of modern life' (see Karim, 2010, 2011). There is no denying the fact that scientific knowledge of development perspective has brought a radical transformation of human society and also at the same time, it has bestowed with enormous control of human beings over nature. This part of development has often disregarded the indigenous knowledge system and thus clearly discounted the indigenous people. But recently, there has been a positive realization in that many academicians, anthropologists and IKS proposers have started to say that development models should integrate local knowledge, and they have to redefine local knowledge for better protection of the natural resource management of this planet earth (see Karim, 2010, 2011). Based on that, we can provide enormous empirical evidence from a number of researchers who have been working on traditional communities in different parts of the world which may be reflective of 'practicing indigenous knowledge', having found its suitability in respective societal situations.

Indigenous Knowledge and Cross-cultural Situations: Ethnographic Examples

We have plenty of examples from anthropological literature that indicate how people around the world have long been using their indigenous knowledge for natural resource management in diversified situations. Many anthropologists and ethnologists seek to discover the life and living of the indigenous people in different phases of human civilization (e.g. Lee, 1968; Newman, 1965; Barth, 1960; Vayda, 1969). Among these, we can proceed with the Kung San foraging people living in Kalahari Desert on both sides of the border between Botswana and Namibia in the southern part of Africa (see Lee, 1979). There are enormous evidence in anthropological literature (see Barth, 1960; Newman, 1965) where horticultural and pastoral people have been found to use indigenous techniques for efficiently producing food in their own economic system. We can cite here a good example of a horticultural community named Gururumba which employed their indigenous techniques to adapt to the environment in the Upper Asaro Vallay in New Guinea (see Newman, 1965). It is a small community of 1,121 people living in an area of 30 sq. miles. In this community, every adult is involved in garden production and the social prestige of a family in that community is fully linked to the neatness and productivity of their respective family-farms. Crop production among the Gururumba is rotated in more than one plot, where they produce different crops in different gardens depending on the suitability of soil and permissive ecological situation. They do not use any fertilizer for the soil, and since rainfall is abundant, the Gururumba peasants also do not use any artificial irrigation in their farming (for details see Newman, 1965).

3

Like the Gururumba horticulturists, there is another indigenous group of people called the Bakhtiari, who subsist their livelihood on pastoralism to make an effective living in an area of arid lands up the hills of south Zagros of western Iran. The pastoral life of Bakhtiari is simultaneously based on two seasonal migrations to find their grazing field and also at the same time, they build two settlements in their seasonal cycles: in the summer, they build houses on the top of mountains and they return to their winter quarters in the low-lying land-surface when there is harsh bleak of snow-storms and ice-falling (see Barth, 1960).

There are other indigenous societies living on slash-and-burn agricultural system and these have long prevailed in many parts of the world (see Bodley, 1975). To be more specific, we can refer to Roy Rappaport's (1968) study which was conducted among the Tsembaga Maring people in the northern slope of central highlands of New Guinea. The most efficient technique of Tsembaga farming is the slash-and-burn system which allows them to procure enough calorie in-take throughout the year without having any pressure on resources. But one significant problem that they face in regard to their agriculture is the presence of many edible insects and weeds which they neutralize through their own indigenous techniques (see Rappaport, 1968 for details). Where the slash-and burn agriculture persisted among the Tsembaga people, it did not however, continue among the CHT[2] groups of people in Bangladesh due to an inflow of migratory settlement to this part of the region from the densely populated mainland areas of the country where they have acute demographic pressure.

An example of indigenous farming community, is discussed in an ethnographic study conducted by the author in two villages named Dhononjoypara and Gopalhati in the northern part of Bangladesh where he had found a radical shifting of traditional farming to a mechanized one to increase production at large (see Karim, 1990). People in the aforementioned villages have for a long time been practicing traditional agriculture by using local manure called *paosh*[3]. The lands in those villages have long been irrigated with handmade irrigation equipment called *jant*[4] and *chetri*[5]. Cropping patterns in Dhononjoypara and Gopalhati clearly reflects a close adaptation to considerable seasonal variation following Bengali calendar to make it adjustable to regular agricultural transplantation and harvesting. With this traditional farming technique, the farmers in these villages have been producing local varieties of rice and other agricultural products (see Karim, 1990 for details). Since agriculture is the principal occupation of the majority of people in Dhononjoypara and Gopalhati, consequently there is heavy pressure on land and there is great effort on the part of the farmers to intensively utilize the land. Due to an extreme pressure of population on the villages, the farmers have to shift from this traditional farming of modern cultivation by introducing the HYV seeds to maximize their crop production. During my revisitation of the villages in 2011 and 2012, I found that the villagers have been utilizing their total agricultural land for multiple crop production. Many villagers reported that they can no longer keep their land fallow any more as their forefathers did in the past. This is because of their food shortage and heavy demand for food as they now have to feed more people in the family.

In providing more specific examples of indigenous knowledge, we have further references showing the diversities in the way of life for survival. In a research on 'Sustainable Irrigation Management', in relation to Sri Lankan peasants, Mahinda Wijeratne (2009) mentions that farmers in a few districts of Sri Lanka have long been using their indigenous knowledge in irrigating agricultural land. The study reveals that ancient irrigation management system which prevails in Sri Lanka has employed indigenous knowledge in balancing their ecological resources. This research has further shown that the farmers have invented a water control system named *bisokotuwa* to preserve water in the reservoir and to release it subsequently to the outlet as per requirement. Similarly, they have also invented another type of water reservoir by employing their indigenous knowledge named *diyakata pahana* to measure the water contents which may be released later on the basis of its availability (see Wijeratne, 2009 for details). It allows them to avoid mechanized irrigation and also at the same time, the farmers do not have to wait for rain.

Abebe Shiferaw and his associates (2009) have written an article presented at the IUAES inter-congress under the title, 'Reorganizing Farms Knowledge in Development Initiatives' which provides us with the techniques of indigenous bee-keeping system in south Ethiopia. After describing a brief history of bee-keeping, the paper analyzes the social, medical and economic values of honey in southern Ethiopia and examined academically various aspects of the bee-keeping practices that have been prevailing in the region genealogically. In the meantime, a modern bee-keeping system has been introduced in the region to replace the older system. The authors forcefully opine that the development of modern bee-keeping should simultaneously reinforce the traditional technique and suggest for an integration of both systems.

Liu Jinlong's (2009) paper on traditional forestry related knowledge (TFRK) in China is another fascinating writing which emphasizes on TFRK as the most important cultural wisdom for protecting the forest resources in the country. The paper argues that to protect forest resources for sustainable development, the country should allow proper use of TFRK. The paper further says that it is also essential for preserving human civilization and diversities. In the recommendation section, the author suggests for a proper integration of scientific and traditional forestry-related knowledge for a better transformation of society.

Zenaida M. Agngarayngay (2009) of Mariano Marcos State University of the Philippines conducted a study to know how gamet or *porphyra* spp has been selected as an expensive seaweed delicacy in Northern Philippines. In the past, seaweeds were gathered from the wild, but recently the processing of this valuable food item is done through machinery as an improved technique. As a nutritious food and containing enormous iron and calcium, it has great commercial value at the national and international levels. While most technologically developed industries have been able to maximize its production, they have failed to preserve its age-old method of sun-drying which provides natural nutritional value. The paper finally recommends an improvement in this gamet's post-harvest technique of drying which will bring the farmers more earnings even during the rainy season. In another study among the Chepang community in Nepal, there is plenty of uncultivated plant species which is part of their culture, benefitting them in multilateral ways. These uncultivated and semi-domesticated plant-species play significant role for Chipping's survival and economic well-being. Their indigenous knowledge allows them to preserve their uncultivated land, meeting food-crisis during slack food production. These are nutritious and are used to supplement as alternatives to food crops. But many of these species are now gradually being eroded and for that reason, the author suggests for having special initiatives for their preservation (see Aryal et al., 2011 for details).

Another paper by Aida Luz Lopez Gomez (2013) has its basis on biodiversity conservation in Mexico and it has been incorporated in this volume to explain the indigenous traditional knowledge associated with conservation of biological diversity (see Gomez, 2009). In the paper, Gomez expresses her concerns over the decay of traditional knowledge for biodiversity protection and suggests that utilization of indigenous traditional knowledge in the conservation of biodiversity is quite significant, but it is suspected that there will be an appropriation of it by industrial plants and international corporations for their own interest. But it is expected that local knowledge for biodiversity conservation relates to the life and living of the local people, who in the real sense, are the 'keepers' or caretakers of it. It provides important contribution for generating its incremental expansion. In the same line of thinking, Prasad (2009) rightly suggests rediscovering the traditional knowledge for biodiversity conservation which is essential for sustainable environmental development. M.S. Umesh Babu and K. Lenin Babu's (2009) paper on "Inventorization of Greenhouse Gases at Administrative Unit" has been presented in the World Congress; and it suggests for environmentally friendly and green energies like solar and hydro power to be introduced for commercial and domestic activities. Based on the field data collected from southern India, the paper further suggests for better livestock and agricultural management strategies like Systematic Rice Intensification (SRI) and decomposition of residues instead of burning on field for use as manure.

A Theoretical Debate to Upholding Traditional and Modern Knowledge

There is consistent debate where many sociologists, anthropologists and researchers often put forward their arguments with an anthropocentric viewpoint, saying that, human entire control over nature and they should not be worried about their environment, or depletion of resources as such because they may find out their destiny eventually (see Buttel & Flinn, 1977; Dunlap & Catton Jr, 1979). These theorists belong to two dominant sociological schools named 'Dominant Western Worldview' (DWW) and 'Human Exemtionalist Paradigm' (HEP) and they seem to be quite ethnocentric in their attitudes to justify that the development paradigm will bring radical transformation to human societies and human beings will remain the principal driving force to control their destiny (see Dunlap & Michelson, 2002; Buttel & Flinn, 1977). Their viewpoints indirectly advocate a total transformation of the traditional indigenous way of life, to make it more advanced, and technologically efficient to control human destiny.

A group of sociologists and anthropologists are known to belong to the NEP (New Ecological Paradigm) school, however, they most logically express their concern that the carrying capacity of this planet earth limits the ecological resources and it can never be replaced (see Schnaiberg, 1975). This group of theorists link population issue relating directly to the sustainable environmental protection.

The author agrees with the views of the New Ecological Paradigm and arguably mentions that the main reasons for a shift from the indigenous way of life to the development paradigm is simply due to the increase in population. Many anthropologists and demographers (e.g., Pimentel, 1983, 1993; Karim, 2010, 2011) put forward their arguments in this line of assessment in regard to the depletion of environmental resources. It is logical to say that the earth has a certain carrying capacity in terms of its available resources. When the carrying capacity has exceeded, people have to find alternatives to boost production for their survival and this is what is actually happening in the case of shifts from natural indigenous living to more controlled development paradigm.

As recently as 1993, David Pimentel edited a book titled 'World Soil Erosion and Conservation', where he clearly mentioned that due to over-population there will be a sharp decrease of the per capita availability of land which in effect creates food shortages and malnutrition in different parts of the world. The environmental depression is further intensified due to soil erosion in the agricultural sector, where 75 billion metric tons of soil are removed from the field through wind and, mostly affecting the cultivable land (see Myers, 1993).

One important step for resource management has been formulated in the name of Framework for Evaluation of Sustainable Land Management (FESLM) undertaken by Food and Agriculture Organization of the United Nations. It suggests five important aspects for making land sustainable which are as follows: (i) maintain and enhance production (ii) reduce the level of production risk for security (iii) protect the potential natural resources and prevent soil degradation and water quality (iv) make it more economically viable and (v) make it socially acceptable (see Smyth et.al., 1993 as quoted in Tisdell, 1994). As part of land management, FESLM encourages increasing agricultural production which certainly requires adopting mechanized cultivation but it does not however, consider the loss of land fertility and other impacts of it as the fault of human beings. We have an example in the farming system in the Barind regions of Bangladesh where labor-intensive and monsoon-dependent traditional farming system has been replaced by intensive ground water irrigation. Torturous irrigation and indiscriminate lifting of ground water cause important consequences for the local people who become the victims of arsenic disease. Additionally we find that an indigenous group of people named the Santal having their predominant traditional dependence on this eco-environment of Barind region, had to emigrate from this region to settle down in some peri-urban localities of Rajshahi City by accepting conversion to Christianity as alternative to their economic survival (see Karim, 2012).

Conclusions: Synthesizing Traditionalism and Modernity as a Policy Alternative

Although both traditionalism and modernity are diametrically opposed to each other, a few sociologists and anthropologists have suggested that there may be an integration of the two ideas as they seem to be essential for environmental protection as well as keeping it economically and socially sustainable (see Tisdel, 2000; Karim, 2011; Cleveland and Daniela, 2002). Many modernists however, are often very much reluctant to accept traditionalism as a way of life and instead, always advocate modernism at the extremity. I

9

would rather say that if we want to make our environment healthy and habitable and if we prefer to live in a traditional God-gifted atmosphere, indigenous way of living can never be ignored fully. For that reason, I have consistently argued in the foregoing discussion that the demographic pressure in the real sense puts us in a critical situation to create major environmental problems and to overcome this unbearable situation, and then we have no other alternative but to keep our population at a replacement level.

We should continue in using our environmental resources, alternatively by reverting to traditional way of life. Side by side, we may also integrate the development model by making it suitable way for the traditional societies. In this context, I take the views of Paul Sillitoe (2002) and C. Prasad (2009) who recognize the significance of indigenous knowledge and based on them, I propagate for an integration of both traditional indigenous mechanisms and modernist approaches to emerge as a suitable synthesized model for future sustainability. Accordingly, this paper has suggested a creative model below showing a geophysical coexistence of the two systems which might be adopted by both developed countries as well as the less developed Third World nations for their environmental protection.

Table 1.1 A Suggestive Model for Reverting To the Indigenous Farming System

Total Suggested Use of Cultivable Land	Farming Method	Purpose(s)		Plans Regarding Population in the Global Context
Fifty percent (50%) of the total cultivable land	Modern intensive cultivation	Scientific cultivation	Diverse food production with huge amount of HYV rice production	a) Population in the third world and poor countries must be kept at the replacement level. b) There should be controlled population policy in many rich and developed nations c) Controlled population in many Asian and Middle Eastern countries.
Twenty five (25%) percent of the total cultivable land	Mono-cropping or Double cropping	Indigenous Cultivation	Indigenous food production as indigenous technology permits	a) Population in the third world countries and many selected underdeveloped countries must be brought at the zero level replacement b) Optimum population in many rich and developed nations (optimum population for many Asian and Middle Eastern countries as well as East Asian countries).
Twenty five percent (25%) of the cultivable land	Keeping it fallow for the whole year.	To maintain land fertility and nutrition		a) Population in the third and many selected countries must be at zero level b) Controlled population for many rich and developed nations c) Controlled population in many rich Asian and Middle-Eastern countries

Endnotes

[1]   The term indigenous knowledge has been used by different writers and it has been defined on different variability with differences in notion and definition. It is often termed as local knowledge, rural people's knowledge, indigenous technical knowledge, traditional environmental knowledge, people's science and folk knowledge (see Grenier, 1998; Sillitoe, 2002:8).

[2]   The meaning of the abbreviated word CHT is Chittagong Hill Tracts, an indigenous region located close to Chittagong city in the north-eastern part of Bangladesh. A total of 12 tribal groups of people, most of them having their own linguistic dialect similar to the south eastern Bengali language (for further details see Grierson, 1919; Karim, 1989).

[3]   'Paosh' is a kind of fertilizer prepared from cow-dung which is usually thrown as garbage. It provides nutrients for the land and it does not have

any chemical reaction which may damage the fertility of the soil.

4   *Jant* is irrigation equipment which has traditionally been used in rural Bangladesh. It looks like a long sized scoop of seven or eight feet long.

5   *Chetri* is another irrigation tool which looks like a bellow to suck water from a ditch.

Global estimates of tropical deforestation range from 69,000 km in1980 to 10,000 to 165000 km in the late 1980s (see Skole & Tucker, 1997).

References

Agngarayngay, Z.K. 2009. Gamet: Food for the Gods and Faith in the Resiliency of the peoples of Amiana. Paper presented at the 16th World Congress of the IUAES held at Kunming, China, 2009.

Agrawal, A. 1995. Dismantling the divide between indigenous and scientific knowledge, Development and Change. 26:413-439.

Aryal, K, Pashudati Chaudhary and E. E. Kerkhoff. 20009. Why Certain Uncultivated plan species become part of human culture? A Case from Indigenous Community, Chepang of Nepal. A paper presented at the 16th World Congress of the IUAES held at Kunming, China, 2009.

Babu, M.S. and K. Lenin Babu. 2009. Inventorization of Greenhouse Gases at Administrative Unit: A Case Study of Madya district, Southern India. Paper presented at the 16th World Congress of the IUAES held at Kunming, China, 2009.

Barth, Frederic. 1960. Nomadism in the Mountain and Platean Areas of South-west Asia: The Problems of the Arid Zone, UNESCO.

Bodley, John H. 1975. Victims of Progress. Menlo Park, Calif: Cummings.

Buttel, Frederick H. and William L.Flinn. 1977. "The Independence of Rural and Urban Environmental Problems in Advanced Capitalist Societies:Models of Linkage" *Sociologica Ruralis* !7:255-279.

Cleveland, David A. and Daniela Soleri. 2002. "Indigenous and Scientific Knowledge plant breeding" in Paul Sillitoe, Alan Bicker and Johan Pottier (eds) Participating in Development:

An Approaches to Indigenous Knowledge. London and New York: Routledge.

Dunlap, Riley E. and William R. Catton Jr. 1979. "Environmental Sociology" Annual Review of Sociology 5:243-273.

Dunlap, Rieley E. and William Michelson, (eds). 2002. Handbook of Environmental Sociology. Westpor, Conn: Greenwood.

Gomez, Aida Luz Lopez. 2009. Indigenous Traditional Knowledge and Biodiversity Conservation in New Mexico: Necessary Consideration on Epistemic Faivaoss and New Citizenship, Paper presented at the 16th World Congress of the IUAES held at Kunming, China, 2009.

Grierson, George Abraham.1903. Linguistic Survey of India (in 11 volumes). Delhi (India).

Grenier, Louise. 2011. Working with Indigenous Knowledge: A Guide to Researcher. Ottawa

Jinlong, Liu. 1998. Traditional Forestry Related Knowledge and Its Implications for China's Forestry Development—development of an anthropological perspective. A paper presented at the 16th World Congress of the IUAES held at Kunming, China, 2009.

Karim, A.H.M. Zehadul. 1989. "The Linguistic Diversities of the Tribesmen of Chittagong Hill Tracts: A Suggestive Language Planning", *Asian Profile* (Hong Kong), Vol. 17, No. 2, April 1989.

Karim, A.H.M. Zehadul. 1990. The Pattern of Rural Leadership an Agrarian Society: A Case study of the Changing Power Structure in Bangladesh, New Delhi: Northern Book Center.

Karim, A.H.M. Zehadul. 2010. "Agro-based Food Production System in Bangladesh: A Socio-Demographic Impact Assessment from Asian Examples". Paper presented in the International Conference on Ecological Discourse. Tamkang University, Taiwan. December 16-18, 2010.

Karim, A.H.M. Zehadul. 2011. "Impact of a Growing Population in Agricultural Resource Management: Exploring the Global Situation with Micro-level Examples". Paper presented at the IUAES conference held in Perth. Australia, July 5-9, 2011.

Karim, A.H.M. Zehadul. 2012. "Santal Religiosity and the Impact of Conversion: A Staggering Situation." Paper Presented at the International Indigenous Development Research Conference held in Auckland, New Zealand in June 26-29, 2012. It was later published in the IIDRC Conference Proceedings in November, 2012.

Lee, Richard B. 1968. "What Hunters do for a Living or, How to make Out on Scarce Resources" in Richard B.Lee and E.Devore (eds), Man the Hunter. Chicago.

Myers, N. 1993. Gaia: An Atlas of Planet management. New York, Garden City: Anchor and Doubleday

Newman, Philip L. 1965. Knowing the Gururumba. New York: Holt Rinehart and Winston.

Pimentel, David (ed). 1993. World Soil Erosion and Conservation. Cambridge: Cambridge University Press.

Pimentel, David (ed). 1998. "Impact of a Growing Population on Natural Resources" B. Nath, L.Hens, P.Compton & D.Devuyst (eds), Environmental Management in Practice: Vol 1. London and New York: Routledge.

Prasad, C. 2009. Rediscovering Traditional Knowledge for Sustaining Development and Biodiversity Conservation. Paper presented at the 16th World Congress of the IUAES held at Kunming, China, 2009.

Purcell, T.W. 1998. Indigenous Knowledge and applied anthropology: Questions of definition and direction. Human Organization. 57(3):

Rappaport, Roy. 1968. Pigs for the Ancestors: Ritual of the Ecology of a New Evinea People New Faven: Connecticut: Yale University Press.

Schnaiberg, Alan. 1975. "Social Synthesis of the Societal-Environmental Dialectic: The Role of Distributional Impacts" Social Science Quarterly 56: pp 5-20.

Shiferaw, Abebe, Bereket Dindamo, Kahsay Berhe, Azage Tegegne, Dirk Hoekstra. 2009.Reorganizing Farmers' Knowledge in Development Initiatives: Indigenous Bee-Keeping in Alaba Special Woreda, Southern Ethiopia. A paper presented at the 16th World Congress of the IUAES held at Kunming, China, 2009.

Sillitoe, Paul. 2002. "Participant observation to participatory Development: making anthropology work", In Paul Sillitoe, Alan Bicker and Johan Pottier (eds.) Participating in

Development: Approaches to Indigenous Knowledge, London: Routledge

Skole, David and Compton Tucker. 1997. "Tropical Deforestation and Habitat Fragmentation in the Amazon: Satellite Data from 1978 to 1988" In Lewis A Owen and Tim Unwin (eds) Environmental Management. Oxford: Blackwell Publishers.

Tisdel, Clem. 1994. Sustainability and Sustainable Development: Are these Concepts A Help or Hindrance to Economics? Economic Analysis & Policy. Vol. 24, No.2. September.

Trutmann, P. J Voss and J. Fairhead. 1966. Local Knowledge and farmer Perceptions of bean diseases in the central African highlands. Agriculture and Human Values. 13:64-70.

Vayda, A.P. 1996. Methods and Explanation in the study of Human Actions and their Environmental Effects, Jakarta: Center for International Forestry Research and World Wide Fund for Nature.

Warren, D.M.,L.J.Slikkerveer and D.Brokensha (eds). 1995. The Cultural Dimensions of Development: Indigenous Knowledge Systems. London: Intermediate Technology Publications.

Wijeratne, Mahinda. 2009. Sustainable Irrigation in Management through Indigenous Knowledge. Paper presented at the 16th World Congress of the IUAES held at Kunming, China, 2009.

Indigenous Traditional Knowledge and Biodiversity Conservation in Mexico: Necessary Considerations on Epistemic Fairness and New Citizenship

Dr. Aida Luz López Gómez

Abstract

Recent concern on indigenous traditional knowledge protection attended at international forums and—more recently—at Mexican legislative scope, is associated to scientific development and technological innovation that enhance possibilities of its industrial appropriation, as well as to the increase of its economic benefits and the consequent international corporations' interest.

On the other hand, it's been demonstrated that Earth's biological diversity is tie to thousands of peoples' and communities' management along history. That means, indigenous and peasant peoples are not only "keepers" or "caretakers" of biodiversity, but they also make important contributions to generate and increase it.

Of such luck, the subject of the indigenous traditional knowledge associated to biological diversity sends to double reflection. The first one it is located in the land of scientific transference models, where it becomes necessary to create horizontal processes that recognize the validity of all knowledge construction forms, beyond the hegemonic scientific paradigm, which we will call "epistemic fairness processes". The second reflection has to do with the need of an effective citizenship of the indigenous peoples. This means, they can totally exert their minority rights from difference, which is not only related to State's law reform but to the creation of new coexistence cultures, or "intercultural" conditions.

Both reflections are closely related to conceptual debate within environmental education field, as long as it constitutes an alternative culture proposal to face environmental crisis, which is in fact a civilization crisis.

Traditional knowledge (TK) and trade appro-priation of nature

Conservation and reasonable management of biological diversity has become a strategic concern of entire international community, particularly the so-called developing countries, because of the environmental services it provides and the enormous wealth it holds. But, forests, deserts, and rainforests, as well as ecosystems within which biodiversity evolved and reproduced, are not only natural reserves but also territories inhabited by different cultures that have shaped their identities, world views and ways of development by exploiting and transforming its natural wealth.

Several experts have shown that the planet's biological diversity is inextricably linked to management that thousands of peoples and local communities have made of it through history. That means, indigenous peoples and peasant communities aren't just "holders" or "keepers" of biodiversity, but they have also contributed to enlarge it.

Worldwide, it is been recognized that indigenous peoples have adapted properly to fragile ecosystems, have developed significant knowledge of the natural resources around them and have often taken very complex methods and techniques to manage habitat in a sustainable manner. The indigenous peoples themselves are seen as an integral part of nature and almost always require the preservation or restoration of their natural resources as a precondition for participation in other development efforts. Therefore, there is growing interest in integrating the knowledge, skills and traditional practices of indigenous peoples in the strategies for nature conservation.

According to the country study on biodiversity in 1998, within Mexico there are located 64.878 of known species on the planet, which places us as one of the twelve mega-diverse countries. This countries harbor together 70% of the living species on Earth.

Furthermore, Mexico holds sixth place in the list of countries with higher linguistic diversity, with 68 native languages belonging to 11 Indo-American linguistic families, and more than 360 dialect varieties.

Ekart Boege has shown that, in 24 million hectares of Mexican territory, indigenous population is over 80%. Within these regions there are located 50% of rainforests (with 5 thousand species), 50% of cloud forests (with 3 thousand species), and 25% of temperate forests (with 7 thousand species). Therefore, it is possible to recognize that Mexican indigenous peoples are some of the ethnic groups with higher biological diversity in the world (Boege, 2006).

Paradoxically, the socio-economic backwardness characterizing the various indigenous communities, hide an immense cultural wealth and heritage that has been preserved over time through practices that allow the coexistence of its production areas to the maintenance of biodiversity. This conservation strategy is based on the fact that many indigenous communities maintain portions of their forests and jungles with minimal disruption, or down complex farming and agro forestry systems. In those places, besides maintaining a significant genetic diversity of cultivated plants, peoples obtain semi-cultivated seeds, medicinal plants, shade, wildlife and timber (Gómez-Pompa, 1998).

Some researchers have called these systems "rural reserves" and recognize the enormous possibility and potential of these practices for effective conservation. Therefore, they recommend encouraging peasant conservation actions through recognition and compensation policies.

On the other hand, manifestations of various local and international indigenous organizations reclaim their territories and natural resources as the fundamental physical, cultural and spiritual bases of their existence.

These peoples harbor a repertoire of ecological and productive knowledge that are all together local, collective, diachronic, and holistic. Every plant or animal species, soil type or landscape, mountain or spring, usually have an appropriate cultural reference:

a linguistic expression, a knowledge category, practical use, mythic or religious significance, individual or collective experience (Toledo, 2001). This knowledge corpus has been constructed through historically shared social experience, transmitted from generation to generation, usually orally. It is tacit. It is dynamic, constantly evolving to adapt to new needs and challenges communities face.

Traditional indigenous knowledge is also highly specialized at local level, this means, in the context of relations established by communities and their immediate environment. TK reflects the social, economic, and cultural relations; as well as particular cosmology within every village or community.

Victor Toledo refers as elements of TK:
- Kosmos: World vision. Philosophic system.
- Corpus: knowledge about nature (astronomy, physics, biology, and ecogeography). It is local and very specialized on the environmental context of each culture.
- Praxis: Production, medicine, ritual life.

According to Pierina German-Castelli, dimensions that characterize the TK are:
- Symbolic meaning through oral history, given names and spiritual relations
- Refers to cosmological distinctions as environment conceptualization
- Relations based on duty reciprocity to other community members as well as other living forms
- Ecological resources management institutions based on sharing knowledge and community responsibility sense (German-Castelli, 2004).

In return, the economic rationality that has become widespread globally with the development of capitalism and, more recently, the so-called globalization, has reified the natural and human world. Several authors have reported the homogenization processes of production and consumption patterns against a sustainability based on ecological and cultural diversity. The economy affirms the sense of the world in production, and nature is denatured from its ecological and cultural complexity, and turned into single feedstock for capital exploitation. Worse, ecologist concern has not returned its being to nature, but it has transformed it into a new form of capital (nature capital), enlarging and generalizing forms of economic valorization and commercial appropriation.

Enrique Leff affirms that we currently attend to a "conservationist nature exploitation", through which biodiversity appears like potential reserve of genetic richness, tourism resources, CO_2 capture or ancient wisdom (Leff, 2005).

In this context, the growing concern on the protection of TK associated to biological diversity taking place in various international organizations—and, more recently, in indigenous people's rights debate within Mexico—is inextricably associated to development of scientific and technological advances that have increased possibilities of its commercial appropriation and its profitability.

Expropriation of TK for private ownership purposes has taken place since the sixteenth century colonialism. However, this process has accelerated exponentially since the late 1980s, with development of biotechnology.

In the same vein, recent policies aimed to protect biodiversity not only respond to a legitimate concern on biological species loss and its impact on Earth's ecological balance. Biodiversity has emerged as a huge bank of genetic resources that become feedstock of large corporations as pharmaceutical, cosmetic, agrochemical, food, etc., which already exceed the economic value of oil trusts.

The advent of biotechnology, along with information technology and communication, define a new paradigm of science and technology. These technologies are knowledge and information intensive, and they establish new patterns of competition, where knowledge becomes an essential asset, imposing new forms of organization and interaction between firms and other institutions, and facilitating rapid changes in research structures, production and marketing.

Thus, the new biotechnologies tend to cause a profound transformation within productive sectors and between them, and open doors for unlimited exploration of the intangible components (genetic information and TK) contained in biodiversity. Genetic resources are placed in the center of trading and, with them, indigenous peoples and local communities whose TK has become a strategic ally in the initial stages of bio-prospecting. Consequently, pressures begin to emerge for the privatization of both biodiversity and TK associated with it.

A 2007 study (García 2007b) reported that the potential of bio-prospecting processes is related to the worldwide existence of approximately 37.000 different species of wild plants, that may have-or had-traditional therapeutic uses. In 2003 it was estimated that global markets related to these activities reached between 500 and 800 billion dollars per year. And while the pharmaceutical industry had total sales of more than 300 billion dollars for those years, it was estimated that at least 60% of this income came from processes arising from the expropriation of genetic resources and TK.

On the other hand, industries related to phyto-medicine and seed production, obtain all of their sales from biodiversity resources. Other industries, such as those related to personal care and production of flavors and fragrances, although currently derive 16% of its sales from biological diversity, have enormous growth potential due to the increasing trend of the use of natural products to replace chemicals.

At present, the production of patent allopathic medicines commercially used in various countries is based on the chemical synthesis of 120 substances derived from the active ingredients of 90 plant species. 77% of these plants are used in traditional medicine.

Regarding the various industrial uses given to TK, German-Castelli affirms that it has a relevant role for the pharmaceutical industry during the stages of high-throughput screening, used frequently to explore new active substances. Once a component is identified, most companies use TK to guide further research, and some of them use it as a basis for competitive compounds classification. This allows, for example, derive more active synthetic compounds.

In biotechnology, many processes (like fermentation) are based on ancient TK. It has been used also in research of plague control, clime resistance of crops, seed improvement, as well as in cosmetic industry, among others. It is also widely used in marketing because of the symbolic value "natural origin" products in recent decades.

These appropriation processes by the corporate capital have urged to think about mechanisms to protect TK, on the understanding that communities may obtain benefits from their ancestral knowledge through intellectual property instruments,[1] and the recognition that it is fair to repay their contributions to biodiversity conservation. However, the debate on TK regulation implies aspects of various kinds, ranging from economic and operational considerations, to the issue of collective rights of indigenous peoples and the ethical implications behind the privatization of Life. Among the proposals being discussed both nationally and internationally, there is a wide range of options and interests. In particular, there is evidence of two extreme positions: on one side, commercial interest of the biotechnology companies, and on the other hand, social organizations' opposition to the privatization of TK, biodiversity and all life forms.

In the first case, privatization is promoted to protect capital investments, particularly in genetic engineering. A controversial feature of this position is the overflow of the essential concepts of intellectual property, such as giving "invention" status to discovery, and protecting investors rather than the inventor. Besides, extending to the living beings a legal regime originally created for inanimate objects, and assign a status of private property to a public good as is TK.

At the other end of the discussion, there are sectors openly opposed to any form of privatization and monopolization of living beings and therefore biodiversity. They also believe that TK should not be subordinated to the so-called "scientific knowledge" but to be considered as a collective good. In this view, a barrier to the freedom of movement and socialization of TK would prevent the enrichment and development of cultures. This position also warns that any form of privatization of knowledge and biodiversity, whether individual or collective, is a risk, particularly for developing countries.

In between, there is apparently an intermediate position. Within the WTO raised the possibility that member countries make proposals for sui generis intellectual property rights. This

---

[1]   However, note that the central instrument of the processes of appropriation of traditional knowledge are precisely intellectual property rights, a system established to generate private ownership on human knowledge: patents, appellations of origin, collective marks and, more recently, certificates of legal provenance.

framework would recognize the rights of local communities over their biodiversity and the knowledge linked to it. Similarly, in the framework of the Cartagena Protocol, there were statements that consider the inapplicability of market principles and categories for local communities and, therefore, should be a special regime in line with their cultural differences and collective rights.

Thus, Article 8 (j) of the Convention on Biological Diversity (CBD) provides for the creation of a special regime of access to genetic resources for TK protection, urging States to take active measures to respect, preserve and maintain knowledge, innovations and practices of indigenous and local communities; to promote wider use of TK relevant to conservation and the sustainable use of biodiversity with the approval and involvement of the holders of such knowledge, and encourage the equitable benefit sharing. However, in Mexico, there are several restrictions to achieve such protection regime. Firstly, indigenous peoples have no legal personality and have no official recognition to their territories. Secondly, due to diversity and widespread distribution of indigenous population, it is almost impossible to determinate which communities own a specific knowledge.

In essence, the debate on biodiversity conservation and the recognition and protection to TK associated with it, confronts two opposing rationalities:

The first one is an economic system's need to preserve "reservoirs" of biodiversity that are substantial sources of environmental services and potential banks of inputs for the biotechnological industry. That means, it encourages "commoditization" and private appropriation of biodiversity. This economic system has widely shown to prioritize the intensive natural resources use and the accelerated depletion. To it, Indian peoples have the role of "caregivers", environmental services providers or "alternative technologies" suppliers getting, in the best case, a "fair share" of benefits.

In Enrique Leff's words: "Global economic discourse, at the same time that 'recognizes' ethnic differences, displays an strategy to convert them to the credo of market supreme law, and to recode their cultures in terms of economic values" (Leff, 2005).

On the other hand, there is the desire of indigenous peoples, expressed by its various social movements, to be subjects of their own destiny; to exercise the right to a territory recognition that guarantees the material wealth for the development of its culture; to exercise their own manners of social and political organization.

They claim also for the right to use and develop their languages; to practice their own belief systems and knowledge; autonomy to define their own strategies for meeting their needs; recognition of their regulatory systems, and the use both material and symbolic of their natural resources. Indigenous peoples claim, in fact, for a new citizenship status, which means a new relation with State and non indigenous society.

Moreover, TK protection, as it has been proposed so far, on the way of intellectual property instruments, refer to an irreconcilable conflict between the collective nature of knowledge (and its role in shaping the symbolic processes of identity) and its treatment as a commodity in the context of global and corporate capitalism.

Therefore, it is necessary to take actions to protect and revalue TK, not from the instrumental rationality of corporate ownership, but within the logic of indigenous peoples' cultural rights to difference. That is, the right to make decisions over their resources and build their future on different bases. This necessarily entails a critical reflection on the civilization model which sustains the current forms of capitalist appropriation: homogenization of human life forms, based on the scientific and technological development.

From instrumental scientific rationality to wisdom dialogue

The global environmental crisis has been characterized by several authors as a "civilization crisis." In this sense, the construction of a new perspective on environmental issues requires a critical review of knowledge forms and processes that have lead to unilateral and exclusive visions on environmental matters, leaving aside social knowledge and experiences that are invaluable to sustain solidary relationships among human beings, and a responsible link between them and nature.

To Enrique Leff, "This civilization crisis is primarily a crisis of knowledge. Environmental degradation is the result of forms of knowledge through which humanity has built the world, and has destroyed it due to universality, generality and totality pretension. Because its objectification and reification of the world. Environmental crisis is not an ecological crisis caused by a natural history. Beyond matter evolution from the cosmic dimension to the living organization, language emergence and symbolic order, matter and being have become more complex due to knowledge reflection on reality. In our proclaimed knowledge society, science advances by throwing shadows on the understanding of the world and subjugating wisdoms" (Leff, 2006, 2).

From the sixteenth century, science was built as the truth criteria that would support the economic and political development of the modern Western world. Since then, it contributes decisively to the creation of new images of the universe and the place that man occupies in it, as well as new environments for human interaction. However, foundational theories about natural and social realities that have shaped Western thought and its technological development during five centuries are facing today a major transformation process. The conception of the world and the cosmos as a functional machine which components may be known entirely, and therefore dominated, has begun to fade.

Throughout history, scientific knowledge has attempted to demarcate the difference between truth and untruth, leaving the former to the realm of science. Scientific knowledge was meant to be rational and objective, and discover the universal laws that explain the real. In the second half of the twentieth century philosophy of science put in the center of its analysis the need of establishing criteria by which some theories or postulates would be "more scientific" than others.

Discussions on rationalism versus empiricism, induction vs. deduction, verificationism vs falsificationism, rationalism versus relativism, or internalism vs. externalism enroll within this level of reflection. But paradoxically, currently most of these couples seem more to be complementary parts of one whole than irreconcilable antagonisms. The claim of finding the absolute foundations of scientific knowledge has sunk into the discovery that such grounds do not exist. Neither empirical or logic verification seem to be enough to establish a certainty criterion to science.

Despite philosophers and epistemologist efforts, objectivity problem has been solved, along science history, through agreements and conventions settled within each discipline or school of thought, and not by any formula to ensure the absolute reliability of scientific knowledge.

This could not be otherwise: knowledge is organized and transformed through the processing of symbols, ideas, and theories that require language and communication, and that are located in the context of a particular cultural background. In Maturana and Varela's words: "Any reflection, including those on the foundations of human knowledge, is necessarily constructed within the language that is our unique way of being human and being in the human doing. Therefore, language is also our starting point, our cognitive tool and our problem" (Maturana & Varela 1999, 21). Moreover, culture becomes possible through language.

Edgar Morin agrees with this approach by asserting that human cognitive abilities, sustained on observation and systematization of experience, can only develop within a culture that has produced and preserved a language, a specific logic and knowledge capital, as well as certain truth criteria. That is, the human mind develops and organizes knowledge using available cultural means (Morin, 1988).

To Morin, "organizing principles of human knowledge are the same that allow the subjective construction of objectivity. Certainly an isolated subject can imperfectly access to objective knowledge. He needs this inter-subjective communication, confrontation and critical discussions. (And it is the historical development of these inter-subjective processes of objectification what has given birth to the cultural sphere of scientific objectivity)" (Morin 1998, 228).

In addition, ideas and methods of science are not the result of technical development, but of all the social practice. Therefore, the discussion of scientific objectivity is a sterile debate. It is not possible to lay the foundation for absolute knowledge. This is necessarily relative and especially relational. It starts from the relationship between the knowing subject and the world around him, but also from the link among the studied aspects or "parts" of reality and the "Hole" that make up such reality.

According to Victor Toledo, in western scholastic, "we were rarely taught to recognize the existence of an experience, of certain wisdom, in the minds of the millions of men and women who toil nature day after day . . . under conditions that could be described as preindustrial. Today, at the dawn of a new century, these men and women still make up most of the population engaged to manage the planet's ecosystems. And it is precisely due to this scientific research's omission and neglecting, opus and foundation of modern, that industrial civilization has failed in its attempts to make proper management of nature" (Toledo, 2005, 16).

This approach allows recognition of several intellectual traditions which are different in its origins, traits and abilities. Modernity gestated forms of understanding the world and relating with nature that date back to the beginning of the industrial revolution. But globally, they exist in parallel with other forms of relationship with nature that are still in force in contemporary world, although they were originated several thousand years ago. At the beginning of XXI century, there are still about 6 thousand not "Western" cultures, most of them living in rural areas of the world. These cultures have avoided the cultural and technological expansion of global capitalism by resistance or marginalization, and many of them retain management practices of biodiversity that are today a source of interest for nature conservation in Western societies.

In the Western scientific tradition (even that knowledge which seeks to grasp the complexity and interaction of multiple processes that occur in reality) there are several meanings and knowledge missing, those that fall outside the symbolic representation or the language of science.[2]

---

[2] "Interdisciplinarity and Systems Theory emerged as methodological devices for the integration of holistic knowledge. These new approaches seek to reintegrate the fragmented parts of a whole of knowledge that, while it emphasizes on the interrelationships of the processes, it does not abandon the principles of objectivity and unity of scientific knowledge. Both interdisciplinarity and Systems Theory remain within the fence of logocentrism of science, the mathematization of knowledge, the certainty and control over the world" (Leff, 2004: 325).

As noted before, science is a cultural product which in turn coexists and interacts constantly with a variety of ways of interpreting the world, with a plurality of cultures. In the present case, this diversity is expressed in different wisdoms and traditional knowledge of indigenous peoples, to which contemporary science frequently assigns the site of "information providers", facilitating and significantly reducing the costs of research activities by private appropriation processes, but not through the recognition of this wisdom as effective forms of knowledge that can provide valuable insights for the development of alternatives to the civilization crisis.

This recognition implies questioning the epistemological hegemony of scientific knowledge, but also the cultural marginality in which indigenous peoples are still, highlighting the need to effectively incorporate interculturalism and respect for cultural diversity as new forms of citizen coexistence.

Necessary questions are then: How to link the different cultural forms of knowledge generation in the search for appropriate solutions to the crisis of civilization? And what changes must occur in society to make this possible? These questions refer to think the issue of recognition and protection of indigenous TK in both political and epistemic dimensions.

From environmental education, we consider imperative the recognition and "visibility" of conflict and domination processes underlying the commercial appropriation of TK, in the hope that indigenous peoples can transcend the prefixed and exclusionary future that capitalist modernity has assigned to them. As well as affirm the creative diversity of human life. These ideas lead us to believe in a process of constructing alternative knowledge from a wisdom dialogue that has been proposed by several authors.

"Wisdom dialogue arises in the fertility of otherness that opens up a not given future (neither on extrapolation of present or in the rational conduct of a development process based on knowledge) . . . Otherness as the meeting between me and you, of the Self and the Other, opens up a world to what 'can be' in the encounter and dialogue between speaking beings" (Leff, 2004).

New citizenship: The political dimension of wisdom dialogue

Construction of spaces for democratic coexistence is not restricted to the political sphere of social relations, but also to symbolic representation. The mere presence of diverse indigenous peoples or heterogeneous social groups in the same territory is not enough to achieve solidarity and recognition of diversity as a core value in the reproduction of a democratic order. Likewise, it is not enough to seek solutions to environmental problems. It requires communication and interaction strategies of varying scope, which involve all sectors of society (citizens, government institutions, civil society organizations, various levels of government, media, among others).

Thus, wisdom dialogue may transcend asymmetries, that means, those inequity power relations that benefit a social group over the others. While it is true that inequalities affecting Indians arise from the prevalence of economic and political conflicts and consequent social marginalization, they are exacerbated by the lack of recognition of their cultural specificity and the annulment of their right to build own future from the difference. This refers, in fact, to conflict over material resources, but also realizes intercultural conflict. Therefore, the issue is not just to overcome economic backwardness and access to government services, but especially to transform the symbolic representation that the rest of society makes of indigenous people, through educational strategies.

Wisdom dialogue has ethical bases: the "others", the "different ones", have the legitimate right to a proper vision of future, built from its particular identity.

Contact between different cultures may enrich them all. Cultural diversity challenges in any society imply to overcome asymmetries, this means, power relations that discriminate some other cultures by others. Achieve recognition of the right to cultural difference and social equity, and intercultural dialogue as a widespread practice in all institutions and social groups.

Wisdom dialogue asserts that cultural diversity ensures human life on Earth, as long as it enlarges possibilities of adaptive responses to the various environmental challenges on the planet. It supposes pluralism and decision making in complex situations, were interests and thoughts are different. It seeks for social and redistributive justice through effective social participation and political representation.

If, as we said, the economic and political conflict of indigenous peoples is sharpened by de lack of recognition of their cultural difference, it is necessary a new coexistence proposal. That is, a process of citizenship construction on new bases.

Equity: The epistemic challenge of wisdom dialogue

Regarding how to link the different cultural forms of knowledge generation in the search for solutions to the civilization crisis, some authors have made proposals such as epistemological pluralism, which provides elements for a plural rationality and acknowledges that objectivity exist in all human cognitive systems, when these are grouped under a single conceptual framework or constructed on epistemic conditions and optimal dialogue (Olivé, 1997). Under this proposal, it is essential to have an unrestricted notion of truth to avoid an extreme relativism. But what would be such a notion "unrestricted" for real? How do we build it?

César Carrillo asserts that "in the construction of a symmetrical relationship between science and indigenous knowledge, developing appropriate approaches and concepts, new ways of approach, possible equivalences and correlations is [. . .] just a first step. To go further it is necessary the active participation of indigenous peoples. The definition of what indigenous knowledge is, its boundaries and assessment of its dominant elements can only come from the Indians themselves" (Carrillo Trueba, 2006).

We fully agree with the latter. However, we have also insisted that scientific knowledge is a cultural event that occurs in a social context, therefore is also subject to unequal relationships that exist in that context. In the present case, we must consider that relationship between indigenous and non-indigenous society has historically been based on a symbolic representation prevailing discriminatory until today, and it has had many manifestations precisely within science and technology fields.[3]

---

[3] We mean, for example, the disdain with which allopathic medicine refers to traditional medicine, to the imposition of crops and technology for

Therefore, rather than a "symmetrical relationship" between science and indigenous TK, the necessary articulation of wisdoms to address the current civilization crisis should be a new way of thinking about the world, that can only be built on the epistemic basis of equity. That is, from a dialogue of rationalities that, recognizing each other different, show ethical and philosophical attitude to reach "other's" understanding.

Epistemic equity implies to abandon totality pretension of western knowledge. No knowledge system can reach total comprehension of universe, this makes possible listening and respecting other knowledge forms. It is necessary to recognize that "otherness" is a radical fait and it can not be absolutely comprehended. If we recognize that other cultures have the same capacity for constructing knowledge about the world, they can not be treated as "study subjects". Knowing the "other" (that will allways be partial) is only possible through a social relationship where both participate and comprehend simultaneously (see Del Val, 2000).

According to diverse authors, knowledges articulate through language, and communicative conduct. "Languages are synonym of knowledge: cultural knowledge, knowledge about the knowledge of nature from the territory that is inhabited, knowledge of biodiversity and the relationship with it. Languages contain and express the whole set of ideas, they contain the universe of thought that has been produced by humans. Each language is the expression of a particular life world, of a specific world vision and a cultural heritage. The speakers of a language are heirs to the wisdom of their people, and how they have solved requirements of interaction with the world throughout history, containing memory and hope" (Limón, 2008). Thus epistemic equity demands new languages, common meaning construction and new forms to name the world.

---

agriculture opposed to traditional crops, the contempt for rituals, sacred sites and forms of religious organization of indigenous peoples and their cargo systems and authority structures that still lack recognition in "modern" Mexican state, and so on.

Conclusion

For all the exposed reasons, we affirm that the recovery, assessment and promotion of indigenous TK associated with biodiversity, as well as its protection from capitalist appropriation processes that carry out multinational corporations, cannot rely on a "sui generis" intellectual property regime that gives the role of "caregivers" of biodiversity in exchange for a "fair share" of benefits. On the contrary, it is urgent to build new systems of knowledge to articulate necessary wisdom to address the environmental crisis, which restored the dignity of all cultures and recognize that, given the current crisis of civilization, it is necessary, above all, a revolution in thought. It is, in short, to build a world for all forms of thinking the world.

References

Banda, Oscar (2008), *Recursos genéticos y pueblos indígenas*. (México: Grupo Parlamentario del PRD. Cámara de Diputados. Congreso de la Unión. LX Legislatura)

Bello, Álvaro (2004), *Etnicidad y ciudadanía en América Latina*. (Santiago de Chile: Comisión Económica para América Latina y el Caribe, CEPAL).

Betancourt, Alberto (2006). *De la conservación "desde arriba" a la conservación "desde abajo". El interés supranacional en los saberes indígenas sobre ecología*. (México: Fundación Carolina, CeALCI).

Boege, Eckart (2006). "Territorios y diversidad biológica: la agrobiodiversidad de los pueblos indígenas de México" in Concheiro (ed.)

Carrillo Trueba, César (2006), *Pluriverso*. (México: UNAM, Programa Universitario México Nación Multicultural).

CONABIO (1998), *La diversidad biológica de México: Estudio de País*. (México: Comisión Nacional de Biodiversidad)

Concheiro, Luciano (ed.) (2006), *Conocimiento tradicional: ¿un bien público o privado?* (México: Centro de Estudios para el Desarrollo Rural Sustentable y la Soberanía Alimentaria. Cámara de Diputados, LX Legislatura).

García A., Miguel Ángel (2007a), "Documento sistematizado de análisis bibliográfico/documental, referente a experiencias relevantes internacionales." Research report num. 5. *Conocimientos Tradicionales de los Pueblos Indígenas de México y Recursos Genéticos*. (México: Comisión Nacional para el Desarrollo de los Pueblos Indígenas).

García A., Miguel Ángel (2007b), "Análisis de la problemática actual de los Conocimientos Tradicionales asociados a los recursos genéticos, a nivel internacional y nacional." Research report num. 9. *Conocimientos Tradicionales de los Pueblos Indígenas de México y Recursos Genéticos*. (México: Comisión Nacional para el Desarrollo de los Pueblos Indígenas)

German-Castelli, Pierina (2004). Diversidade Biocultural: Direitos de Propriedade Intelectual versus Direitos dos Recursos Tradicionais, Tesis de Doctorado. Universidad Federal Rural de Rio de Janeiro. Instituto de Ciencias Humanas y Sociales. Posgrado en Desarrollo, Agricultura y Sociedad.

Gómez-Pompa, Arturo (1998), Conferencia Magistral presentada en XIV Congreso Mexicano de Botánica, Ciudad de México, octubre.

Leff, Enrique (2004), *Racionalidad ambiental. La reapropiación social de la naturaleza*. (México: Siglo XXI).

Leff, Enrique (2006), "Complejidad, racionalidad ambiental y diálogo de saberes". Ponencia presentada en el I Congreso internacional interdisciplinar de participación, animación e intervención socioeducativa, celebrado en Barcelona.

Limón, Fernando (2008). "Día internacional de la lengua materna y año mundial de los idiomas" in *Diario Expreso*. 1:7.

López, Aida (2005), "Conocimiento Tradicional Indígena: Consideraciones sobre las iniciativas para su protección." Ponencia presentada en el Seminario La investigación del campo mexicano en el siglo XXI desde la perspectiva del Poder Legislativo. Centro de Estudios para el Desarrollo Rural Sustentable y la soberanía Alimentaria. Palacio Legislativo de San Lázaro, 6 de diciembre.

Maturana, Humberto and Francisco Varela (1999), *El árbol del conocimiento. Las bases biológicas del conocimiento humano*. (Barcelona: Debate).

Morin, Edgar (1995), *Introducción al pensamiento complejo*.(Barcelona: Gedisa).

Morin, Edgar (1998), *El método. El conocimiento del conocimiento*. (Madrid: Cátedra).

Olivé, León (1997), "Pluralismo epistemológico: más sobre racionalidad, verdad y consenso" in Velasco (ed.)

Tobin, Brendan (2001), "Redefining Perspectives in the Search for Protection of Traditional Knowledge: A Case Study from Peru" in *RECIEL* 10:1.

Toledo, Víctor Manuel (2000), *Atlas Etnoecológico de México y Centroamérica*. (México: CD-Rom).

Toledo, Víctor Manuel (2001), "El Atlas Etnoecológico de México y Centroamérica: Fundamentos, Métodos y Resultados" in *Etnoecológica* Vol. 6 No. 8, p.41.

Toledo, Víctor Manuel (2005), "La memoria tradicional: la importancia agroecológica de los saberes locales" *en LEISA Revista de Agroecología*, april.

Velasco, Ambrosio (1997), *Racionalidady cambio científico*. (México: Paidós).

Internet-based references

Del Val, José (2000), "Entender y comprender al otro" *México Nación Multicultural*, UNAM [website] (updated 6 June 2007) http://www.nacionmulticultural.unam.mx/Portal/Central/EDITORIAL/pdfs/edito1.pdf

Leff, Enrique (2005), "La Geopolítica de la Biodiversidad y el Desarrollo Sustentable: economización del mundo, racionalidad ambiental y reapropiación social de la naturaleza". *Aprodeh* [website] (updated 28 Feb. 2008) http://www.aprodeh.org.pe/tlc/documentos/documentos_otros/LEFF_Enrique_Geopoitica_Biodiversidad.pdf

The Use of Folk Literature in Aborigine Education: A Review of the UNICEF Project in Malaysia

Dr. Ahmad A. Nasr
Dr. See Hoon Peow

Abstract

This study proposes to review the United Nations Children's Fund and the Curriculum Development Centre, Ministry of Education project of using Orang Asli folktales in the education of Orang Asli school children in Year One to Year Three. The objectives of the project are to attract Orang Asli children to attend school, encourage their reading habits, improve their writing skills, while promoting their cultural knowledge. The study found that the project is a laudable one, and at the very least acknowledges the educational value of Orang Asli folk literature. It also found that the project suffers from a number of problems and weaknesses, which could have been easily avoided by the involvement of professional folklorists.

Introduction

Formal education is the most effective channel by which the indigenous people like the Orang Asli of Peninsular Malaysia can change and improve their lives. Yet schools are, generally speaking, hardly attractive places for the Orang Asli children, and education is often considered unimportant to them and their parents. The Exxon—Mobil and United Nations Children Educational Fund (UNICEF) project for collecting Orang Asli stories and using them in the education of the Orang Asli children is designed to encourage them to read, improve their writing skills, attract them to attend school, and promote their cultural knowledge. The main objective of this article is to review this project.

Orang Asli and Their Problems

The indigenous people of Peninsular Malaysia are known by the collective Malay name Orang Asli (literally: original people). They numbered 105,000 in 1997, and 149,723 in 2005 according to the Department of the Orang Asli Affairs (hereafter: JHEOA)(Annual Report 2005). They are classified by the JHEOA and anthropologists into three major groups, namely Negrito who are made up of Kensiu, Kintak, Jahai, Lanoh, Mendriq and Batek subgroups, Senoi who include Semai, Temiar, Che Wong, Ja Hut, Semaq Beri and Mah Meri, and Proto-Malay who are subdivided into Temuan, Semelai, Jakuri, Orang Kanak, Orang Kuala and Orang Seletar. Each subgroup has its own language and culture and identity. Economically, they have varied occupations such as hunting, gathering forest produce, fishing, permanent agriculture and/or engaged in paid labour. They also are engaged in some trade with the Malays and Chinese middlemen, selling jungle produce.

In the British colonial period, the administration's main task was to protect the Orang Asli as noble savages from outside influences. That made them excellent subjects for anthropological research and convenient target for Chrisian, Bahai and Muslim missionaries. No attempt was made to develop them. They were left to live according to their traditions and customs. During the civil war between the Government and Communist insurgents (1948-1960) the British regrouped the Orang Asli in settlement camps to deprive the insurgents from the help the Orang Asli provided them in the form of food, shelter and intelligence. Later, jungle forts and a Department of Aborigines was established and the Orang Asli were provided with basic health services, education and basic consumer commodities.

This period also witnessed the enactment of the Aboriginal Peoples Ordinance in 1954 (later known as Act 134; amended in 1967 and 1974 to meet the changing conditions) to protect the Orang Asli and indicate the Governement's responsibility towards them. The period also saw the establishment of JHEOA and the Aboriginal Peoples Act 1954, both of which, as Colin Nicholas (1997) rightly points out, are the only government department and the only piece of legislation concerned with Orang Asli. The Act (revised in 1974) recognizes some rights of the Orang Asli such as eduucation and provides them with lands and reserves. It also gives the state governments the right to relocate them, often without consultation and their consent, whenever the lands on which they are grouped are needed for various forms of development such as a dam, an air-port, a highway, sites for universities and even a golf course. In other words, the Orang Asli has no land titles. The National Land Code does not recognize their rights to their customary lands. The Orang Asli's dispossession from their ancestral home lands constitutes the greatest threat to their culture, identity and livelihood.

The JHEOA, since its establishment, is the sole responsible agency for the development of the Orang Asli, be it infrastructural like providing roads, electricity, pipe water and roads, medical by improving their health and wiping out infectious diseases, economic by incorporating them into the national economy, educational by establishing schools, and more recently, "spiritual" by making enormous efforts to convert them to Islam, and thus integrate them with the mainstream national society particularly the Malays. In spite of the improvement in the livelihood of the Orang Asli, they are still left behind, and classified as hard-core poor minority.

The problems of the Orang Asli could be overcome by policy and legal reforms. These include (i) restructuring the role, the abolishment or the control of JHEOA by the Orang Asli, (ii) making development in line with their cultures, (iii) Integrating them in the Malaysian multi-ethnic society as a distinct community and not assimilating them to the Malays by converting them to Islam. Moreover, (iv) the one seat reserved in the Senate is insufficient representation in parliament and States Assemblies, and should be increased to enable them to participate in political decisions, (v) granting titles to their lands by incorporating their lands right in Act

134 and the National Land Code, and (vi) amending Article 153 of Malaysia Federal Constitution to include the Orang Asli as *bumiputra* (literally:prince of earth. Early settlers) to enjoy the privileges accorded to the Malay and the natives of Sarawak and Sabah such as reservation of quotas in terms of employment in public service, trade permits, business licences, and scholarships, education and training. These reforms do not involve a high financial cost and all they need is a political will and Orang Asli's more active mobilization (Nicholas 1997, Lim 1997, Dentan et.al.1997)

The Orang Asli and Education

As mentioned earlier, formal education is the most effective channel by which the Orang Asli can change and improve their lives economically and socially. It is also identified as the most important means for intergenerational mobility. In other words, long-term development of the Orang Asli involves better educational opportunities for their children. Without formal education the Orang Asli will remain trapped in poverty, and continue to be looked upon by the rest of the Malaysians as primitive, lazy, unintelligent and easily manipulated. No wonder then that section 17 (1) of Act 134of Laws of Malaysia (1954 revised 1974) states that "[no] aboriginal child shall be precluded from attending school by reason only of his being aborigine". The section also prescribes a fine not exceeding five hundred ringgits for any person who is found guilty and convicted of acting against that law. Three types of schools were available to the Orang Asli. The first type (primary, mostly covered grades 1-3) are managed by JHEOA and after which children must go to boarding schools ; the second, by JHEOA and the Ministry of Education ; and the third by the Minisrty of Education. The first type was a dismal failure.

In 1991 a group of Orang Asli, including prominent Orang Asli intellectuals proposed a plan for the development of the Orang Asli in the context of the Government's vision of 2020—a vision that aims of making Malaysia a fully developed nation. One of the main proposals was that the Ministry of Education should take over all the schools administered by JHEOA and be responsible for the education of the

Orang Asli. This, incidentally, was the only proposal adopted by the Government.(Dentan *et. al.*, 1997: 155-156) But the take-over, which was completed in the year 2001, had not been successful as some of the Orang Asli teachers submitted their resignations and the teachers who replaced them did not speak the Orang Asli languages (Fui, 1997: 157).

A number of reasons were given to explain the high drop-out rate, which may vary from one Orang Asli community to another. These are lack of interest, boredom, laziness, inability to adapt to schooling life, and cope with lessons, the far location of schools, being bullied and traumatized by the Chinese and Malay classmate (Bidin, 2010). Other reasons are (i) some of the parents' emotional and spiritual attachment to their remote traditional settlement and their unwillingness to move and join the nearest settlements where schools are established, (ii) some parents fear that the teachers might convert their children to Islam (Toshihiro, 2008 :213). Being illiterate, these parents do not know that section 17 (1) of Act 134 of the Laws of Malaysia clearly states that "no aboriginal child attending any class shall be obliged to attend any religious instruction unless the prior consent of his father or his mother if the father is dead or his guardian should both parents be dead, is notified to the Commissioner and is transmitted by the Commissioner in writing to the headmaster of the school concerned." (iii) Due to their negative attitude toward education the parents do not send their children to schools, and if they do, not care about their attendance or performance nor encourage them to do well. (iv) Other factors, according to Nicholas (2006) are structural rather than attitudinal; they are related to poverty, non-delivery of educational assistance, contrast in the pedagogy and culture between the educational system and the Orang Asli traditional learning system, gaps in attendance and imperfection in the (school) system that does not involve participation of the Orang Asli parents in significant way"

Individuals, non-government organizations, the print media and Ministeries have made attempts to solve the problem of the high drop-out rate, and thus bridge the education gap between the Orang Asli and the other ethnic groups. An example of individuals is an Orang Asli secondary school teacher, who preferred to stay with his people and addresses 7-12 year age students when they return from the school hostel to the village, while their parents watch and listen. He advises them to study hard and make their dreams of becoming a doctor or an engineer, for an example, come true (Shadan, 2006). An example of the NGOs is the Rotary Club of Bandar Utama who agreed with The Jehai Orang Asli community in Perak to provide education to Orang Asli children below fifteen years with basic education including books, stationary and food while attending school. They also entrusted some education experts to make a simple syllabus for the long term project which is expected to continue for three to five years (Dass, 2008). The Department of Special Education, Ministry of Education, Malaysia (Japatan Pendidikan Khas Kementerian Pelajaran) collaborated with other government agencies, higher educational institute, and NGOs in organizing a five-day outreach programme which targeted the biggest Orang Asli settlement Hini, Pakan, Pahang. The Orang Asli parents were informed about the importance of education, and information about Orang Asli education, culture and traditions was also gathered. Print media usually highlights the success of Orang Asli students who excel in the primary and high secondary school examinations every year as a means to motivate other students. The highlighting also includes the few Orang Asli Ph.D holders and business men to show that hard struggle pays off (Chin, 2009).

The Minister of Education, in an attempt to reduce the rate of dropouts, established schools in the remote Orang Asli areas, constructed roads and improved the existing ones in settlements. It also aimed at changing the mindset of the Orang Asli parents and creating awareness on the importance of education among them and their children by conducting classes to teach them to read and write and thus improve the literacy rate. The attempt achieved some success. The dropout rate has fallen in the last fifteen years; and the rate has dropped from 29% in 2011 to 26% in 2012. The Ministry of Education is working to reduce the rate from primary to secondary schools to 15% by the year 2015(The Star 23 May, 2012). However, about 80% of the children still do not complete secondary education. In other words, the rate of dropout is becoming higher as they get to higher levels. The number of those who complete school is declining. (Nicholas, 2006) This shows that the efforts of the Ministry and other organizations seem not to produce the desired result, and that there is still need to intensity efforts to reduce the drop rates at various level of education.

Literature Review on the Use of Folklore in Education in Malaysia

The field of folk literature and modern education in Malaysia is almost a virgin field. Studies in the form of conference papers and postgraduate theses dealing with it started in the 1960's. Those related to Malay literature are piecemeal, small scale studies. Only one study explores in details Chinese folk literature whereas studies on Indian folk literature do not, according to our knowledge, focus on its relationship with modern education. As far as the indigenous people are concerned only one study deals with the importance of the Iban folk literature in the process of socialization.

Hussain (1975), Yassin (1983) and Yusoff, Mutalib and Ali (2003) acknowledge in short articles the suitability of folk literature, which include tales, Malay poems and parodies, as a reading material for students, and enumerates the characteristics such material must possess These are educational and psychological values, suitable social and cultural features to the nation promotion of social peace, fighting spirit, patriotism or heroism and promotion of love for one's country and for its people, adventurous spirit, humour and victory of good over evil. Hussain points out that this reading material entertain students and train them to think critically and logically ; he raises important points but does not elaborate them. But these authors have not discussed important issues such as the criteria for the selection of the material, and rewriting into contemporary style before presenting it in an electronic form.

Ramli (2004) is interested in the pre-school children's interpretation of the immoral conduct (lying and aggressive behaviour) of the fairy tales' characters, and whether or not these children change their attitude after learning the purpose of the immoral actions, as well as gender difference in interpretation, if any. She found that most of them condemned the immoral conduct, but some of them changed their mind when they came to know the purpose of the immoral conduct, and that there was no difference in interpretation between boys and girls. Ramli is to be credited for scientifically testing her ideas despite the small scale of the study, which is hardly representative of the populace and consequently the reliability and validity of her findings. Moreover, the tales read to the children are in fact not fairy-tales. Ramli's inability to correctly identify the tales is a common weakness among non-folklorists.

The National Writers' Association of Malaysia (1996) identifies folk literature, especially folktales and literary romances as important and potential resources for children literature. The association divides folktales into four categories, namely myths or folk romances, usually referred to by the term *hikayat*, beast fables, farcical fables in which the characteristics of human are exaggerated, and aetiological fables (about the origin of natural phenomena). These can be included as a reading material in textbooks for children. Before inclusion, the fables are to be properly selected because not all folktales are good, and rewritten in contemporary style. The fables must also be written in the interests of Malaysia's multi-racial society. Moreover, they can be turned into science fiction and thus "[W]e can create our own 'Disneyland' out of them".

Antonysamy (2003) conducted an experiment on four children aged between nine and eleven to explore how learning (a) fable genre, (b) about the genre and (c) through fable enable children to write better, particularly fables and to develop their critical and creative thinking. Antonysamy asked the children to write a fable, and investigate their ability to write it. Then she widened their repertoires by informing them about the attributes of fables and finally asked them to create their own fables. She found out that knowing fables is not enough in helping the learners to write their own fables but learning the features of fables enable them to create their own. Learning through the genre process helps the learners to be more linguistically aware of gender difference by learning how to use pronouns, for example, and to know the implicit meaning of the stories by exploring its creation and eventual interpretation. Antonysamy's experiment reveals the linguistic and literally creational function of fable genre. But it is based on a small sample and thus it is neither representative nor inclusive. Moreover, some of the fables used in the experiment are written literary works and not folktales.

Sutlive Jr. (1979) deals with the folk literature of a non-Malay group—The Iban, an indigenous people of Sarawak. He shows how the analysis of their folk literature enhances one's understanding of their culture and socialization. Hill rice, he points out, is the distinctive feature of Iban culture. As such their folk literature reflects the value of agrarian culture—self-sufficiency, egalitarianism, respect and responsibility, community and co-operation, and luck.

It is worth mentioning that the Malaysian government has been aware of the usefulness of folk literature. In the context of Malaysian national identity and national development. The Department of Information has made use of various forms of Malay folklore, including literature such as love ballads (*dondang sayang*) to explain the government New Economic Policy, national unity (Zain, 1975). The Department of Broadcasting started a project, which lasted for two years, of collecting folk songs and broadcasting them on television and radio, especially after the rise of nationalism in 1955 general election. The Department also distributed folk songs books to the public and organized concerts that presented them (Ramli, 1975). It is noticeable that these efforts were confined to the Malay folk literature and as such neglected the folk literature of the Chinese, Indian and indigenous groups.

See (2010) explores how Chinese folk literature is used in Chinese language education, value transmission and identity formation through a case study on Chinese language textbooks used by the National Type Chinese Primary Schools from the 1960s to the 2000s. He finds out that a wide range of values such as diligence, intelligence, self-sacrifice, harmony, unity, repriority, wisdom, justice, loyalty, modesty are transmitted through folk narratives in the 1960s and 1970s textbooks. He notices that the quantum and the range of values have decreased since 1980s because of the decline in the number of folk narratives. The 1990's witnessed an increase in the frequency of folk narratives followed by a drop in the 2000s with regard to identity formation. See finds out that the content of textbooks is far from charismatic. The identity is reflected through the folk narratives and the attitude and action of the teachers and the textbooks' writers and editors. The changes in the treatment of folk narratives in Chinese textbooks—from different eras in the development of Malaysian education system—reveal the fluid

Chinese identity in Malaysia that is a reaction to the current socio-political-economic landscape in which the Chinese find themselves.

Renganathan *et al.* (2011) carrried out a literacy project which involved folklore, and which they classified as a project on Education for Sustainable Development (ESD). The objective of ESD is to help the Orang Asli children of Semai tribe in Perak state "develop their attitudes, skills and knowledge to make informed decisions for the benefit of themselves and others, now and in the future, and to act upon these decisions". Each literacy activity was based on a theme so that children can participate at any time even if they have missed the other activities, and each session was started with fun activity such as songs or games. The children were encouraged to read books, including story books, donated by some members of staff of the University of Petronas, which is not far from the Community, and deposited in a literacy corner. They were also encouraged to do small projects of their own choice. It is worth noting that the small projects chosen were folklore. The ten year old boys chose to document a local game, the twelve year old girls preferred to write a recipe on local dishes, the thirteen and fourteen year old ones described in writing a traditional dance called "tarian sewang", while others were interested in the history of the village and interviewed some of the elders in their community. It is also worth mentioning that though the main language of instruction was Malay and literacy materials were in Malay and English language, the children were also encouraged to speak in the language they felt comfortable with, and whenever necessary they were asked to translate to their own Semai language. Renganathan and his colleagues are to be commended for including story books to their literacy corner, and for their conscious effort to bridge the Orang Asli experiences and knowledge with that of the mainstream.

The use of folk Literature in the UNICEF Project

UNICEF (2007) is doing a lot with regard to the Orang Asli childern's education. In addition to using outreach programs and workshops to show the Orang Asli the benefits of early childhood education, it also supports training of teachers and schools' administrators of Orang

Asli children by focusing on "inclusive learning environment, tailoring grading systems and strengthening parenting". The project of using the folktales in the education of Orang Asli school children in Year One to Year Three is a result of a corporation between UNICEF and the Curriculum Development Centre, Ministry of Education (MOE). The objectives of the project are to attract them to attend school, encourage their reading habits, improve their writing skills, while promoting their cultural knowledge. (UNICEF 2007; Argonza 2012) It started in the year 2007 with a workshop in which twenty Orang Asli teachers participated.

The stories were published in two volumes under the title *Koleksi Cerita Rakyat Masyarakat Orang Asli* (Collection of Folktales of Orang Asli Communities) and distributed to ninety four Orang Asli schools in the states of Pahang, Perak, Selangor, Kelantan Johor, Negeri Sembilan and Terengganu with 13,000 children involved in earlier 2010. The cost of the print and distribution of the two volumes was paid by Exxon Mobil in conjunction with the International Literacy Day as UNICEF is not funded by the United Nations organization and depends entirely on voluntary contributions. Teachers from the ninety nine schools were trained in the technique of story-telling such as the use of body gestures, facial expression, mimicking characters' voices. UNICEF is planning to expand the book project by including folktales from the remaining Orang Asli tribes and turning some of the folktales into animation for the children to enjoy while learning about each other cultures.

According to Norhayati Mokhtar (Telephone interview, 15 Jan 2013), the Assistant Director of Ministry of Education, who is also the projector coordinator, initially they hoped to collect stories from each tribe. However, only twelve stories were collected from five Orang Asli tribes—four from Temuan and two each from Mah Meri, Jakun, Semai and Semalai in the states of Pahang, Perak, Selangor, and Negeri Sembilan respectively by primary school teachers.

The project improved the attendance among the students. For example, some of the *Orang Asli* students who form the majority of the 187 students at SK Sungai Bumbun and who do not attend classes for up to a year, have recorded about 80% attendance. The books also encouraged the students to communicate with each other because they discussed the stories after reading them (Nettleten, 2008).

The project was well commended by students, teachers, schools' administrators and an official from the Ministry of Education. For example, Nur Rafiha, a third grade student at the Tasik Cini Primary School, "like[s] the folktales because they are funny, and I get to act, and read and write." (Nettleten, 2008). Teacher Sontey Degu from SK Sungai Juda (A) holds that the story books keep the culture and beliefs of her community alive for the younger generation. Maisita Udang, a teacher of Malaysian language and moral education opines that the story books enliven her classes and increases her students' linguistic proficiency. She uses the books for comprehension and grammar, and story-telling session (Arfah, 2010). The principal of Tasik Cini Primary School, Akit bin Huat thinks that the project really does help because story-telling is a way to entertain the children, and helping them to remember the way of life in their own community and making them interested. Moreover, Norhayati Mokhtar opines that the using of folklore can help the school children "develop pride in their ethnic identity, provide positive role models, develop knowledge about cultural history and build self-esteem" (Argonza, 2012).

UNICEF is to be credited for preserving *Orang Asli* folklore. The folktales published in the two volumes are *Orang Asli folktales*, and would be recognized as such. Unlike other some *Orang Asli* stories, legends and myth, the folktales would be saved from expropriation, from being perceived as Malay stories like the stories about the trickster, the tiny mousedeer, *Sang Kancil* and about the fool *Pak Pandir*, which are now commonly considered as Malay stories. Moreover, the legend of Hang Tuah is now regarded as an all Malay chronicle in spite of the fact that the main protagonist himself Hang Tuah is being recorded in earlier history books as being a member of *Orang Laut* community, the native of Malacca. As such, *Orang Asli* cultural heritage, including their oral traditions, should be protected by UNESCO as cultural property and accorded a rightful esteem. Interestingly, one of the *Orang Asli* tales collected here is a *Sang Kancil story*, which seems to confirm that *Sang Kancil* tales were *Orang Asli* tales (Vol. 1 Story 5, *Tortoise and Sang Kancil*). However, in this story instead of being the usual benevolent trickster that tricks the big and evil animals, this time *Sang Kancil* instead tricks the poor tortoise. But the tortoise has his revenge too by tricking *Sang Kancil* back! The character Pepaner is also actually an *Orang Asli* version of the Malay fool Pak Pandir. According to the teacher (Telephone interview Jan, 2013), who collected this tale, the Semelai are proto Malays, hence the closeness in culture.

It is not our intention to investigate here the extent to which the stories succeeded in inculcating the values mentioned at the end of each story, as that falls beyond the scope of this article. Rather, we would deal with the technique used in the collection of the folktales and the writing of some of them from memory in the Malay language, their illustrations, titles, suitability for children and the values which are supposed to be inculcated into the Orang Asli students. We would argue that though the folktales captured the imagination of the Orang Asli students, who like children all over the world, are story lovers, and thus, improved their attendance in Grade One to Grade Three; their interest in school education and improved attendance would not be sustained in the long term. In our view the dropout rate would continue in the upper grades in future and that due to a number of reasons, the Orang Asli will be lagging behind the rest of the population. We would also argue that the publication of the stories in the Malay language would not develop pride in the ethnic identity.

The teachers were not given any training in the techniques in collecting folklore. This is probably due to ignorance, as no expert in folkloric studies was consulted. This lack of training and experience is evident in the quality of the stories collected. There was only minimum planning before the stories were collected. The teachers did not plan for example what types of story to be collected. Basically, they were asked to collect what they could get. Some of them produced their stories from their childhood memories; others asked their parents or the elderly in their tribes. None of the teachers interviewed (Telephone interview in Jan, 2013) actually "collected" the stories in the folklorist way. All of them collected the stories by using the traditional recording method of pen and paper—a device used by the eighteen century fieldworkers—rather than using the recording equipments. Worse still, they summarized the stories, and some recorded the stories in the Malay language instead of the narrator's language. The points recorded were later elaborated into a full text which was given in turn to an expert in the Malay language to edit. Unfortunately, all the drafts of the stories were destroyed! As such we have not been able to compare them with the final product and detect and comment on the changes made by the expert in the vocabulary and content of the stories.

The writing of some of the stories from memory in Malay language and the translation of others in that language resulted in some omissions that affected the flow of narration. For example, in the story *Why Tapah Eats Keli* 1[1], the story ends suddenly without mentioning what *Tapah* had done to *Keli* at first instance after he found out what *Keri* had done. Instead the story ends immediately with a swear from *Tapah* that he will hunt *Keri* from that day on. In the stories, *Why Lemurs is Thin* and *Pepaner Catch Birds with Glue*, the woman marries the stranger immediately after they met! There are also illogical story lines in these two stories. In *Why Lemurs is thin*, the lemur becomes so hungry after waiting for a few days for the woman to come down from the tree, that he eats part of his own body. That is why lemurs are thin. But what about the woman? Does not she have to eat for a few days? In *Pepaner Catch Birds with Glue*, Pepaner is supposed to be normal human, mistaken to be supernatural. But his new wife (princess) gave birth to a son with white blood! There is nothing in the story to suggest that his new wife is supernatural either. Talking about the wife, the story does not mention what happened to his old wife after the opening of the story, after she taught him how to catch birds with glue. These are probably the result of poor recording and translation. In addition, two stories refer to kings and sultans, which imply that the Orang Asli societies are not stateless. In the story of Sentenah, the kind hearted Sentenah who isgood in cooking ended up marrying the *Raja* (King); replacing the wicked queen. In the story of Pepaner, the Sultan was cheated by Pepaner. However, these are the result of liberal translation into the Malay language, which the translators conveniently translate village or group chiefs into kings (*rajas*) and sultans.

Some of the titles of the stories are arbitrarily chosen. For example, five of the tales are aetiological, explaining a natural phenomenon: why the water of River Bebur is black, why lemur is thin, why *kancil* cannot look up to the clouds, and tortoise's main

---

[1]   *Tapah* and *Keli* are two types of common fish in Malaysia.

food is anthill mushrooms, why *tapah* hunts and eats *Kali* and his descendants, and why spotted dove is seen near houses. The first is titled the legend of Besar River; the second, and the fourth, the titles are in the same question form. The third, Tortoise and *Kancil*; the fifth, *my dayang spotted dove*. This shows that the collectors' or the editors' choice is random. A title derived from the values conveyed by the story would have been better.

The illustrations in the books leave much to be desired. They are amateurish as teachers are used to draw the illustrations rather than professional illustrators. According to Norhayati Mokhtar they did consider using professional illustrators, but in the end they thought using teachers will be more appropriate for education purpose. Worse still, some of the illustrations do not reflect the Orang Asli cultures such as the people's clothing and the houses they live in. One of the teachers who collected one story makes the same observation about the illustrations in the book in the interview.

When telling a story, a narrator usually takes into consideration his/her audience. If the audience is composed of children he/she would choose animal tales for example and not stories suitable for adults. A look at the stories of the two volumes reveals that the story titled *Pepanar* catches birds with glue is clearly not intended for children. In the story *Pepaner's* wife taught him how to catch birds by applying glue to branches, however he applied the glue onto his own body instead and went up the tree. Many birds were glued to his body, and he was carried by the birds and fell on the roof of the palace. The sultan mistook him to be supernatural and married his daughter to *him*. Later, it was found out that *Pepaner* was only normal human. The sultan was very angry and ordered him to be burnt alive! Before, execution he was tied and kept in an empty house. The sultan left for another business, his mother passed by the house and found *Pepaner*. *Pepaner* tricked her into releasing him and let him tie her. The sultan returned and burned the house, and his mother was killed. It is worth mentioning that the editors were more concerned with the two ghost stories, which may be too scary for the children and finally decided to include them because the stories were part and parcel of Orang Asli folklore. The illustrations of these two stories and another two that make reference to ghosts are rather scary. One may question the suitability of using scary tactics in educating young children these days.

However, there are also examples of good and suitable stories in the collection. In *Tatak Ungku's Punishment* the dog save his master despite being ill treated is a very good moral story (type 101). It teaches children loyalty and at the same time being politically correct with the animal rights movement. The Cinderella like story of *Senternah* (type 510A) tells how a happy and kind poor girl end up marrying the king and live happily ever after, is like a standard fairytale.

Mere instruction in morality is not sufficient to inculcate and nurture values in children Values need to be presented to them in an attractive way that stirs their imagination. Stories are an irreplaceable means for doing that. The number of values embodied in each of the twelve stories as assumed by the editors is either three (nine stories) or four (three stories). The important values are thinking or acting cleverly when or before doing something to avoid bad consequences, or solve problems (repeated six times), all actions whether good or bad have consequences (repeated three times), friendship, honouring a promise, honesty, being careful or aware of strangers, kindness to animals (repeated twice), followed by those which are mentioned once. They are trustworthiness, cleanness, perseverance and patience, co-operation, thrift, valuing others' help, holding high values, being thankful for what one has, listening to advice, not to ridicule others, not to enslave others especially children, not to take others' right, not to trick/cheat people, not to be persuaded easily by others, not to delay doing things, not to be lazy, not to waste food, and not to take advantage of others' misfortune. One may ask which of these values are given priority and regarded important by the tribes concerned. There does not appear to be any organization or pattern in the distribution of the values. The easiest and most convenient explanation will be that the stories are not collected systematically and the values are fixed to them later, after whatever has been collected.

The folktales, as we mentioned before, are published in the Malay language, the national language of Malaysia. An Orang Asli teacher from Mah Meri tribe points out that students with poorer skills in the languages do not understand the stories, and she always has to spend time explaining the stories in Mah Meri language in order to sustain their interest and enable them to learn something. One of the present writers, who learned and was educated in the Malay language from primary to secondary school level, finds that the stories recorded are not easy to read. But choosing the Malay language is commended by a mathematics teacher to year three students at SK Sungai Bumbun (A) on Carey Island. According to her, choosing the Malay language was the right decision as "it is the best medium to promote integration among school children . . . [because] all pupils understand it". Choosing the Malay language is in line with the Government's policy to integrate the Orang Asli specifically into the Malay. The term 'integration' is often used interchangeably with 'assimilation'. It is no wonder then that "[T]here is no state-sponsored actions to protect and promote Orang Asli traditions and languages, be it in the education system or in the mainstream government". And the JHEOA's regroupment policy has broken down features of the Orang Asli cultures, which are incomplete with the Malay practices, including their languages, and thus assisted the process of their assimilation.

The policy of assimilation seem to be based on the argument that the Malay are the majority and all are Muslims, that the Orang Asli are ethnically close to the Malay, speak the Malay language, follow Malay customs and rituals, view the external world through the Malay culture, look similar to the Malay and share the same ancestor with them (Kasimin, 1991:268, f.27). The last two characteristics, which refer to the Orang Asli major group known as the Proto-Malay are discredited by Lye Tuck-Po (2001:218) because the label Proto-Malay suggests that "the Orang Asli are incompletely evolved Malays"; it is derived from R.O. Winstedt's dual classification of Malay groups, namely Proto-Malay, that is the first wave of Malays and Deutro-Malays i.e the second wave of Malays. All these characteristics, including the discredited one, do not justify the assimilation of the Orang Asli into the Malay sector of the mainstream society at the expense of their roots, identity, legacy, history, languages and culture. Ali (2010) rightly argues out that the concept of 1 Malaysia, a unifying slogan for all Malaysians, is definitely against the assimilation of indigenous peoples and their languages, and that Islam urges us to tolerate each others' language. Allah says, "O mankind We have created you from male and female, and made you into nations and tribes, that you may know one another . . ." (The Qur'an 49:13). From this he concludes that "[A]ll languages in Malaysia can exist alongside each other, and that there is no need for linguistic assimilation, isolation or hegemony." (Ali, 2010: 10) In other words, the Orang Asli can be integrated with their fellow Malaysians without abandoning their roots. He goes on to suggest ways and means of sustaining minorities' languages and prevent them from falling into oblivion. For example, literates in these languages should write the folk literature which may be translated later to address wider audience. Also anthologies of folktales should be published, and, to encourage publishers to print them, the Government should purchase them for school libraries. The Dewan Bahasa dan Pustaka (The Institute of Language and Literature) should play its part by publishing such anthologies. It is worth mentioning that the author's suggestions concern indigenous languages spoken by a sizable number of people, which may still be saved. The fate of other languages according to him is uncertain or worse doomed to die "since Malaysian language (Bahasa Melayu) is a patent force in uniting the various ethnic groups". The process of assimilation of the Orang Asli then is implemented at the expense of their roots, identity, legacy, history and cultures. As such the folktales would not develop in the students' pride in the ethnic identity as the Assistant Director of the Ministry of Education claims.

Conclusion

Despite weaknesses in the UNICEF project, it is still a laudable one. It at the very least, acknowledges the educational value of Orang Asli folk literature. Some of the problems and weaknesses in the books produced and the quality of the education provided could have been easily and largely enhanced by the involvement of professional folklorists in planning, management, and training in the project.

References

Ali, Haja Mohideen bin Mohamed. 2010. The maintenance of Malaysian's minority languages. <http://www.mymla.org/files/cmm2010_papers/ICMM2010-p.27.pdf> Accessed on 12.6.2012.

Anshar, Asmi. 2009.Orang Asli deserve much better. *New Straits Times* 04.11.2009.

Antonysamy, A. C. 2003. Learning genre, learning about genre, learning through genre: a case study of four young learners reading and writing fables. Unpublished Dissertation for the Degree of M.Ed. University of Malaya, Kuala Lumpur

Arfah, Sharifah. 2010. "Storybook add novelty to school" New Straits Times 21.11.2010.

Argonza, Erle Frayne D. 2012. "Folklore to improve literacy: Oral tradition in Asia" <http://unladtan.wordpress.com/2012/5/24/folklore-to-improve . . . Asian/> Accessed on 12.6.2012.

Bidin, Zainin. 2010. "Dropouts among the Orang Asli (indigenous) school children in Malaysia: Attitude or policy?". A paper presented at the annual meeting of the 54th Annual Conference on the Comparative and International Education Society, Chicago, Illinois, Feb.28, 2010. <http://citation.allacademic.com/meta/p_mlaaparesearch_citation/4/0/0/4/4/p400444_index.html?phepsessid=72365dbt> Accessed on14.6.2012.

Chin, Koh Lay. 2009. I remember when I was caned twice for every error. *New Straits Times*.28.6.2008.

Dass, Francis. 2008. Helping hand for a forgotten people. *New Straits Times* 23.1.2008.

Dentan, Robert Knox.*et al.* 1997. *Malaysia and the "original people": A case study of the impact of development on indigenous peoples.* Boston, Toronto, Sydney, Singapore: Allyn and Bacon.

Hussein, Khalid. 1975. Menggunakan Tradisi Lisan Sebagai Bahan Bacaan BagiMurid-murid Sekolah dan Orang-orang Dewasa (Use of Oral Traditions as Reading Materials for School Children and Adult), in Osman, M.T. (Ed.) Tradisi Lisan Di Malaysia (TRANSLATE), Kuala Lumpur: Belia dan Sukan Kementerian Kebudayaan.

Jabar, Badrul Hizar Ab. 2008. Orang Asli dapatbantu (Orang Asli received aid). *New Straits Times* 22.12. 2008.

Kasimin, Amran. 1991. *Religion and social change among the indigenous people of the Malay peninsula.* Kuala Lumpur: Dewan Bahasa dan Pustaka.

Laoimbang, Adrian. 2009. "Call to do away with development of Orang Asli" Indigenous People's Network of Malaysia. 09.08.2009. Evangeline Majawat. 09 August 2009 Evangeline Majawat.

Laws of Malaysia. 1954. Act, 134. Aboriginal Peoples Act Revised 1974. Kuala Lumpur: Dicetak oleh Pengarah Percetakan dan Diterbitkan Dengan Perinta Pada.

Lim, Hin Fui. 1997. *Orang Asli, forest and development.* Malaysian Forest Records No.43. Kuala Lumpur: Forest Research Institute Malaysia.

Lye, Tuck-Po. 2001. *Orang Asli of Peninsular Malaysia: A comprehensive and annotated bibliography.* CSEAS Research Report Series No.88. Koyoto, Japan: Centre for South-East Asian Studies, Koyoto University.

National Writers' Association. 1966. A Survey of Local Sources for the Productionof Children's Literature in Malaysia. Paper presented at Seminar Kebangsaan Sastera Kanak-kanak Malaysia Umur 11-16 (5-12 Sep 1966: Kuala Lumpur).

Nettleton, Steve. 2008. Using folklore to promote and enhance education for Orang Asli children. <www.unicef.org/malaysia/reallives_8744html> Accessed on 12.6.2012.

Nicholas, Colin. 1997. The Orang Asli of peninsular Malaysia. Kuala Lumpur : Centre for Orang Asli Concerns.

Nicholas, Colin. 2006. The state of the Orang Asli education and its root problems. <http:www.coac.org.my/codenavia/portals/coacv2/images/articles/OA%20education.pdf> Accessed on 14.6.2012.

Nicholas, Colin. 2004. Orang Asli and the Bumiputera policy. In Richard Mason and Amin S.M.Omer (Eds). *The Bumputera policy: Dynamics and dilemmas.* Special Issue of Kajan Malaysia. *Journal of Malaysian Studies.* 21(182), 315-329.

Nicholas, Colin. 2004. Stories of people: Asserting place and preserve via Orang Asli traditions. <http://www/coac.org.my/

codenavia/coacv2/code/main/main art.php?parentID=114002 26426398&artID=115483> Accessed on 24.06.2012.

Ramli, D. 1975. Penggunaan Tradisi Lisan Khasnya Yang Bermusik Untuk TV DanRadio Ddalam Konteks Pembangunan Negara (The Use of Oral Tradition on TV and Radio, Especial Folk Music, in the Context of National Development),in Osman, M.T. (ed.), *Tradisi Lisan Di Malaysia*, Kuala Lumpur: Kementerian Kebudayaan, Belia dan Sukan.

Rebganthan, et. al. 2011. Living literacy :The Orang Asli literacy project" *Arts and Social Sciences Journal* Vol.27. <http:astonjournal.com/assj> Accessed on 14.6.2012.

See, Hoon Peow. 2010. The Use of Folk Literature in Modern Education: The Case of the Chinese Textbook. *Unpublished Dissertation for the Degree of Doctor of Philosophy. International Islamic University, Malaysia, Kuala Lumpur.*

Shadan, Adham. 2006. The spirit of Alang Pendak. *Kosmo* 6.6.2006

Sutlive, Vinson H. 1979. Iban Folk Literature and Socialization: The Fertility of Symbolism, in Becker, A.L. & Yengoyan, A. A. (ed.), *The Imagination of Reality: Essays in Southeast Asian Coherence Systems*, Norwood: ABLEX Publishing Cor.

Toshihiro, Nobute. 2008. *Living on the periphery: development and Islamization among the Orang Asli.* Koyoto, Victoria: Koyto Area Studies on Asia, Centre for South-East Asia Studies, Koyoto University.

The Star. Fewer Orang Asli Dropouts. 2012, 23 May http://thestar.com.my/news/story.asp?file=/2012/5/23/nation/11339037&sec=nation. Accessed on 22.6.2012.

UNICEF. 2007. Permanent Forum on Indigenous Issues, Sixth session Report. <http://www.un.org/esa/socdev/unpfii/documents/6 session unicef.pdf>. Accessed on 22.6.2012.

Yassin, Fatimah Md. 1983. Cerital Rakyat Sebagai Alat Pendidikan: Satu Analisa IsiYang Becorak Etika (Folktale as Educational Instrument: An Ethical Analysis), paper presented at Benkel Pengkajian Tradisi Lisan Bercorak Cerital (3-6 Oct 1983: Kuala Lumpur).

Yusoff, N., Mutalib M.A. and Ali, R.M. 2003. Menyemai Nilai Melentur BudiDalam Tradisi Lisan Kanak-knak (Transmitting Values

Through Children's Oral Tradition), paper presented at Seminar Za'ba Mengenai Alam Melayu (12-14 August 2003).

Zain, A.N. 1975. Penggunaan Tradisi Lisan Dalam Kegiatan Jabatan Penerangan. Dalam Konteks Pemupukan Identiti Kebangsaan (The Use of Oral Tradition in the Activities of the Department of Information, in the Context of Formationof National Identity), in Osman, M.T. (ed.), Tradisi Lisan Di Malaysia, Kuala Lumpur: Kementerian Kebudayaan, Belia dan Sukan.

Women as Defenders of the Earth: Voluntary Restoration Activities with "Our Patch" Group in the Torrens River Catchment

Dr. Nor Azlin Tajuddin

Abstract

Discussions about women and climate change have tended to focus on women's vulnerability, leading to the portrayal of women as victims only rather than in their other capacity as agents of change (Terry 2009). Additionally, there is spatial bias, as many discussions concentrate on women in the global South and rural areas. This paper takes an opposite direction whereby it examines women's contribution towards a more sustainable environment, particularly to efforts aimed at improving water quality, as well as biodiversity of an urban river. Based on an ethnographic study about the Torrens River catchment in South Australia, I explore people's perceptions and responses to river pollution. While my study does not directly deal with the issue of climate change, it is always there in some form. I begin, therefore, with an exploration on how freshwater resources worldwide are projected to be impacted by climate change as reported in selected scientific studies. I then overview a few well-known 'green goddesses' in history, and discuss briefly how they have changed environmental thinking and practice both locally and globally. Finally, drawing from my ethnographic data, I present three stories of women volunteers in the Torrens River catchment highlighting their unique knowledge and expertise in river restoration works in which they are so passionately engaged. I conclude with a brief reflection on how the stories of these women relate to the ICW's pledge and action plans to defend 'the integrity of the planet'.

Contextual background

This paper is based on my PhD research, which was aimed at unpacking the meanings of pollution by comparing people's responses to two urban rivers—the Klang River in Kuala Lumpur, Malaysia, and the Torrens River in Adelaide, South Australia. The research is not explicitly designed to address people's perceptions of, and responses to, the impact of climate change. Nonetheless, both water and climate are intricately and directly linked to one another.

Methodologically, I conducted various periods of fieldwork in Kuala Lumpur and in Adelaide throughout 2006 and 2008. I used traditional ethnographic methods during this time, such as participant observation and in-depth open-ended interviews. However, in this paper I focus solely on the experiences of women participants in Adelaide. My participant-observation activities included walking along the river systems and observing how local women and men made use of the river, the way in which various types of pollutant discharged into the river, as well as the cleaning-up operations. I also participated in various environmental workshops and seminars, and river restoration activities. During my fieldwork in Adelaide, I gradually began to notice that women had played an active role in their capacities as catchment officers or volunteers in protecting the Torrens River catchment.

The Setting

The Torrens River originates in the Mount Lofty Ranges, 55 km north-east of Adelaide, Australia. It flows 85 km from its headwater through a few small towns in the upper reaches, and meanders through Adelaide city centre before it drains into the Gulf of St. Vincent at Henley Beach. The Torrens River drains a total area of 1278 km. Like many other rivers around the world, it has been highly modified to meet human needs, such as dam construction, transportation, flood mitigation control, and other land use practices. Such rampant land use practices combined with population growth put a strain on the catchment's eco-system, thus contributing to the declining river health. In this regards, the Torrens River has been identified as a polluted river in the local official documents as well as popular media.

Water and Climate Change

There is an increasing accumulation of journal articles and reports stating projected impacts of climate change on freshwater resources. The most authoritative publication is by the United Nations Intergovernmental Panel on Climate Change (IPCC), which has allocated a chapter on water resources in its Second (1995), Third (2001), and the latest, Fourth Assessment Reports[1](2007). In 2008, the IPCC released a separate technical Paper on 'Climate change and water'. Similarly, the theme for the 9th International River Symposium in Brisbane, Australia,—'Managing rivers with climate change and expanding populations'—generated hundreds of papers on the subject matter, as well as on other river issues more generally. Taken together these bodies of work signify the critical state of affairs to protect freshwater resources as the climate changes over time.

The IPCC 2008 (Bates et al., p. 4) report suggests that 'the negative impacts of future climate change on freshwater systems are expected to outweigh the benefits'. The bio-physical negative impacts, amongst others, include: 1) increased precipitation intensity and variability, which are, in turn projected to increase risks from floods and droughts; 2) a warmer temperature, leading to higher evaporation rates; 3) a decline in water supplies stored in glaciers and snow cover in the long term; and 4) a rise in sea-level that is projected to extend areas of salinisation of groundwater and rivers' estuaries (Bates et al. 2008, p. 3).

---

[1]   The IPCC Assessment reports were produced by the IPCC Working Group II which assessed the impacts (negative and positive consequences), vulnerability and adaptability of socio-economic and natural systems to climate change.

The climate change impacts on the above hydrological and ecological systems are also projected to have multiple and simultaneous effects. For example, increased temperatures and more intense rainfall are expected to exacerbate existing water pollution problems; such as 'toxic algal blooms are *likely* to appear more frequently and be present for longer due to climate change' (Bates *et al.*, 2008, p. 91). This is significant in the context of Torrens River, as most of my participants in this study, for instance, had mentioned to me the presence of the algal bloom was an important indicator of river pollution. Higher intensity and variability of flood and drought can disrupt the functions and operations of existing water infrastructure, such as hydropower dams, flood mitigation and irrigation systems (Bates et al. 2008, p. 4). Consequently, other effects emerge indirectly—these have profound effects on human well-being as well as to the ecology. The water quantity and quality is affected by a more variable climate, for instance, would affect food availability as well as water supply, outcomes that in turn increase the risks and problem of malnutrition, poor sanitation, and water-borne diseases.

According to IPCC, Australia is already experiencing climate, change causing stresses to both natural and economic systems. All of the eastern states and the south-west region of Australia have moved into drought since 2002 (Bates *et al.*, 2008, p. 90). The drought has caused severe water depletion. Unsurprisingly, water supply has been identified as one of the 'most vulnerable sectors' to the effects of climate change (Bates *et al.*, 2008, p. 90). A recent study conducted by Australia's national science research agency, the CSIRO (Commonwealth Scientific and Industrial Research Organisation), further confirms the inextricable link between climate and water resources. The study assessed the impacts of climate change on the country's 325 river catchments (alongside other threats, such as the conditions of the catchment and population growth). Based on climate change vulnerability, the catchments were classified into 'very low', 'low', 'moderate', 'high' and 'very high'. By contrast with other catchments, the Torrens River is acutely vulnerable to the climate change as it is classified as 'very high' alongside six other catchments in the continent (The Climate Institute 2008; Preston 2008b). Assuming there is non-action to reduce global warming and the greenhouse effect, the CSIRO projected substantial reductions in rainfall patterns in the Torrens catchment—decreased 6 per cent by 2030; and further 16 per cent by 2070 (The Climate Institute, 2008; Preston, 2008a).

The evidence presented here strongly suggests immediate actions need to be taken to protect our freshwater resources that are currently already under pressures due to increasingly competing demands, pollution, and over extraction. Most of the international, regional and local scientific reports are already trying to highlight high-end technical adaptations (such as adopting solar energy, building embankments), as well as economic frameworks such as carbon trading to offset the impact of climate change. However, WWF's work with local governments and communities in six catchments worldwide suggests that better catchment management and simple resource-neutral technologies can substantially improve catchment adaptability to existing water scarcity and pollution, and ultimately climate change. For instance, community catchment participation programs, such as the enactment of river restoration by removing exotic trees, replanting indigenous vegetation and protecting riparian zones from cattle grazing, can have immediate benefits for nature conservation, as well as to improve people's livelihood and well-being (WWF International 1996).

Women as Changed Makers of the Earth

We can find many exemplary women as powerful agents of change for a better and sustainable earth in the modern history of environmental advocacy and movements. I chose three stories of remarkable women, as their stories and struggles provide an insight into inter-connections between land, forest and water. Many would associate the world famous Chipko Movement with its women who formed the backbone of the movement. On 26 March 1974, Gaura Devi and 27 other women of the Reni village captured world-wide attention in their struggle against deforestation of their Himalayan forest (Bandyopadhyay, 1999). Gaura, the head of the village women's organization, successfully led the all-women-action group preventing the cutting of their forest trees by loggers.

Some narrations claimed that they hugged the trees, while others mentioned simply that they stood guard against the loggers. Notwithstanding the variation of stories, the act of the Reni women became a landmark event that further spurred the movement's struggle against deforestation. On the other hand, Vandana Shiva, the author of *Water wars: privatization, pollution, and profit*, highlights the wisdom of these women's struggle against deforestation which is hidden in many discussions about the Chipko movement and its women. In particular, despite her formal academic credential (she holds a PhD in Physics), she attributed her 'big water lesson' to the ordinary rural women of the Himalaya like Gaura Devi. She learnt from those women that 'as you log the forest, you get floods and droughts. Springs dry up. That's where the water crisis comes from' (Clarke, 2002).

Vandana Shiva and Rachel Carson have been listed as among the *Fifty key thinkers on the environment from all over the world*, and from ancient times (such as Buddha and Aristotle) to the present day by a panel of key experts (Palmer, 2001). Vandana Shiva, who has also participated in Chipko movement, is well-noted for her advocacy work against unsustainable environmental practices, as well as social injustice, due to the impact of globalization and economic exploitation. Shiva has received various environmental and humanitarian awards locally and internationally attesting to her significant contribution for the benefit of human society and ecology. Among others, she has founded the Research Foundation for Science, Technology and Ecology and Navdanya, a women-centred environmental movement in India. She has also written hundreds of journal articles and books reporting scientific findings and advocating for better environmental management and practices. As an environmental activist and advocate, scientist, and prolific writer, her expertise has been sought worldwide on various issues, such as water, sustainable agriculture, and climate change. She has also been acknowledged 'for placing women and ecology at the heart of modern development discourse' (The Right Livelihood Award Foundation, 1993, p. 1). Similarly, Rachel Carson, another remarkable woman scientist, challenged the status quo during her time particularly against the American corporate and scientific establishment. While battling against her deadly cancer, Rachel

Carson wrote *Silent Spring*, which sparked a storm of controversy worldwide alerting the public to the hazards of chemical <u>pesticides</u> misusing on the environment. In one of the chapters—*Rivers of Death*, she highlights numerous incidents of how the spraying of DDT on the land destroyed fish populations and other species in the United States and Canada. The book was instrumental in the banning of pesticides such as DDT, spurring the establishment of the Environmental Protection Agency, and the birth of modern environmental movements in the United States (Lytle, 2007).

The work of and biography about these passionate and charismatic women are both inspirational and influential in calling for action, as well as influencing policies and practices related to environmental protection and sustainability. They have certainly inspired me. There are many inspirational women who are less renowned; however, and in the following section I present three remarkable stories about women as caretakers of the Torrens River catchment.

The Unsung Heroines of the Torrens River Catchment

Whilst I have met and worked with many women environmentalists in Malaysia and Australia, the stories of three women volunteers of the 'Our Patch' catchment groups in the Torrens River catchment are the focus here.

Our Patch is one of the South Australian government's action-oriented programs aimed at protecting local environments. It encourages individuals or groups (communities, businesses and schools) to adopt and care for a local patch of the environment, usually a creek or river. Our Patch members are made up of people who volunteer their time, energy, knowledge, expertise, skills, and labour geared towards improving the water quality and restoring biodiversity of the catchment. The main activities, among others include landscaping, particularly along the riverbanks, removing exotic or introduced species, replanting native species, and promoting and delivering environmental education projects.

I am using pseudonyms in presenting the stories of 'Jane' and 'Amber', and 'Karen'. Jane and Amber belong to the Friends of the

St. Peters Billabong Our Patch (FOB) whilst Karen belongs to the Vale Park Our Patch (VPOP) group. These are two neighbouring catchment groups located less than ten kilometers from Adelaide city centre. According to one of the catchment officers whom I have interviewed, these two groups have been active members of the 'Our Patch' program managed by the Adelaide and Mt Lofty Natural Resource Management Board. Within the context of the Our Patch activities, these women embodied a strong sense of care in improving the water quality and biodiversity of the Torrens. Anthropologist Kay Milton has argued that human actions are 'fundamentally emotional; without emotions there is no commitment; no motivation, no action' (2002, p. 150). Deep emotional connections to the Torrens River as well as its flora and fauna, motivated these women to undertake on-the-ground river restoration work within their local councils in close collaboration with their male colleagues and the council's officers. The most striking on-the-ground work shared passionately by these three women was tree planting and weed removing activities. Equally important, each of these women brought in their unique skills and expertise for the betterment of the Our Patch program and consequently contributed to efforts in the catchment restoration.

Jane: The 'Working Bee' Manager

Jane, now in her early sixties, has lived in St Peters since 2000, and explained that she bought her current property because of its location overlooking the billabong[22] She identified herself as a semi-retired academic. Jane spends a week or two in her laboratory in a local university in New South Wales every two months; otherwise, the rest of the time, she works 'in a voluntary capacity looking after the Billabong in St Peters River Park' (Interview: Adelaide, 22/11/07).

Jane made plain her interest in the management and ecological issues of the Billabong: 'I was very interested in how the billabong was managed. [. . .] There were a lot of weeds, and there were obviously

---

[2] Billabong literally means a small lake—a stagnant pool of water attached to a waterway. St Peters Billabong was formed when an old section of the Torrens River was isolated from the main stream in the 1970s, due to problems with bank erosion.

some work that needed to be done'. She was inspired to work towards the restoration and revegetation of the St Peters Billabong 'to a condition that is as near as possible to the pre-European vegetation' as she believed that the pre-European vegetation provide habitat for plant and animal biodiversity. Initially, she volunteered to be one of the council members of the Friends of the St. Peters Billabong in 2002. Soon she realized the need for a more integrated approach and on-the-ground work to restore the Billabong. Together with Tim, a dedicated male member of the group, they initiated the Friends of the Billabong Our Patch group in 2005 under the auspices of the Adelaide and Mt. Lofty Natural Resources Management Board and the City of Norwood, Payneham and St Peters Council. According to Jane, the earlier committee was disbanded and integrated into the Friends of the Billabong Our Patch or also known as FOB, 'so it fulfils the original role of the committee plus an additional role of the on-the-ground work'.

Her years of experience in academic institutions helped her as the current Convener of the FOB in managing the group, usually in cooperation with Tim. They planned for the ongoing restoration and educational activities in regards to the Billabong. She co-ordinated internal group meetings, as well external meeting with the local councils and catchment officers, whereby at times the meetings were conducted in her house. She also continued to develop good rapport with different local stakeholders such as the Our Patch Project Officer, the mayor and environmental officers of the local council, and local green environmental groups. Competing for limited grants is a common task for many non-governmental organizations like FOB. When I was first introduced to her by the FOB Catchment Officer, she was busy at home working with Tim preparing a proposal for a community grant application to be submitted to the local council. Attempting to increase membership of the FOB was also one of her concerns. This was evident as soon as I finished interviewing her during my fieldwork in 2007, as she quickly invited me to be a member of the FOB and asked me to join its 'working bee' days whenever possible.

Indeed, Jane emphasized that an individual becomes a 'friend' by attending a working bee. In this context, the working bee is simply referring to a group of people working together in on-the-ground conservation activities that constitute the core of Our Patch under the supervision of experienced and knowledgeable members. The most frequent tasks are tree planting, watering, and hand weeding, which were suitable for volunteers of all ages. However, these activities depend on the weather and seasonal factors, as well as the Billabong's environmental needs. Generally, hand weeding notorious plants and watering native plants are the main activities in summer. In autumn, the volunteers plant native trees as the cooler weather permits the growth of plants. Heavier tasks, such as cutting and removing harder woody weeds were done by the Council staff.

The regular FOB working bees were generally scheduled from 10am to noon or 2pm to 4pm of the second Sunday of each month. In the week of the upcoming working bee, Jane would send an email to inform members about the event. As a member of the FOB, I continue to receive emails though I have completed my fieldwork. In each email, Jane noted the specific activities in which the members would be involved during the working bee day, simultaneously reminding them of the usual details including, asking them to wear suitable clothes, as well as to bring their own small weeding/digging tool. One of her emails reads (Personal Communication, 9 July 2008):

FOB Our Patch working bee on 13th July

Hi FOB,
Planting day! Sunday 13th July.

Come for any time, at any time between 10am to 1pm, or 2pm to 4pm, or both!!! This weekend is our big chance. Last FOB working bee, the soil was still very dry and, as a group, we did more weeding than planting. Now planting conditions are perfect, although the weather may not be. We have hundreds of tubestock plants. [There are] easy jobs and hard jobs (I promise that those who got the hard jobs last month will be able to do some more satisfying work!). If you wish to straddle the lunch break, please bring a sandwich or a plate of something simple to share, and join us at my place.

See you there,
Jane

Jane regularly sent the monthly inspirational emails motivating the members to sacrifice part of their weekend for the benefit of environment. As the membership of the FOB group is small, she rigorously seeks help from other environmental groups for extensive restoration works. During my fieldwork in 2007, she organized and supervised groups such as Conservation Volunteers Australia, Work for the Dole, and Youth Conservation Corps in the restoration work at the Billabong.

Apart from contributing her leadership skills, Jane is also an efficient and dedicated on-the-ground bee worker. Jane oversees every single detail in all of the FOB activities, starting from setting up the Our Patch signage near the Billabong, to preparing gardening tools and tea breaks. During my first working bee day in the summer of 2007, she explained briefly that I could make use of gardening tools such as hoes, trowels, watering cans, and weedy bags, for planting and removing activities. Jane then passionately and patiently guided me on how to distinguish between native and introduced plants, since they looked pretty similar at first glance. I was reminded to refer back to her or to leave the plant in case I was in doubt whether it was a 'good' or 'bad' one. I was particularly moved to observe her commitment to do the on-the-ground-work, for example, in removing the ground cover weed plants. She held the identified weed close to the soil, and then pulled it out with the roots intact, shook off the soil, and finally put it in the weedy bag. She even tied herself to a rope, to work on the steep slopes of the Billabong. On other occasions, she carefully planted native water plants along the water edges of the Billabong. She explained that the plants can function as water filtration for the incoming pollutants into the Billabong. The Billabong itself served as a wetland purifying the water flows from the Second Creek (one of the Torrens' River tributaries) before the water discharged back into the Torrens through an underground pipeline.

In her own spare time, Jane also frequently worked at the Billabong, since the working bee activities were only a monthly occasion. Indeed, she has immensely contributed her time, energy, and labour for the management of the Our Patch group, as well the restoration of the St Peters Billabong to improve water quality and biodiversity.

Amber: The Local Artist

'Amber' is a 45-year-old local freelance artist. She had a degree in Fine Arts and used to teach Art in secondary school. She has lived in St. Peters town for more than twenty years; her house is about 10 minutes walking distance to the St. Peters Billabong and the Torrens Linear Park. Both Jane and Amber were neighbours. Like Jane, she bought her land due to its proximity to the water courses.

Having a house close to the Torrens increases Amber's opportunity to have a personal, physical connection with the Torrens River. She has walked along the Torrens for the past twenty years. She even used to canoe in the river. However, canoeing 'gradually got phased out' in the section of the Torrens at St. Peters because of the level of pollution. She and other river users were no longer able to engage in recreational activities which exposed them to a direct physical contact with the polluted water. She was perceptive about the changes in the water quality of the Torrens and shared her disappointments:

> There are times when you see the disgusting froth at certain times of the year, I think more in the summer. And there's a lot of green algae that grows on the surface (of the Torrens) certain times of the year, during summer. And it seriously looks disgusting, absolutely disgusting (Interview: Adelaide, 20/11/07).

When I continued to probe about pollution at the Torrens, Amber talked about the need for people to be 'aware of what gets washed into the river and have an understanding of it.' She listed several items of pollutants such as 'the oil from cars', 'sort of industrial stuff', and 'detergents and things like that' that washed into the Torrens. She also declared 'There's a problem with introduced street trees and the leaf litter and that sort of thing from the trees'. For Amber, introduced leaves contribute to river pollution. Hence, she valued indigenous trees more highly than introduced species. She called for more planting of native trees, especially eucalyptus trees to line the streets, in the immediate area of the river banks, as well as the whole catchment area.

Amber has 'walked her talk'. Not only has she proposed the idea of the need to plant 'appropriate native trees', she has also actively been involved with the Billabong restoration project since the establishment of FOB, as Jane had approached her to become a FOB member. She was also inspired by her father, who was one of the founding members of the Conservation Foundation. Indeed, she has volunteered herself tirelessly in efforts to restore the Billabong. In fact, I met her the first time when she was busy weeding alone in the Billabong area. During my fieldwork, she never failed to turn up during the working bee days. I worked together with Amber, mainly doing weeding, as it was a summer season. Like Jane, Amber patiently guided me on how to distinguish introduced and native plants, while she herself pulled the noxious weeds. She shared her passion:

> It's just a natural thing for me to actually get down there [the Billabong area] and help out; it's just so beautiful too to see the vegetation, just the beauty of seeing the whole process of it all being revegetated; it's so wonderful to help out (Interview: Adelaide, 20/11/07).

Amber's distinct contribution to the preservation of native plants and animals was evident in her community environmental artwork at the Billabong. Amber's artwork is a colourful snake mosaic, approximately five metres in length, that was surrounded by two semi-circular carved brick paths. Her own river restoration work on the Billabong inspired her to embark on this artwork project. This was because while doing planting and weeding around the slopes of the Billabong, she frequently found colourful tile pieces, ridges of plates and varieties of tableware pieces. The fragments found were not unusual, as the Billabong (which was once part of the Torrens) was formerly a rubbish dump. Amber also observed that the area near the Billabong was very barren. Though the Our Patch group had gradually planted many native trees around there, she still thought 'that wide area is still very barren, so it's the perfect spot to start with some artwork and then bring the plants around it' (Interview: Adelaide, 20/11/07).

She explained the evolution of ideas of her artwork design through a series of drawings and thinking about 'how to use these recycled materials' found in the billabong. She kept thinking simultaneously about colours and shapes of the recycled materials, the curves of the land, and the meandering line of the river—taken together, she reflected, they resembled the movement of a snake. She also thought 'to have a couple of paths in an interesting way, so the curved paths became a part of it [the artwork], then the snake winding through the path, and gradually the design will evolve' (Fieldnote: Adelaide 20/11/07).

The paths were another highlight of the artwork. There were made of reddish brown bricks; each of the bricks was engraved with a specific message or a motif. One of the engraved bricks read: 'The snake represents the life-giving force of the river'. Another reads: 'This artwork is dedicated to the volunteers of Our Patch whose tireless work is transforming this special place'. More significantly, each of the bricks was engraved with the motif of a native plant or animal found in the Torrens River catchment—a further reflection of Amber's concern for the protection of native flora and fauna. The motif was carved by students from the nearby East Adelaide School. I was touched when I read one of the carved bricks, which said on the top of the brick 'Declam' (the name of the student who carved the brick), then engraved below—'Long neck turtle', and finally a carved turtle motif.

It was a very long process putting all the plans and actions together, which involved various parties in the township to materialize the community artwork. This included: excavating and collecting colourful waste fragments from the Billabong and the adjacent Torrens Linear Park by the year four students and teachers of the East Adelaide School (as well Amber and Jane themselves); preparing and submitting the artwork proposal for funding; contacting and discussing the execution of the artwork with contractors; carving the bricks; and finally putting the snake mosaic and path bricks adjacent to the Billabong.

Nonetheless, it is a rewarding and truly a community project. I can verify this as I observed the proud faces of Amber, Jane and Tim (as FOB members), the mayor and environmental officers of the local council, the students, parents and teachers of the East Adelaide School, as well Our Patch and Natural Resource Board Management officers during the launching of the Billabong's snake mosaic. The snake mosaic is more than a community art project. It is implicitly an environmental education project aiming to promote the protection of the Torrens River, its surrounding environment and its biodiversity, as well as to promote a sense of belonging and a sense community among its inhabitants. Indeed, emotionally motivated to become practically and creatively engaged, Amber has fully used her talents and creativity for the benefit of her community and ecology.

Karen: The Native Trees Planter

Karen, in her mid-forties, holds a degree in Botany and Zoology from the University of Adelaide. Amber suggested Karen become one of my interviewees, as she was a 'key person' in the revegetation work at Vale Park. Amber was right, as I discovered that Karen was responsible for the establishment of the Vale Park Our Patch (VPOP) group in 2000. Once I finished interviewing Karen, I wrote in my fieldnote book—'a dedicated Our Patch volunteer', 'energetic' and 'passionate with native plants'. This was evident when I called her to set the date for the appointment; she excitedly suggested that the interview should be conducted at her revegetation site, as it is next to the Torrens Linear Park. Once I reached the site, I could immediately detect that the section of the Torrens at the Vale Park area was among the most densely vegetated, especially along its water edges, by contrast with most of the suburbs I had visited in the middle and downstream sections of the river.

Karen indicated that the two most significant restoration works conducted at the Vale Park patch were to revegetate native plants and 'to catch leave litter polluting the river'. Hence, the interview was mainly focused on the sharing of her existing and future revegetation works, as well as her knowledge of different varieties of plants species in the Adelaide region. Karen valued native plants for their biodiversity (biological diversity) and aesthetic values. This was evident in her enthusiastic sharing of her revegetation work:

> I'm trying to make a grassy land here [adjacent to the Torrens Linear Park]. I'm going to call it wildflower fields. I'm trying to plant [them] here. We got lots of lovely things. In spring it looks gorgeous. We have native grasses, lilies, and orchids. I want to improve the biodiversity, so . . . more little plants—all the tiny little plants underneath the big trees. They attract a lot of biodiversity—all the butterflies and insects—more plants more, more food. And you get the whole change is going—more plants provide more shelter for the birds (Interview: Adelaide, 18-02-08).

She identified 35 bird species along the Vale Park area, most of which were indigenous to the area. She proudly listed 'quite a range of birds', including red tails, honey bees, pipe cormorants, parrots, and kookaburras. Big trees, such as gum trees, provided 'little heavens' for the birds, as they nested in the hollows of tree branches or trunks. Subsequently, she pointed out that 'the river has its own ecology and the river bank has its own ecology'.

Kren made an explicit connection between pollution and the presence of introduced plants. She vocally declaimed:

> We also picked up leaf litters. In [a] lot of cases native leaf doesn't produce like the European poplar leaf, which is all right in northern Europe. Over there the water is very cold; here, the water is warm. So the leaves break down quickly. So we have a huge load of leaves that drop into the river, soft leaves that drop into the river; and they cause pollution downstream. They rob the water of oxygen and we tend to get blue green algae (Interview: Adelaide, 18-02-08).

Evidently, the leaves of this introduced plant were considered undesirable in the riparian zones, as they contributed significantly to the pollution problem of the Torrens. She continued to give a lengthy scientific explanation on how the introduced plants cause harm to the ecology of the river. Karen and the VOP members then spent their energy and time to pick up leaf litter as part of the effort to improve the river's water quality.

Extensive time and energy in restoring and improving the Torrens River heightened Karen's knowledge of her locality and native plants. More importantly, she willingly shared her knowledge with her community. Shortly after an hour of the interview had elapsed, she invited me to walk along with her around the dried riverbed of the Torrens River at Vale Park. Like a park tour guide, she gave explanations of the various native grasses and trees they have planted along the edges, as well as in the dried riverbed. I noted informative colourful labels including notes on known Aboriginal uses, she attached to some of the native plants that grew along the river. She also initiated a public art work of wooden poles erected near the riverbank inspired by Aboriginal arts and symbols displaying the water and wildlife environment.

Karen's practical and ongoing contributions to assist the improvement, restoration and sustainability of the Torrens River did not go unnoticed by her local council, as she was nominated for a prestigious United Nations of Australia World Environment Day Awards (individual category). She was eventually selected as one of three finalists nationwide, but did not win the award. Nevertheless, the Walkerville Council, her nominator, was 'extremely proud of her outstanding achievement'. The council provided a lengthy list of her contributions in its submission for the award. Amongst others, Karen has been involved in the removal of approx. 30,000 litres of weeds and rubbish from the river, has supervised the planting of more than 12,000 native plants along the river, has also helped plant a further 1,200 locally native plants in special educational gardens (outdoor classrooms) around Vale Park Primary School, and has voluntarily taught numerous classes at schools and has been guest speaker on various topics in relation to plants and environmental issues. She has also researched and designed extensive biodiversity resources (such as a DVD and Plant and Wildlife Manual Sheets) for the use of schools, Our Patch groups and local councils, and shared her expertise on revegetation projects with the other Our Patch groups along the river at Gilberton, Walkerville, Windsor Gardens and St. Peters (The Corporation of the Town of Walkerville 2006, p. 9).

I was moved when I learnt from Amber that Karen had been in hospital after a long battle with an illness and, as a consequence, might not be able to participate in an interview session. Nonetheless, she agreed to meet me and spent approximately three hours discussing various environmental issues, later walking along the Torrens River. Indeed, her botanical knowledge, courage, determination and passion are an asset to her community, evident in her emotional ties to the river reinforced by practical, on the ground activities.

Conclusion

The ICW's toolkit on climate change states that climate change begins locally, thus, the process of adaptation must start in the local community. The toolkit also suggests action plans to reduce the effects of climate change, among others, women need to 'plant more trees' and 'set up tree planting projects' (ICW, p 3.) In this paper I have discussed how local women have responded to the environmental issues that affect the Torrens River catchment via their involvement in a catchment group. These ordinary but outstandingly visionary women have a different set of skills and knowledge, but share striking similarities in their dedication to Our Patch tree planting projects and their caring for the Torrens River catchment. Each one of these women has assumed a leading role in her community, reinforcing messages about sustainability, biodiversity, and the protection of flora and fauna. Implicitly, these women also have built a strong network among themselves, as well as a partnership with men and local authorities, to achieve a more sustainable environment. They have clearly prepared plans to defend themselves against the projected vulnerability to climate change.

A further reflection on what it means to act locally reveals that being the queen of our domestic spaces allows us to care for the environment in our own comfort zones. Practices that contribute to conservationist practices relating to the use and management of water, and interdependent resources, are often rooted in traditional, local, indigenous practices, and customs. I believe these beliefs and practices should be encouraged. My mother is my role model. For instance, I have observed my mother for several decades religiously keeping the water that she used to wash the rice, and then pour the water onto the plants she grows. She simply says, "It's a *petua* (a Malay word for traditional tip) for the plants to grow healthier and quicker". I gradually learn to interpret it as a smart practice of water conservation. Indeed, we can all become heroines—either well known or famous like Gaura, Rachel and Vandana or the unknown ones like Jane, Amber and Karen to facilitate change for a more sustainable Earth.

References

Bandyopadhyay, J 1999, 'Chipko movement: Of floated myth and flouted realities', *Economic and Political Weekly*, vol. 34, no. 15, pp. 880-882.

Bates, B, Kundzewicz, ZW, Wu, S & Palutikof, J (eds) 2008, *Climate change and water: Technical paper of the Intergovernmental Panel on Climate Change*, Geneva.

Clarke, NP, *Interview with Vandana Shiva: Discussing "Water Wars"*. Available from: http://www.inmotionmagazine.com/global/vshiva3.html [2 September 2010].

International Council of Women (ICW), *Women defending the integrity of the planet: Toolkit of resources for community education to reduce the effects of Climate Change*. Available from July 2010]

Lytle, MH 2007, *The gentle subversive: Rachel Carson, Silent Spring, and the rise of the environmental movement*, Oxford University Press, Oxford.

Milton, K 2002, *Loving nature: Towards ecology of emotion*, Routledge, London.

Palmer, JA 2001, *Fifty key thinkers on the environment*, Routledge, London.

Preston, J 2008a, 'Evaluating sources of uncertainty in Australian runoff projections', *Advances in Water Resources*, vol. 31, pp. 758-775.

Preston, J 2008b, 'Screening climatic and non-climatic risks to Australian catchments', *Geographical Research*, vol. 46, no. 3, pp. 258-274.

Terry, G 2009, 'Introduction', in *Climate change and gender justice*, ed. G Terry, Practical Action Publishing in association with Oxfam GB, Bourton, pp. 1-10.

The Climate Institute, *Climate change and water*. Available from: http://www.climateinstitute.org.au/images/climatechangeandwater.pdf [2 September 2010].

The Corporation of the Town of Walkerville 2006, 'Our Community', *Walkerville News*, p. 9.

The Right Livelihood Award Foundation, *Vandana Shiva*. Available from: http://www.rightlivelihood.org/v-shiva.pdf [2 September 2010].

Liminality and Menopause: The Urban Malay Women's Perspective

Dr. Nurazzura Mohamad Diah

Abstract

This paper discusses the menopause experience of urban Malay working women in Kuala Lumpur. It attempts to bring to the fore the importance of liminality as a concept which has rarely been used to help explain menopausal experiences among women. The notion of liminality sheds some lights on how modern urban working Malay women accommodate and adapt themselves to an environment which is seen as imposing some threats and/or danger to their well-being compared to the rural women. In this study, loosing youthful looks and vitality and losing the ability to reproduce, both of which are connected, have the potential to create discomfort, and can be seen as an assault to self-identity. This study employs participation observation and in-depth interviews with a sample of thirty women aged 48-55. They are formally educated and work in professional paid jobs. Data analysis was performed using the qualitative process. This study shows that menopause is a problematic and chaotic life stage for most urban working Malay women. Their dual obligations to both family and work complicate their experience, particularly if they have typical menopausal symptoms such as 'hot flushes' and fatigue. Pressures from work as well as the desire to portray a youthful and attractive appearance, contribute to their acceptance of biomedical interventions particularly in the form of Hormone Replacement

Therapy (HRT). In general, the experience of liminality throughout the time of menopause while still working has led urban Malay women to seek help from the medical professionals to create a new sense of order in their lives.

Introduction

Malaysia has created a remarkable history in its development. From being a small nation well-known with its tin-mining and rubber industry, today Malaysia has embarked into an industrialized nation. Industrialization in Malaysia has tremendous impact on women. This repercussion is also seen elsewhere around the world. Rural-urban migration is rampant in Malaysia where women were exposed to modern lifestyle. More importantly, educational opportunities have changed women's position in the society. Due to 'the revolution of rising expectations' (Ariffin, 2000:37) among educated women, more women has join the paid work force and consequently has altered their traditional roles. Like other women around the world, women in Malaysia have two roles. They are wife and mother at home and employees outside the home. In attempting to discharge each of the two roles and to bring together the contradictions inherent in them, women encounter various challenges.

Despite Malaysia a small nation that moving forward in its economic endeavour and despite women are required to actively participate in the nation, they are facing with difficulties of trying to co-ordinate and balance home-life with work. The strain of having to cope with traditional wifely duty and paid work plus managing their health in their middle-age leads to life discordance. Today, Malay society has changed and specifically Malay women themselves. They have lived and experienced variety of living circumstances that requires them to be active and productive in the private and public realm. Their lives are filled with various challenges and pressures like managing the household, being a productive employer and at the same time managing their own health. These triple burdens to some extent have created uncomfortable condition like fatigue, depress and stress. In addition to their uncomfortable situations, their menopause experience is becoming difficult today as compared to the experiences of their own mothers due to the fact that Malay women today are actively participating in an income generating job, plus managing their roles as mothers/wives and employees.

This study however argues that menopause is not at all an easy transition life stage for urban Malay women. They have great concern about their declining physical appearances, sexual attractiveness and productivity; menopause is seen as a threat to their work performance, self-worth and general well-being.

Cross-Cultural Studies on Menopause in Asia

Menopause is a subject which gains relatively little attention in anthropology (Agee, 2000; Beyenne, 1986; Kaufert, 1982). The rareness of anthropological research on menopause is best explained through the relative importance placed of menstruation and pregnancy as significant events in the life cycle of a woman as compared to menopause. Menstruation and pregnancy are positive signs of womanhood and reproductivity compared to menopause. The onset of menstruation in many societies marks the reproductive ability and maturation of a woman, whereas menopause is often seen as a symbol of decrepitude and decay (Posner, 1979). Since menstruation is a physical transition associated with being a woman, it is discussed among women more openly than is the case with menopause. In the anthropological literature on menopause, there has been a general agreement that social and cultural factors have strongly shaped women's menopausal experience (Lock, 1994; Chirawatkul & Manderson, 1994; Rice, 1996). Menopause is a process of ageing that comes with emotional, psychological and physiological changes similar to menstruation and pregnancy (Daniluk, 1998). These events are associated with hormonal and bodily changes coupled with a range of emotional and psychological factors that vary across cultures.

In general, there have been relatively few anthropological studies on menopause conducted in Asia. The existing literature shows heterogeneous data on menopause due to geographical location, health care systems and women's conditions (Punyahotra & Limpaphayom, 1996; Boulet et al., 1994). One of the earliest and most famous anthropological studies about menopause in Asia was by Flint (1975) who studied women in Rajput, India. Flint studied menopause and status change at mid-life. She found that menopause marked the end of *purdah* (veil and social isolation) and that women were given the freedom to participate in activities previously denied to them. Flint explained that women of Rajput considered menopause as a reward that entitled them to greater freedom. In reality, she noted, Rajput women hardly had any menopausal symptoms. By contrast, it has been shown that Western women who suffer from role loss and empty-nest syndrome regard menopause as a punishment. Two studies by Beyenne (1986) and Rice (1996) record similar findings. Nonetheless, Sharma and Saxena (1981) who studied Indian women in Varanasi City, India found that 61 percent of women were having hot flushes, 58 percent had night sweats and 67 percent complained of insomnia. This finding disagrees with the statement above by Flint, that women of Rajput are barely affected by the symptoms. The high percentage of Varanasi women inflicted by hot flushes is similar to most Western women who are disturbed by menopausal symptoms.

Like Flint, Chirawatkul and Manderson (1994) found similar results with Thai women who did not regard menopause as an upsetting event. Culturally, Thai women were highly valued and they regarded menopause as a biological event associated with ageing. Nevertheless, the researchers indicated that this perception has gradually changed among some modern Thai women. These women experienced menopause negatively and thus they resorted to medical treatment. One of the reasons offered was that the women were confident with biomedical treatments which they saw as controlling infectious diseases. In addition, since pregnancy and childbirth were under the surveillance of medical treatment, this was viewed as appropriate for other women's health treatments as well. Although modern women seek medical treatment, Chirawatkul and Manderson found there were no available studies specifically on HRT among Thai women.

A study among Hmong women who migrated to Melbourne, Australia, by Rice (1996) has also associated menopause with ageing. In Rice's study, Hmong women welcomed menopause and perceived it as a positive event with few symptoms. Rice reported that Hmong women who lived in Melbourne experienced a process of cultural adaptation to the Western society. However, she had not, at that time, explored the possibility of younger generation Hmong women adopting different attitudes towards menopause as a result of exposure to Western ideas.

Lock's (1993) well known study focused on Japanese and North American women. She explored the divergent sociocultural factors of ageing women which range from the physiological changes and cultural understanding of menopause. She found Japanese women reported fewer menopausal symptoms compared to Western women. Lock's interesting findings outline a number of contributing factors that influence menopausal experience like women's social status, gender roles, personality, life history and state of health. All of these have an effect that, in part, determines their menopausal experiences and position in the society. In comparison with Kauferts's (1985) study on women in Manitoba, Lock found Japanese women reported low menopausal symptoms.

Study Design

The choice of studying urban Malay women as the research participants did not stem from pragmatic deliberations alone. Urban Malay women have experienced tremendous social and cultural change, over the past twenty to thirty years, and it struck the researcher as something that would not only be interesting to study but also something not sufficiently researched before. In addition, it would be more appealing being an insider despite the unique challenges confronted by anthropologists who work within their own cultures. Using qualitative approach, this study investigates how urban working Malay women accommodate and adapt themselves to a new life stage. In-depth interviews and participant observation helped to unravel the complexity of this topic, which in Malay society is considered private and sensitive and dealt with in silence.

A sample of thirty women aged 48-55 participated in this study. They are formally educated and work in professional paid jobs. All of them are in their menopausal stage. They all worked outside their own homes in either the public or private sector as managers and administrators. The women were all in a relatively high socio-economic group, having obtained either a diploma or bachelor's degree mostly from local universities. Most women had between one to five children with three of the women having had six children. Thirteen women were grandmothers. Many had children who were married, but the majority of their children were still studying either in a secondary school or university.

Interviews were conducted in an environment where the participants were most comfortable, where it was easily accessible for the women and where they were able to respond freely. Some women chose to be interviewed in their homes and others in the menopause clinic. Other interviews took place in beauty salons, hospitals, community halls and business premises. Interviews were conducted in a conversational way, using open-ended questions. The interviews were conducted in English or the Malay language, depending on the respondent's preference. However, the interviews conducted in Malay language were then translated into English. Interview transcripts were analyzed through the qualitative process. Pseudonyms were used throughout to protect the privacy of the women who participated. Permission to quote from the women was granted to the researcher.

The Rites of Passage

This article begins with a brief discussion about Arnold van Gennep's anthropological work *The Rites of Passage* (1960) which has contributed to my thinking around Malay women's transition through menopause. van Gennep's work provides a theoretical framework which can be applied to the life stage (or lifecycle), thus allowing an understanding of how women undergo a process which sees them separating from one stage of their life, transitioning to the next and will later see them being incorporated into a final stage (old age). While moving from one phase to the other involves changes in roles and status, it is during the transition (liminal phase) that women in my study are living, in what might be termed a 'limbo'. Needless to say, the majority of the women in my study have negotiated this liminal phase by turning to methods (particularly in the form of Hormone

Replacement Therapy) that helped them retain aspects of their youthful and healthy selves.

van Gennep has provided a model to analyze life crises according to certain recurring patterns. The central idea of van Gennep's work is to identify the *process* of acquiring a new status that is the movement from one status to the other. He is not focusing on the nature of the position (being a wife, mother or grandmother) or role in society (Draper, 2003). He found that the process involves three stages: *rites of separation, transition rites* and *rites of incorporation* all of which transform social identity. During *rites of separation,* a person is detaching his or her former status into a new one. For example, marriage which is a common rite of passage in every society is religiously sanctioned and performed to achieve the distinction between the world of staying single and moving into the realm of becoming a family person. Menopause may well be a transition that people would rather not acknowledge; in some circumstances it may not rate as important enough to warrant attention, particularly as it involves a transition in older women from reproductivity to being unable to reproduce. Ironically, while older urban Malay women may no longer be able to reproduce they are still extremely productive members of society.

In the *transition rites,* van Gennep described this stage as one in which a person may have been detached from the old status, however not yet attached to the new status. Draper (2003) described this stage as one in which the individual occupies a non-status, a kind of no-man's land seen as potentially harmful. The stage is seen as being *betwixt and between* the former status and an uncertain future. Transitional rites are puzzling periods. Allan (2007) uses the concept to explore the liminal period in her study which focuses on the experiences of infertile women in a British fertility clinic. The women in her study found they were living *betwixt and between* as there was no certainty as to whether they would become pregnant and there was a high risk they may fail to conceive. In some societies, often during the liminal stage, the human body is itself the object of ritual process. A young person, for example, may be required to undergo procedures like circumcision among the males (Bloch, 1986) or scarification (K. L. Little, 1951). The healed wounds permanently signify the status change from boyhood to manhood. Having completed the initiation rites, a person can now move into the next stage—incorporation. The last stage, *incorporation* is when the passage from one status to another is perfected. This phase involves the reintegration of the transformed individual into the social group to which the person previously belonged. The individual is once again in a stable stage and is expected to comply with the customary rules that bind the new status.

Rites of Passage of Urban Malay Women

Arnold van Gennep's three stages of passage is important to describe the lives of urban Malay women. The model below developed by the researcher gives a simplified overview. It would appear that Malay women undergo separation, transition and incorporation at two major junctures of their lives. First at menarche, the first menstrual bleeding, which typically is the time when a girl leaves childhood and enters adulthood; second, when a woman stops menstruating and she moves, less obviously from middle-age to old age. In reality, both of these transitions do not happen overnight and there is a period of transition.

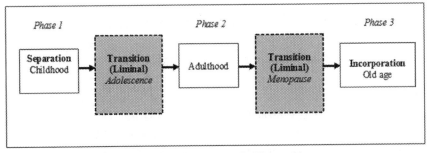

Figure 5.1 Three stages of a Malay woman's life transition

In the case of adolescence, during phase one, *separation*, we see the end of the urban Malay female's period of childhood. Here they begin the transition into the adult world. In general, their socialisation begins through imitating their mothers. During their childhood the Malay girls are taught feminine tasks like cooking, washing, looking after the younger siblings and cleaning the house. In addition, Malay girls are also taught to behave softly and politely (Omar, 1994). When Malay girls reached puberty and become adolescent, they are trained to be a 'proper Malay woman' (Omar, 1994: 28). There are three things that are emphasized in order to become a proper Malay woman: learning household tasks; refining appropriate female behavior; and the inculcation of *adat* (customary law) and religious belief. The *incorporation* phase clearly marks the transition to a confirmed status—following adolescence this is adulthood and following menopause this is old age. The new status brings new identity either as an adult woman or as an old woman (a grandmother and an infertile woman). In most Asian countries, grandmothers deserve and expect respect from their children and grandchildren; they are also regarded as wise and experienced persons (Bart, 1969; Omar, 1995; Rice, 1996). Old age is regarded as a phase when old woman are free from their many daily responsibilities and the woman turns herself into a consultant on all matters, particularly women's health and childrearing practices.

Menopause and the Liminal Life of Urban Malay Women

Although van Gennep highlighted the idea of liminality, it was anthropologist Victor Turner (1974) who was most interested in the liminal phase to explain ritual and performance. Liminality is defined as a stage in the transition when an individual moves from one status to the other, but is not fully secure in the other status (Draper, 2003; MacNeil, 1997). Turner (1974: 231-232) wrote:

> . . . margin (or *limen*—the Latin for threshold, signifying the great importance of real or symbolic thresholds at the middle period of the rites, though *cunicular*, "being in a tunnel", would better describe the quality of this phase in many cases, its hidden nature, its sometimes mysterious darkness).

This concept is useful to clarify the condition of my participants who are caught in between—on one hand there is the desire to look young, beautiful and sexually attractive as they used to, but at the same time their bodies are no longer as they were in youth. Liminality has also been used to explore other social contexts, for instance in the area of health and illness. Liminality has been applied to help explain the condition of sick people, particularly those suffering from chronic or serious illnesses like cancer (M. Little, Jordens, Paul, Montgomery, & Philipson, 1998; Luxford, 2003), disabled people (Murphy, Scheer, Murphy, & Mack, 1988), schizophrenia (Barett, 1988), stroke (Becker, 1993) and infertility (Allan, 2007). In the study of advanced prostate cancer among fifteen men in Israel, Navon and Morag (2004: 2345) found that men who had undergone hormonal treatment reported themselves as 'neither or nor beings'. The men also indicated that they were neither ill nor fully recovered. They felt living in betwixt and between. Similarly Luxford (2003) who investigated the experience of older women with breast cancer in Australia reported that liminality occurs when women were uncertain as to whether they had benign breast disease or not. They were uncertain about whether their health status was 'healthy' or 'sick'. Luxford argued that the liminal experience of her participants has created a sense of uneasiness between the women and their bodies. In other words, the previously predictable and familiar relationship between the women's selves and their bodies has been disrupted.

Douglas (1966) wrote that during the liminal period, a person has no place or status in society—temporarily there is no *sense of belonging*. She argues that the individual between statuses is ambiguous, and it is this ambiguity during the liminal phase that is susceptible to potential danger:

> Danger lies in transitional states, simply because transition is neither one state nor the next, it is undefinable. The person who must pass from one to another is himself in danger and emanates danger to others. The danger is controlled by ritual, which precisely separates him from his old status, segregates him for a time and then publicly declares his entry to his new status. Not only is transition itself dangerous, but also the rituals of segregation are the most dangerous phase of the rites (Douglas, 1966: 97).

Bloch and Parry (1982) have characterized the liminal phase as disorder, chaos and pollution which turn the social order upside down; the danger also means the matter is out of place (Douglas, 1966). People who are living in a liminal state are regarded as living 'outside' the normal boundary because 'they have been declassified but are not yet classified: they have died in their old status and are not yet reborn in a new one' (Murphy *et al.*, 1988: 237). Thus, interacting with them is seen as problematic or/and unpredictable. This was evident in some of the stories told by the children of women undergoing menopause:

> I guess my mother has entered another world. A world of tiredness and inefficiency. Just like my late grandmother who had entered the same world. Previously my mother was very active and energetic. She cooked and cleaned very fast. She participated in women's activities in the neighbourhood. Now she seems very tired, rarely wants to go shopping or travelling and she is forgetful. She prefers to stay at home or to visit her grandchildren who live nearby. Lately my mother is becoming very sensitive. We have to be very careful of what we say or do at home. I try to minimize speaking to my mother. I fear my words will hurt her even though I didn't mean it—(Azman, 29 years old).

> I don't understand why lately my mother is grumpy. I noticed she has a fluctuating mood. Sometimes she's OK, she's nice to us. Sometimes she's not stable, always pissed off. We are all the prime target of her anger. My father advised us not to argue with our mother as it will make her more 'unstable'. I guess the older you grow, it's like that— (Kamal, 26 years old).

The children were clearly confused about what was going on and why their mothers acted outside the realms of their normal behaviour. Since the Malay culture (and other cultures as well) do not embrace menopause as a rite of passage, women's productivity has been suppressed. Reproductivity has come to an end and there is no cause for celebration. Although men may not live as long as women, they are still seen as sexually active and productive as they age, at least throughout their fifties and sixties. In other words the ageing process is not as detrimental for them. Women who live longer are the opposite—supposedly asexual and weak (Wolf, 1991). The stories of Sharifah and Balkis I presented below are indicative of the kinds of chaotic lives that may be experienced in the menopausal stage. Sharifah aged 51, a hairdresser and a part-time beauty instructor in a private college suffered particularly from hot flushes which came on frequently while she was at work:

> I cannot tolerate hot flushes. One day when I was trimming my customer's hair, my hot flushes came. The heat came from my tummy and *zupp* goes straight to my brain. It was so very hot that I felt my brain was burning! I can't think. It really upsets me! I cannot work. It is hot inside me! I took a deep breath and pretend nothing happened in front of my customer. I can't. Another day, I accidentally cut my fingers. It was too hot! Every time I had this hot flush, I stop doing my work because the heat is intolerable. This situation happens several times. Every time it occurs, I apologised to my customers. I would rest for five minutes until the heat subsides. Then, I continued my work. There are also times when I can't do my work at all. I have to ask my assistant to help with my work. Similar situations also happen while I am lecturing my students in the college. Since most of my students are between 20-30 years of age, many express their concerns about my condition. I didn't tell them it was hot flushes. I told them I'm not well. Sometimes I have to dismiss the class early or I will postpone the class if my condition is worse. I felt weak and tired. I have to manage my business, giving lectures, taking care of the family as well as managing my body. It's too much. I hate giving excuses and apologising to people because of my condition. Not once, but many times! I felt my body has worn out *lah*!

In a similar vein, Balkis 54, an income tax officer told me that she easily got tired and sometimes snapped for small reasons, both at home and in the workplace. She told me how her children and her co-workers were the targets of her fluctuating moods. She scolded her children for not helping her in the kitchen, for not keeping the house tidy and for not appreciating her. In the office for example, Balkis once snapped at co-workers who stared at her. Some co-workers who talked loudly even made her feel irritated. As a result her younger co-workers minimized their communication with her. She became furious when a co-worker labeled her as a *kondem* (a colloquial expression which means useless) woman. Balkis was seen as less productive and less professional in her work. She took longer time to prepare paper work, was unable to meet deadlines, and once in a while she misplaced important documents. Balkis felt that her co-workers felt negatively towards her and other colleagues who were also menopausal.

According to Balkis they were seen to be not as efficient as the more youthful members of staff. Balkis also felt that both her children and co-workers were scrutinizing her appearance. This made her feel self-conscious and she decided to change her old style and try to be more fashionable in order to keep up appearances in the office. Azaliah aged 50 told me:

> I have a bad crying spell. Sometimes for no reason, I feel sad and started to cry. I'm confused. This usually happens at home or in my office. When I cried at home, I lock myself in my room and spend at least 15 minutes crying. In my office, I usually go to the *surau* (praying room) and cry. One day, my husband said, 'Look at you. Just like our youngest daughter, a cry-baby in your fifties'. I was not like this before. Some friends said sensitive is part of being old. I'm not old yet!

The 'danger' that is triggered by menopause for the individual presents predominantly as a threat to mental health and well-being. This form of danger is also clearly illustrated from two other studies. One study focuses on suicide among the Gisu women of Uganda.

Here we see an example of an ultimate 'danger' with women feeling so worthless at this stage of life that they take their own lives. La Fontaine (1960) discovered that the suicidal rate among Gisu women increased when they reached the end of childbearing years. Woman's position in Gisu society clearly depended on their ability to fulfill maternal roles. A woman in that society is an asset to the community only while she is capable of reproducing. However, when women stop reproducing, they are regarded as a liability to the community and subjected to rejection by both husbands and families.

Correspondingly, menopausal experience has entailed personal, physical and emotional changes among Italian-Australian working class women studied by Gifford (1994). The women in Gifford's study described menopause as a time of vulnerability, fear and insecurity. The women were depressed, sad and nervous and this was linked to the stress associated with becoming an 'old' woman. Retirement meant women had to leave their jobs and this event meant they were isolated from their co-workers and friends. The role as an 'old' woman that they were expected to undertake in Italy was not possible in Australia because their children lived far away and they were no longer consulted about childrearing practices. They also encountered difficulties when their adult children left home, gained employment or got married.

What makes menopause impose a kind of 'danger' to women's well-being though? In the previous examples we see a threat to the integrity of the self and this has been evident in the stories recounted in this article by the women themselves. The topic of menopause is surrounded by taboo and secrecy (Agee, 2000; Im & Meleis, 2000). Sheehy (1998) called menopause a 'silent passage'. I believe it is a passage of ignorance. Some of the participants in my study had no idea what was really happening to them. They were not aware of the symptoms which had been with them for many years and some wondered what all the fuss was about with menopause. The symptoms of menopause were considered a part of 'women's lot in life'—a woman must accept the so called 'deficiencies' of her female body. In this context for a woman to claim special status would be to threaten the integrity of men's privileged position in society. The freedom of not having the possibility of having to reproduce may potentially allow a woman to take a more prominent position in society.

In the context of Malay society for example, although menopause has never been associated directly as an issue that contributes to divorce rate, it may be associated with changing relationships between men and women. Women may no longer be interested in sex; they may focus more on their children and on being a grandmother. One suggestion may be that this might lead husbands to find other ways (particularly marrying younger woman) to fulfill their needs. This sentiment has also been expressed by the women in my study. The story of Sharifah earlier gives a picture of how bodily changes may affect a husband's expectation of a woman's sexual activity. Although none of my participants talked about their husbands' intention of marrying younger women because of their condition, some of them did say that their husbands once in a while jokingly said they wanted to marry another woman. Nevertheless, most of them did express the fear of their husbands marrying someone else. Maisarah said:

> When I reached this age now, if I don't do anything or deal with my menopause symptoms, my heart sometimes says 'What if my husband finds another one [wife]?' I've heard . . . stories from friends at the office, on TV, magazines and newspapers this thing can happen to a woman like me, at this age. Because my husband is a building contractor, he always goes to the site and there are many young Indonesian girls there working. When I think about this, *takut jugak*! (I'm scared too).

Like Maisarah, Rozana warned me:

> Better do something before it is too late! I want my marriage to last long like my own parents. *Takut jugak kalau suami lari* (I'm afraid too if my husband run away) because of me!

Both Maisarah and Rozana described how *takut* (scared/afraid) they were thinking their husbands would look for younger women. They saw that it was important for them to keep their marriage intact, particularly at this stage of their lives. They were concerned that serious symptoms associated with the menopause could affect the marital relationship. This was a prominent issue of concern for the majority of women in my study. They had become 'worried' people thinking about their marital lives. Although, none of my participants experienced divorce in their middle-age, the feeling of insecurity regarding their marriage for those who had husbands, was definitely an issue. I am aware that the there are many factors that contribute to divorce, and I am not suggesting that menopause contributes to divorce per se. However, the symptoms of menopause can contribute to stress within the marital relationship and this was related to me by the women I spoke with, many of whom feared the possibility of their husbands divorcing them.

Urban Malay Women Creating a New Sense of Order in Their Lives

One thing that I realised that most of the women in my study approached the liminal stage with a particular kind of attitude—to 'put up a good fight' (M. Little et al., 1998: 1491) in approaching the uncertainty of menopause:

> Putting up a good fight is socially endorsed. Patients will often say, when someone explains that there is nothing that can be done to cure the disease, "I can't simply give up. There must be something I can do to fight this thing". Relatives and friends will say in hushed (and often slightly disapproving) voices "He's given up. He just doesn't seem to want to fight it any more", as though the effort of will could indefinitely prolong life.

The culture of putting up a good fight is endorsed not only by the women in my study but also by others who have suffered from cancer and AIDS (Sontag, 1990). In order to create a new sense of order in their lives, many of my participants have chosen to follow the medical path to fight against this uncertainty. At this particular point, I wish to emphasize that there is an increasing influence of Westernization and medicalization in the lives of urban Malay women. Urban Malay women did not succumb to the problems associated with menopause but turned to medical help particularly by consuming HRT to alleviate menopausal symptoms and restore their health conditions. As Habibah said:

> There are lots of medicine out there to help us with menopausal symptoms, why fret? Go and get one. Don't sit down and cry because we have *all these things* [menopausal symptoms].

There is an urgent need for urban Malay women to overcome uncertainty as they are juggling between two roles simultaneously. My participants feel they have to work through the liminal phase, both metaphorically and literally, as they have to move on with their lives *and* participate in the paid work force. While women like Sharifah, Balkis, Azaliah and Habibah are participating actively outside the house to improve their living conditions, I have argued more generally that the workplace has become 'the site of tension and anxiety' (Morris & Symonds, 2004: 314). The workplace has become the ground where women undergoing menopause are scrutinized by other women who judge the other's capacity to work adequately. Some women felt uncomfortable, inferior and inadequate when menopausal symptoms, particularly hot flushes or mood swings, came on suddenly in the office. The lack of support the women felt they received both at home and in their workplace added to the pressure of juggling their maternal roles and worker roles. Based on the selected narratives of Balkis and Sharifah I have illustrated what Kittel and colleagues (1998: 621) term 'keeping up [the] appearances' in terms of managing their menopausal bodies. Because menopause is an emotionally draining experience and women need to feel good about themselves, most women in my study have decided to get treatment in the form of HRT in order to reclaim control of their bodies as well as to overcome the symptoms so that they can perform their motherly duties at home and work in the office with the least amount of disruption.

Conclusion

In sum, while women undergo rites of passage from one phase to the other with societal acknowledgement and rituals particularly coming of age, birth, marriage and death, menopause is a process for women where there is no formal or specific way of acknowledging this transition. Like other transitions, particularly from adolescence to adulthood which involve elements of liminality, menopause is also similar. As I have described in this article, the menopause process is characterized by liminality or uncertainty. This situation has been described by many of my participants as problematic and chaotic. There is, as Douglas notes, a danger to the individual and the social order—this danger relates to how women's identities are challenged. In terms of the social order it is that women should transition easily and silently from one status to another. However, in modern societies this is not the case—women are expected to maintain roles of productivity as well. The social order needs them as productive members of the society (young/middle aged) and as older persons (grandmotherly and wise). Interestingly, menopause as a passage is silent in order to support the social order. There is no cause for celebration like childbirth, wedding or funeral. Clearly loosing youthful looks and vitality and losing the ability to reproduce, both of which are connected, have the potential to create discomfort, and can be seen as an assault to self-identity. In addition, a previously healthy person may become 'unwell' by virtue of the symptoms associated with a 'normal' phase of the lifespan. Thus, the experience of liminality throughout the time of menopause has led most urban Malay women to seek help from the medical professionals to create a new sense of order in their lives.

References

Agee, E. (2000). Menopause and the transmission of women's knowledge: African American and White women's perspectives. *Medical Anthropology Quarterly, 14*(1), 73-95.

Allan, H. (2007). Experiences of infertility: liminality and the role of the fertility clinic. *Nursing Inquiry, 14*(2), 132-139.

Barett, R. J. (1988). The 'schizophrenic' and the liminal persona in modern society. *Culture, Medicine and Psychiatry, 22,* 465-494.

Bart, P. B. (1969). Why women's status changes in middle age: the turn of the social ferris wheel. *Sociological Symposium*(3), 1-18.

Becker, G. (1993). Continuity after a stroke: implications of life-course disruption in old age. *The Gerontologist, 33*(2), 148.

Bloch, M. (1986). *From blessing to violence: history and ideology in the circumcision ritual of the Merina of Madagascar.* Cambridge: Cambridge University Press.

Bloch, M., & Parry, J. (1982). Introduction: death and the regeneration of life. In M. Bloch & P. Jonathan (Eds.), *Death and the regeneration of life.* Cambridge: Cambridge University Press.

Boulet, M. J., Oddens, B. J., Lehert, P., Vemer, H. M., & Visser, A. (1994). Climacteric and menopause in 7 South-East Asian countries. *Maturitas, 19*(3), 157-176.

Chirawatkul, S., Patanasri, K., & Koochaiyasit, C. (2002). Perceptions about menopause and health practices among women in northeast Thailand. *Nursing and Health Sciences, 4,* 113-121.

Douglas, M. (1966). *Purity and danger: an analysis of concepts of pollution and taboo.* London and New York: Routledge.

Draper, J. (2003). Men's passage to fatherhood: an analysis of the contemporary relevance of transition theory. *Nursing Inquiry, 10*(1), 66-78.

Flint, M. (1975). The menopause: reward or punishment? *Psychosomatics, 16,* 161-163.

Gifford, S. M. (1994). The change of life, the sorrow of life: menopause, bad blood, and cancer among Italian-Australian working class women. *Culture, Medicine and Psychiatry, 18,* 299-319.

High, R. V., & Marcellino, P. A. (1994). Menopausal women and the work environment. *Social Behaviour and Personality, 22*(4), 347-354.

Im, E.-O., & Meleis, A. I. (2000). Meanings of menopause to Korean immigrant women. *Western Journal of Nursing Research, 22*(1), 84-102.

Im, E.-O., & Meleis, A. I. (2001). Women's work and symptoms during midlife: Korean immigrant women. *Women's Work, Health and Quality of Life,* 83-103.

Kaufert, P. A., & Gilbert, P. (1986). Women, menopause and medicalization. *Culture, Medicine and Psychiatry, 10*, 7-21.

Kittell, L. A., Mansfield, P. K., & Voda, A. M. (1998). Keeping up appearances: the basic social process of the menopausal transition. *Qualitative Health Research, 8*(5), 618-633.

La Fontaine, J. (1960). Homicide and suicide among the Gisu. In P. Bohannan (Ed.), *African homicide and suicide* (pp. 94-129). New Jersey: Princeton University Press.

Little, K. L. (1951). *The Mende of Sierra Leone*. London: Routledge & Kegan Paul, Limited.

Little, M., Jordens, C. F. C., Paul, K., Montgomery, K., & Philipson, B. (1998). Liminality: a major category of the experience of cancer illness. *Social Science & Medicine, 47*(10), 1485-1494.

Lock, M. (1994). Menopause in cultural context. *Experimental Gerontology, 29*(3-4), 307-317.

Luxford, Y. (2003). Troublesome breasts: older women living in th eliminal state of being 'at risk' of breast cancer. *Health Sociology Review, 12*, 146-154.

MacNeil, M. (1997). From nurse to teacher: recognizing a status passage. *Journal of Advanced Nursing, 25*, 634-642.

McCrea, F. B. (1983). The politics of menopause: the 'discovery' of a deficiency disease. *Social Problems, 31*(1), 111-123.

Mernissi, F. (1987). *Beyond the veil: male-female dynamics in modern Muslim society*. Bloomington: Indiana University Press.

Morris, M. E., & Symonds, A. (2004). 'We've been trained to put up with it': real women and the menopause. *Critical Public Health, 14*(3), 311-323.

Murphy, R. F., Scheer, J., Murphy, Y., & Mack, R. (1988). Physical disability and social liminality a study in the rituals of adversity. *Social Science & Medicine, 26*(2), 235-242.

Navon, L., & Morag, A. (2004). Liminality as biographical disruption: unclassifiability following hormonal therapy for advanced prostate cancer. *Social Science & Medicine, 58*(11), 2337-2347.

Omar, R. (1994). *The Malay women in the body: between biology and culture*. Kuala Lumpur: Fajar Bakti Sdn. Bhd.

Omar, R. (1995). Menopause and the rural Malay women. In R. Talib & T. Chee-Beng (Eds.), *Dimensions of tradition and development in Malaysia* (pp. 475-488). Kuala Lumpur: Pelanduk Publicatons.

Rice, P. L. (1996). Only when I have borne all my children!: the menopause in Hmong women. In P. L. Rice & L. Manderson (Eds.), *Maternity and reproductive health in Asian societies* (pp. 261-275). Amsterdam: Harwood Academic Publishers.

Sheehy, G. (1998). *Menopause: the silent passage*. New York: Pocket Books.

Sontag, S. (1990). *Illness as metaphor and AIDS and its metaphor.* New York: Picador.

Turner, V. (1974). *Dramas, fields, and metaphors: symbolic action in human society.* Ithaca and London: Cornell University Press.

van Gennep, A. (1960). *The rites of passage* (M. B. Vizedom & G. L. Caffee, Trans.). Chicago: The University of Chicago Press.

Wolf, N. (1991). *The beauty myth.* London: Vintage Books.

Traditional Monarchy and Modern Democracy

Dr. Ahmad Nizar Yaakub

Abstract

Yogyakarta is the last remaining sultanate which has a real political power. The hereditary Sultan holds the power as governor based on the special status of the province (*daerah istimewa*). Since the fall of the Suharto administration, Indonesia has seen a tremendous democratization process happening at all level of governments. As such, this paper aims to investigate the polemic of the Susilo Bambang Yudhyono central government planning to conduct democratic election on the position of governor of Yogyakarta like other provinces in Indonesia in order to uphold democracy. This paper also tries to explain the reactions of Yogyakartans on the election plan. It will later discuss the trade-off and concession made by both conflicting parties in solving the tension. The paper views that the monarchical system can co-exist with democratic system in the current situation in Yogyakarta provided the people can express their freedom of rights despite their differences in opinion towards Yogyakarta administration system. At the same time, Yogyakarta is moving towards a limited monarchical system while strengthening democratic system.

Introduction

In a democratic state an individual or a group can show their competing interests and values through a free and fair democratic election. However, democratic election is still a minimum definition for democracy but at least it is the begining for a society to have a democratic leader who will govern them (Dwi Harsono, 2012). The fall of an autoritarian leader under Suharto in 1998 marked the begining of the democratization process in Indonesia. According to Rakner and Fritz (2007) the democratization process can be divided into three parts namely liberation, transition and consolidation. The liberation stage begins with the fall of an authoritarian regime or monarchy system. The transition stage can be seen from continous competitive elections held by the government. The consolidation stage is when the society recognises and accepts the practice. The Indonesian leaders after Suharto have made efforts to enact democratic reforms through democratizing presidential elections, releasing many political prisoners, freeing the press, allowing the establishment of labour unions, conducting free and fair elections, and enforcing new human rights standards.

Meanwhile, a state that is ruled by a person who inherited the power from the family is known as a monarchy. Sultan Hamengku Buwono X inherited his power to rule Yogyakarta from his late father Sultan Hamengku Buwono IX. A monarch is often believed by the people to be ". . . divine, or has a divine ancestor, or is divinely appointed . . ." to rule and protect the religion, people and land (Lipson 1997, p. 187). The Javanese traditionally believed the Sultan or King had gained *kesaktian* (supernatural power) and *wahyu* (mandate from heaven) to lead the state and to ensure the continuing loyalty and support from the people (Loveard, 1999). The Javanese also believed the Sultan in Yogyakarta had a spiritual bride known as Nyai Roro Kidul, the Queen and Guardian of the Southern Ocean. The temporal and spiritual powers of the Javanese Sultans and Kings have been the inspiration for modern leaders in Indonesia. The first five Indonesian Presidents were also said to have consulted spiritual advisers to assist them in making important decisions (Mydans, 2001, p. 10). In the context of having a connection with *kesaktian*, all Indonesian Presidents from Sukarno to SBY have been known to have made frequent visits to holy places, tombs, caves, mountaintops and ancient ruins in Java. President Suharto was imagined by many Javanese to have indirectly gained *wahyu* to lead the nation through his wife, Raden Ayu Siti Hartinah (Ibu Tien), a descendant of the Mangkunegaran royal court in Solo, Central Java. However, since Ibu Tien's death in 1996 President Suharto was said to have lost the *wahyu* (Mydans, 2008). Besides Indonesia, there are still a few countries like Kuwait, Brunei Darussalam and Oman that are run by absolute monarch. The most common form of monarchy today is constitutional monarchy where the monarch is a symbol of unity but with limited power. The monarch has to accept the role of parliment and cabinet in running the state. Countries with a constitutional monarchy can be found in northern Europe including Denmark and United Kingdom and several Commonwealth members including Australia and Malaysia.

From here, the paper is divided into four sections. The first section will highlight the role of Yogyakarta Sultanate in helping the Indonesian revolutionery movement to gain independence from the Dutch and Sultanate's inclusion in the Indonesian Republic as a Special Province. The second section explains the role of the Sultan as the hereditary monarch and the position of the governor during the Suharto regime. The third section discusses the tensions between Sultan Hamengku Buwono X and the Yogyakartans with the SBY central government on the Sultan governorship and Paku Alam IX vice governorship. The final section discuss the Bill passed by the *Dewan Perwakilan Rakyat* (DPR) (People's Representative Assembly) on the issue of the special status of Yogyakarta especially on the post of governor and vice governor.

Yogyakarta Sultanate and the birth of Indonesian Republic

The Yogyakarta Sultanate and Surakarta Sunanate were formed after the split of the Mataram Sultanate based on the Treaty of Gyanti on 13 February 1755. Pangeran Mangkubumi (later known as Sultan Hamengku Buwono I) became the Sultan of Yogyakarta while Paku Buwono III became the ruler for Surakarta Sunanate. During the Dutch colonisation of Indonesia a small *Kadipaten* (principality) of Pakualam under the ruler of Paku Alam I was established south of Yogyakarta on 17 March 1813. Around the same time, a special political contract was made between the Yogyakarta Sultanate and the Dutch whereby the post of a *rijksbestuurder* (resident) was formed to help the Sultan of Yogyakarta run the everyday administration of the Sultanate. According to Baskoro and Sunaryo (2011, p. 34), during the Japanese Occupation of Indonesia, the position of Sultan Hamengku Buwono IX and the post of *sumotyokan*(resident) was maintained in Yogyakarta Sultanate. When the Japanese felt that they were losing the war, they allowed the Indonesian nationalist leaders under Sukarno and Mohd Hatta to proclaim independence for the Republic of Indonesia on 17 August 1945.

Faced with the formation of the Republic, Sultan Hamengku Buwono IX and Paku Alam VIII showed their support for the establishment of the new Republic of Indonesia. The new government under President Sukarno and Vice President Mohd Hatta recognised the support of Sultan Hamengku Buwono IX and Paku Alam VIII support by officially appointing both, on 5 September 1945, as the Governor and Vice Governor of Yogyakarta respectively. Yogyakarta was then given its status of Special Province. The independence following the Japanese retreat was short-lived as the Dutch military forces came back to reclaim their colonies. Since the Indonesian nationalist government and military forces were not yet strong the capital city of Jakarta was quickly occupied by the colonial forces during the first Dutch military offensive, in early 1946. As such, Sultan Hamengku Buwono IX offered the Indonesian nationalist government to use Yogyakarta as its capital city (Tuti Artha 2009, p. 74). He even contributed a large sum of money to the new government to fund its adminstration and military forces. During the negotiations between the Indonesian and the Dutch governments, Sultan Hamengku Buwono IX was one of the members of theIndonesian delegation. When the negotiations failed, the Dutch followed up with its second military offensive on 21 December 1948, successfuly occuppying Yogyakarta and capturing Sukarno and Mohd Hatta.

The Dutch did not arrestSultan Hamengku Buwono IX and decided to establish an Indonesian federal state of Central Java with Sultan Hamengku Buwono IX as the puppet Head of State with the capital still in Yogyakarta. However, the Dutch colonial government in Jakarta was furious when the Sultan refused to accept the offer as the Head of State. In fact, the Sultan was secretly planning with the remaining Indonesian military forces to conduct a major military action against the occupying Dutch military forces in Yogyakarta. The main objective of the military action was to raise the moral of the Indonesian military forces and to let the world outside know that the Indonesian nationalist government had not surrendered, and continued fighting Dutch military forces (I Gusti Bagus Saputera 2007, p. 373). General Sudirman, Commander of the Indonesian military forces, directed his officer Lieutenant Colonel Suharto to work secretly on military actions with the Sultan. On 1 March 1949, Indonesian military action had raised the moral of the remaining Indonesian military forces in Java and other islands dug in, continuing on with guerilla warfare. The Indonesian military forces managed to liberate Yogyakarta from the Dutch military forces although only for six hours. During the military action, the Sultan had allowed his *keraton* (palace) to be used by retreating Indonesian military forces as a hideout from the Dutch. This incident received international community attention, especially the United Nations (UN). The UN demanded the Dutch government negotiate with the Indonesian nationalist leaders and give back independence to Indonesia. Finally, the Dutch government agreed to UN demand and began withdrawing from all of Indonesia, excepting from Dutch New Guinea (Irian Jaya). Indonesia gained independence from the Dutch on 27 December 1949 after several round of negotiations.

After independence, Hamengku Buwono IX continued to serve as governor of Yogyakarta and as cabinet member of the Indonesian government. In addition he served as Minister of Defense and Homeland Security Coordinator from 1949-1951 and 1953, Minister of Economics, Finance and Industry from 1966-1973 and, Vice President from March 1973-1978. He refused to accept the nomination by the *Majlis Permusyawaratan Rakyat* (People's Consultative Assembly) for the second term as Vice President citing ill health. Some scholars argued that he was disillusioned with the Suharto government and its increasing authoritarianism and corruption. His refusal to accept the nomination was taken personally by Suharto. Sultan Hamengku Buwono IX died in 1988 and was succeeded by his son Hamengku

Buwono X as Sultan of Yogyakarta. However, the new Sultan was not appointed as the governor of Yogyakarta. Instead, the Suharto government promoted Paku Alam VIII from vice governor to the post of governor. It was argued that, like his father the young Sultan despised the rampant corruption in the Suharto government and wanted to protect his family name rather than persuing his personal desire (Loveard 1999, p. 74).

Sultan Hamengku Buwono X and the fall of the Suharto regime

The 1997-1998 Asian economic and financial crisis had considerable impact on Indonesia as it suffered economic meltdown when the Rupiah currency depreciated sharply against the US dollar. This situation worsened when mass demonstrations were held all over Indonesia demanding Suharto to step down from office. The main reason was that the Indonesians lost their trust on Suharto leadership. In Javanese culture, trust is highly valued and considered as a strength. Indonesians can no longer tolerate *Korupsi, Kolusi dan Nepotism* (Corruption, Collusion and Nepotism) which were reportedly rampant during Suharto rule.

During the early *reformasi* (reformation) period, SultanHamengkuBuwono X participated in the street demonstrations with university students to oppose the Suharto's rule and to force him to step down as President (TutiArtha 2009, p. 56). The Sultan wanted to play an important role in the *reformasi* movement through peaceful demonstrations and to emulate his father's early involvement in the struggle for Indonesian independence. He also got Paku Alam VIII to issue a joint declaration to support the *reformasi* movement and strengthen national leadership which favors the people side on 20 May 1998. The joint declaration was read by the Sultan in front of his palace witnessed by several hundred thousand people. When JusufHabibie replaced Suharto, HamengkuBuwono X was instrumental with four others in the Ciganjur Declaration which demanded the government to conduct early elections. With the death of PakuAlam VIII on September 1998, HamengkuBuwono X was installed by the Indonesian government under JusufHabibie as governor of Yogyakarta on 3 October 1998.

The resignation of Suharto in 1998 ended three decades of authoritarian rule in Indonesia. Suharto handed the presidential power to his vice president, Jusuf Habibie who later took the oath as President on 21 May 1998. The post-Suharto period is called *reformasi* since Jusuf Habibie undertook more open and liberal political and economic reforms. Stemming from this there is still greater freedom of speech in contrast to Suharto's rule. In February 1999, the government passed the 'Political Parties Law' which among others laws allowed for the establishment of more new parties from the existing three parties (Golkar, PPP and PDI-P). Moreover, Pancasila is no longer a requirement as an ideology for these newly formed parties. In May 1999, the central government passed the 'Regional Autonomy Law' which open the process of decentralization of the Indonesian government. Provincial governments are now allowed to play bigger role in governing their provinces. There is a legislative body in every province called *Dewan Perwakilan Rakyat Daerah* (DPR-D) (Regional People's Representatives Assembly). In 2000, the Provincial Administration of Yogyakarta brought up the issue of RUUK DIY to the central government, and that it should be discussed at the DPR. However, the matter was not discussed due to the sensitivity and difficulty of the issue. In 2004 the Regional Autonomy Law was revised to include the leaders of local government (governors, regents and mayors) to be elected by popular election for five-year term.

Conflict between Sultan Hamengku Buwono X and the SBY government on the governorship post.

The Regional Autonomy Law passed in 2004 had opened the door for further discussion on the stalled RUUK DIY issue especially on the election of Governor and the Vice Governor. Under the Law No 32 of 2004, the SBY government issued a three-year term (2004-2007) on the post of the Sultan as governor while the DPR discussed the RUUK DIY. Since the three-year term for Sultan Hamengku Buwono X as governor ended in 2007, the DPR has yet to approve on Yogyakarta's special status to date. As such, SBY issued a decree to renew another three-year term for the Sultan as governor until 2010. Again the Sultan received a year term extension two times from 8 October 2010 to 7 October 2011 and from 8 October 2011 to 7 October 2012 as Governor and Paku Alam as Vice Governor.

A conflict of interest began when the SBY government decided to up hold the democratic process in Indonesia on the election for the post of governor in Yogyakarta. To date only Yogyakarta has not conducted any elections on the post of Governor and Deputy Governor, as was held by Sultan Hamengku Buwono X and Paku Alam IX respectively. As commonly accepted in democracy the leader must represent the voices of the people and the people have the freedom to choose their leader. The conflict heightened when SBY stated at the Indonesian cabinet meeting in early February 2010 on the special status of Yogyakarta that there should not be a monarchical system within a democratic country.

There was also a growing concern over the Sultan holding the post of governor when the Sultan might not be able to act as governor if he is sick, too old or too young. The direct appointment of the Sultan opened the opportunity for unlimited and uncontrolled power centralised around the royal family. Moreover, there was no formal institution to demand accountability of the Sultan if he made mistakes or failed to provide public goods demanded by the Yogyakarta society. The whole purpose of the SBY government decision to hold elections for the post of governor is how to serve the people better and to efficiently provide the public goods needed by the society, founded on accountability, rather than automatic appointments lacking meritocracy.

With regards to a democratic general election in 2004 and again in 2008 the Sultan decided to run for election for the post of President against SBY and other candidates. The Sultan seemed to receive some strong support from the people in Java who made up the bulk of the Indonesian population. The Sultan finally became a confirmend candidate in both presidential elections. Both heavyweights in the election ring represent different political parties where the Sultan is a member of the Golkar party while SBY is the president of the Democrat party. These elections have strained personal relations between the Sultan and SBY.

At the same time, the Yogyakartans reacted differently when majority of them wanted the post of Governor and Deputy Governor not to be contested and passed down to the Sultan and Paku Alam IX respectively. According to a survey conducted by Golkar Party and sponsored by the Yogyakarta DPR-D, more than 70 percent Yokyakartans wanted direct appointment of their governor, not appointments through election (The Jakarta Post, 2010). Moreover, Yogyakartans strongly respected the Sultan and Paku Alam IX as they symbolise the image and values of *Kejawen* (traditional Javanese culture) which is an important aspect of their lives. After all Yogyakarta is known as the cradle of Javanese culture. A famous UNESCO World Heritage site, the Buddist temple of Borobudur and the Hindu Siva temple Parambanan are also located near Yogyakarta. In addition to these historic symbols, Yogyakartans are also proud of the role of the Sultan as the protector of tolerence between different religions in Yogyakarta. According to Dwi Harsono (2012) the Yogyakartans believe that the Sultan posesess ". . . values such as *dhana* (generous), *sila* (good attitude), *ksanti* (calm and patience), *virya* (courage), *dhyana* (contemplate), *paranidhana* (good determination), *bala* (powerful) and *juana* (well-informed to new knowledge)".Culturally, the traditional Javanese believe that the throne is a revelation from the *pengeran* (god) (Dwi Harsono 2012 cited in Nusantara 1999, p. 91). In Javanese, the meaning of Hamengku Buwono is 'leader of a Javanese Universe' and Paku Alam means 'Nail of the Universe'.

It is surprising therefore that the majority of Yogyakartans were enraged by the comment made by SBY at the cabinet meeting on the Sultan position of governor. From Yogyakarta perspectives it was done without consideration and sensitivity, especially considering the deep sorrow of the Yogyakartans who had just suffered the eruption of Mount Merapi in October 2010. Hundreds of Yogyakartans lost their lives in the eruption including Mbah Marjan, royal keeper for the Mount Merapi. Moreover, the eruption also destroyed thousands of homes and flaten several thousand hectares of agricultural lands. It is important to point out that in Southeast Asian cultures it can be observed that during times of great and common strife, such as during a natural disaster, there is an expectation of togetherness and teamwork to follow. SBY's insistence on the democratization during this time is a huge insult that cuts much deeper than power relations may normally play out to. This could subsequently be viewed as a vulnerability that SBY should never have exposed.

As a result of either the insult or the vulnerability, the Yogyakartans staged protests and demonstrations on the streets against the SBY's decision to force direct elections for the post of governor and vice governor in Yogyakarta. In the same light, the Yogyakartans also staged silent protests in a more traditional way known as *Pisowanan Agung* where they gathered silence at the Sultan's keraton near North Alun-Alun. *Pisowanan Agung* is staged when Yogyakartans want to show protestation on certain issues in support of the Sultan, or also when waiting for any major decision from the Sultan. For example, in 2008 about 150,000 people staged *Pisowanan Agung* at the Sultan's keraton to hear his decision to run for President in the Indonesian general election. Again on 17 December 2010 around 50,000 people staged *Pisowanan Agung* near the Sultan's keraton to protest SBY on the issue of election for governor and vice governor. The Yogyarkartans argued that the founding fathers, Sukarno and Hatta had awarded a special status to Yogyakarta on 5 September 1945 in return for its service and contribution to the republic during the struggle for independence. As noted above, on the special status issue, the Sultan and Paku Alam were automatically appointed as Governor and Vice Governor. To people there, the SBY government failed to understand the history of the rights they held.

Similarly with the reaction of Yogyakartans, the Sultan took offense and refuted SBY's infamous aforementioned statement to the cabinet meeting on Yogyakartan democratic practices in Indonesia. SBY argued that the administration of the Yogyakarta province is inherently the same with other provinces. The only difference is that the governor is appointed (passed down from father to son) and not elected through election, and therein lies the problem for the republic. Moreover, as governor the Sultan is accountable to the central government as well as the DPR-D in Yogyakarta. Later on, the palace or *keraton* acted more accomodating to the demand of DPR on the many changes made to the Bill as long as the concept of 'Sultan for governor and governor for Sultan' is uphold by the DPR (Muryanto and Susanto 2010). With regard to republic claims of possible abuse of power by the Sultan or royal family, it was countered by the fact that actually the Sultan had limited power because he was supervised by the DPR-D whose members are elected in a democratic manner that should appease the SBY government.

The continued insistence of the SBY government did not ease tensions, rather heightening them. The Sultan and Yogyakartans later called for *jajak pendapat* (referendum) to be carried out on the governorship issue. Both wanted referendum to be carried out like in East Timor during Jusuf Habibie era where East Timorese were allowed to vote on their future. Furthermore, Yogyakartans living near the compound of the Sultan's *keraton* established an independent referendum committee (Susanto 2010). At the peak of the tensions Yogyakartans calling for Yogyakarta to break away from Indonesia. Moreover, Gusti BendaraPangeran Haryo Prabukusumo, the younger brother of the Sultan called on Yogyakartans to be vigilant after a bomb was thrown at the house of a village head Mulyadi in the Sidomulyo village on 1 June 2011. Mulyadi was an active proponent of the automatic appointment of Yogyakarta's Sultan to governor.

Solution to the conflict

Waves of progress in negotiations have been felt since then. The DPR continued to deliberate on the Bill of Yogyakarta's special status until mid-2012. Finally, the SBY government, DPR, DPR-D and the Sultan reached some agreements by July 2012 on the issue of the post of governor and vice governor of Yogyakarta. The Bill on the special status of Yogyakarta was passed by the DPR on the 31 August 2012 after almost nine years of deliberation. On 3 September 2012 SBY signed the Bill just three days after the DPR passed it. This Bill is now known officially as Law No. 13 of 2012 on Yogyakarta's Special Status. On 10 October 2012 the Sultan and Paku Alam IX were sworn in as appointed Governor and Vice Governor of Yogyakarta for the 2012-2017 term of office. The swearing in was done by SBY at Yogyakarta State Palace Gedung Agung under Article 27(1) of the Bill which stipulates that the swearing in of governor and vice governor must be done by the President of Indonesia.

The Bill was a major compromise between the SBY government, the Sultan, the DPR and DPR-D on the special status of Yogyakarta especially on the sensitive matter of governor and vice governor. Finally, it would seem, the monarchy system can coexist with democracy in Indonesia through some trade-offs. The Bill allows the Sultan and Paku Alam IX to be appointed without election as governor and vice governor respectively, but there are several administrative requirements and phases before they can be governor and vice governor that will be discussed next.

This paper highlights some of the important adminstrative requirements and phases. For example, the Sultan and Paku Alam must be at least 30 years of age before they can be appointed as governor and vice governor respectively. In the case where the Sultan is under-age, Paku Alam will be appointed acting governor until the Sultan reaches the required age. This rule also applies to Paku Alam as vice governor. However, if both the Sultan and Paku Alam are still below age then the provincial government will be run by the provincial secretary until both of them reaches the required age. In the case of the Sultan and Paku Alam are mentally or physically unfit then the Bill requires both royal households to find their successors (Max Sijabat 2012). In this context, currently the Sultan is facing a problem because the Yogyakarta Sultanate tradition allows only male to succeed him. He has no son but five daughters. He further reluctant to appoint a crown prince. The most likely sucessor for the Sultan is his younger brother Gusti Bendoro Pangeran Haryo Prabukusumo.

Other requirements include that the governor and vice governor of Yogyakarta need to have at least a senior high school level of education, good health, be god-fearing and be loyal to the state of Indonesia. These requirements need to be verified by the DPR-D as demanded by the Bill under Article 14. The role of DPR-D was a trade-off by the SBY government so that the appointment of the Sultan and Paku Alam to the posts of governor and vice governor still remains democratic. The verification by DPR-D needs to be done every five years as the term in office of the governor and vice governor requires it. The difference with other provincial governors and vice governors is that they can only serve for two terms while the tenure for the Sultan and Paku Alam is limitless.

Meanwhile, the Bill under Article 16 stipulates that the Sultan and Paku Alam must not be members of any political parties because as governor and vice governor by default they need to be non-partisan presumably so s not to overly influence the democratic system. Due to this stipulation, the Sultan had to resign from the patron boards of the Golkar Party and cut his relations with the National Democratic Party which he co-founded earlier. The concession under Article 16 to some extent benefited the SBY Democratic Party because the Sultan and his late father had allied themselves with the rival Golkar Party. At the same time, the Sultan has been seen as the likely candidate as a running mate to Aburizal Bakrie from the Golkar Party in the 2014 presidential election. Article 16 to some extent can be argued as depriving the political right of the Sultan because democracy in Indonesia ensures that every individual has the right to membership of any political party (Aritonang 2012).

Another administrative requirement is that the two royal households will be given upkeep funds. This is done in order to maintain and preserve the cultural heritage of the sultanate and the principality. The fund is allocated to the provincial government from the central government, directly, without going through DPR-D approval or review. At the same time, the two royal households are allowed to maintain control over their royal household lands.

Conclusion

The conflict between SBY government with Sultan Hamengku Buwono X and Paku Alam IX on the special status of Yogyakarta especially on the positions of governor and vice governor was finally solved by SBY's relenting on the matter of direct elections, allowing for appointment. The trade-off on the Bill negotiated by all the principal parties ensured that the monarchy system can co-exist with democracy in Indonesia. The Bill allowed the continuation of the automatic appointments of Sultan and Paku Alam as equivalent to governor and vice governor, but there are some adminstrative requirements and phases that they must comply in order to take up the posts: minimum age level, sufficient education, non-partisanship are imposed, while special funds are allocated for the upkeep of the royal household. These requirements would ensure that the DPR-D and Yogyakartans can oversee and monitor the succession of governor and vice governor in the spirit of democracy.

References

Aritonang, Margareth S. "House set to force Sultan to resign from Golkar". *The Jakarta Post*. http://www.jakartapost.com. 28 August 2012. (Accessed on 20 December 2012).

Baskoro, Haryadi and Sunaryo, Sudomo. *Wasiat HB IX Yogyakarta Kota Republik*. Yogyakarta: Galangpress, 2011.

Dwi Harsono. *Reign to the People: The Application of "Democratic Monarchy" in Yogyakarta*. Paper presented at the Annual Conference of IAPA (KAN) in Malang.http://staff.uny.ac.id. June 2012. (Accessed on 20 December 2012).

I Gusti Bagus Saputera, S.H. *Merdeka Melalui Diplomacy: Perjuangan Ide Anak Agung Gde Agung*. Denpasar: Yayasan Usaha Pekerja, 2007.

Lipson, Leslie. *The Great Issues of Politics*. Prentice Hall: New Jersey, 1997.

Loveard, Keith. *Suharto: Indonesia's Last Sultan*. Singapore: Horizon Books, 1999.

Maulia, Erwida. "SBY denies controversial statement on Yogya". *The Jakarta Post*. http://www.thejakartapost.com/news/2010/12/02/sby-denies-controversial-statement-yogya.html3 May 2010. (Accessed on 8 June 2012).

Max Sijabat, Ridwan. "Monarchs remain in control of Yogyakarta under new law". *The Jakarta Post*. http://www.thejakartapost.com 14 August 2012. (Accessed 28 January 2013).

Muryanto, Bambang and Susanto, Slamet. "One-year tenure extension for Yogyakarta governor".*The Jakarta Post*. http://www.thejakartapost.com/news/2011/10/10/one-year-tenure-extension-yogyakarta-governor.html 10 October 2010. (Accessed on 3 May 2012).

Mydans, S. "Indonesia Draw Mystical Connections to Suharto". *International Herald Tribune.* http://www.iht.com/articles/2008/01/25/asia/indo.php. (Accessed on 13 October 2008).

Mydans, S. "Mystical connundrum in Indon politics". *New Straits Times.* 22 August 2001.

Nusantara, A. Ariobimo (ed.)*Meneguhkan Tahta untuk Rakyat* (Confirming to Reign for the People). Jakarta: Grasindo, 1999.

Rakner, L. Menocal, AR and Fritz, V. *Democratisation's Third Wave and the Challenges of Democratic Deepening: Asseeing International Democracy Assistance and Lessons Learned,* ODI Working Paper No 1, London: Overseas Development Institute, 2007.

Susanto, Slamet. "Yogyakartan's administration status gets mixed response".*The Jakarta Post.* http://www.thejakartapost.com12 April 2010. (Accessed on 3 May 2012).

Tuti Artha, Arwan. *Langkah Raja Jawa Menuju Istana.* Yogyakarta: Galangpress, 2009.

Malay Cosmopolitanness and Reciprocity: Between Adat and Religion

Dr. Rosila Bee Mohd Hussain

Abstract

This article discusses how Malay postgraduate students prepared themselves to undertake overseas study and the various new challenges with which they need to deal upon arrival. It explores some situations relating to their efforts to reinforce their ethnic and religious identities in relation to their interactions with others. What is highlighted throughout this experience is the fact that decisions made by the Malay students prioritise their religious identity compared to other forms of identity. Discussions indirectly show how the Malay postgraduate students reveal they are still negotiating their traditional culture/adat and new environment. The idea of reciprocity between traditional culture/adat and new/modern culture is much anticipated in their adjustment process. This study is part of an empirical research conducted among the Malay postgraduate students in Western Australia.

Introduction—An overview of Malay *Adat*

In discussing Malay society, it is essential to develop an understanding of the cultural formations and constructions of Malay *adat* (traditional customs)[1]. According to Zainal Kling (1997, p. 8), *adat* represents a 'commonsense' construction of everyday life. Overall, Malay *adat* emphasizes peace and harmony, based on the precept of altruism (unselfishness) and proper respect for another's feelings, status and position; it acknowledges change, but it establishes the means through which change is incorporated and accommodated and reintegrated. As the Malay folk model, *adat* provides the means by which identity is sustained. Apart from Zainal Kling's work on *adat*, Syed Hussein Alatas (1996) has distinguished aspects of the 'New Malay' and 'Old Malay' by observing how the New Malays have claimed that Islam and their unique *adat* (culture) were features of their identity. Alatas referred to the New Malay as Malays with a new consciousness who 'will be selective of positive and negative influences that have been left in the past' (1996, p. 6) and he characterised the New Malay as rational, moral and selective. This means the New Malays maintained their identity and culture but ridded themselves of regressive traditions by being rational and selective.

The content of *adat* alters from one place to another, though it is a concept which at the most general level has been described as 'unify(ing) the mind of the Malay world' (Zainal Kling, 1989/1990, p. 115). In other words, *adat* has often been recognized as both 'traditional' and 'stable'. When analyzing *adat* in the contemporary context, we must take into consideration the fact that *adat* must be analyzed in a wider context and in relation to the historical influences of colonial rule and the present-day post-colonial situation (Hisashi Endo 1999). The 'traditional' *adat* and the 'modern' concept of 'culture' and 'development' are considered to be two sides of the same coin. The more culture and development are emphasized, the more *adat* is transformed in accordance with them (Hisashi Endo 1999, p. 22). In fact, Hooker (1970, p. vii) has also pointed out that *adat* is not a quaint system of customary law, but is a living system, enshrined in law reports, statutes, and administrative minutes.

A description of *adat* by Wilder (1982, p. 117) is summed up by a Malay proverb: 'other pools, other fishes; other fields, other crickets' *(Lain lubuk, lain ikannya; lain padang, lain belalang).* That is to say,

---

[1]   Peletz (1987) describes *adat* as 'customary law'.

every community has its own accent, custom, personality and history. Another significant Malay proverb on *adat* is 'Better to let one's child die, but not one's custom (*Biar mati anak, jangan mati adat*). This is the 'tightness' about which Provencher (1971, pp. 205-206) wrote when he warned that Malay communities only looked 'loose' to a 'cognitively naïve Westerner'. In other words, the typifications as 'loose' or 'tight' would seem to depend on what exactly is being examined when we are considering the whole community of the 'Malay people'. This article attempts to consider the position of *adat* outside the Malaysian context and the extent to which Malay postgraduate students in Western Australia view *adat* as relevant to their everyday life.

Malay *adat* also is characterized as the basis of social formation when discsussing images of altruism or indecision among the Malays (Zainal Kling, 1997). In such cases *adat* as inculcated by the Malays may in reality dictate that not all decisions can be achieved on the basis of consensus; instead differences are discussed through negotiation until consensus is achieved. This importance of achieving consensus could be found in another Malay proverb, '*Bulat air kerana pembetung, bulat manusia kerana muafakat*' (**Water is round because of its culvert, man is integrated because of their consensus or agreement—this is the closest translated literal meaning I would suggest**). What is emphasize in this article on Malays outside Malaysia is the subjective construct of *adat*, not just its formulation as an ideological concept. Whether *adat* is the same as 'ideology', there is no definite answer to this. However, according to Eagleton (1991, pp.1-31), the term ideology can refer to a wide range of meanings, and not all are compatible with each other, as each involves different conceptual strands. Some of the definitions of ideology listed by Eagleton that can be used to relate *adat* in some ways are:

(a) The process of production of meanings, signs, and values in social life;
(b) Ideas which help to legitimate a dominant political power;
(c) Identity thinking;
(d) The medium in which conscious social actors make sense of their world;
(e) An action-oriented set of beliefs.

In this article, I explore how Malay students have understood *adat* through their personal experiences and socialization process. In other words, it is suggesting that the Malay *adat* could be viewed as functioning ideologically, but it is not an ideology by itself.

Objectives and Methodology

This research was conducted using methods selected used in sociology and cultural anthropology. Ethnographic approaches were used including interviews, participant-observations and recordings made in series of interactions between participants in various social settings. It emphasizes confidentiality and voluntary participation based on informed consent. Informants were recruited primarily through snowballing technique and all of the thirty respondents involved in this research are pursuing their masters or doctoral degrees.

As an insider and researcher among the Malay-Muslim student community in Western Australia, some of the experiences encounters also reflect back to my own personal experiences as a student studying abroad. This insight is also used in my reflexive analysis of the feedbacks and experiences of the Malay postgraduate students involved in this research (Goffman 1989, p.125).

On Malay Cosmopolitanness and Reciprocity—A Review

In this research among Malay students outside Malaysia, I have explored the idea of cosmopolitan identity. Cosmopolitanism, derived from an ancient Greek term meaning 'citizen of the world', captures a receptive and open attitude towards the other (Kendall, Woodward & Skrbis 2009, p. 1). Kristeva (1991, p. 13) has proposed an alternative basis of identity for the new cosmopolitan by suggesting that, living with the other, with the foreigner, confronts us with the possibility (or not) of *being an other*. It is not a matter of our being able to accept the other, but of *being in her or his place*, and this means to imagine and make oneself for oneself. I argue that constructing a cosmopolitan identity is not as important to the Malay students compared to their ethnic and religious identity. They are aware of the idea of cosmopolitanism, but treat it as referring to people who have contacts with the wider world. The idea itself does not bear any considerable meaning to them and is felt to be more 'economically' rather than 'culturally or morally' oriented.

Hannerz (2004) has emphasized cosmopolitanism as referring to a willingness to engage with the others. Therefore, cosmopolitans are those individuals who make their own individuality the locus for determining what they want to accept and what they want to reject. In this case, cosmopolitanism is an international outlook wherein the individual picks and chooses from all the cultural traditions to which s/he has been exposed, negotiating an individual intercultural stance among all of those. What my discussion shows is that continuing communication among Malays when abroad militates against that individualist stance of wholesale cosmopolitanism. Besides its function of promoting solidarity, it also has the policing function of community surveillance and enforcement of religious observance and customary behaviour in accord with Malay-Muslim standards. As pointed out by one of the respondents, it displays the dangers of cosmopolitanism. So, the very success of Malay-Muslim identity maintenance and adjustment runs counter to many cosmopolitan ideals. In the case of the Malay cosmopolitannes, I would characterize them as 'rooted cosmopolitans'. This rooted-cosmopolitan idea rests on a complex tension between the particularity of local place and dwelling, on the one hand, and universalistic dispositions, on the other (Szerszynski & Urry 2006).

Hannerz (1990) also highlighted issues relating to the conceptualization of Malays as cosmopolitans. He raised the question of who is a true cosmopolitan. Does it refers to someone who exhibits a culturally open disposition and interest in others, or whether they simply want some experience of 'home plus' when going abroad? Generally, the term cosmopolitan, describes just about anybody who moves about in the world. But among such people, some would seem more cosmopolitan than others, and others again hardly cosmopolitan at all (Hannerz 1990). Hall (2002, p. 26) further discussed cosmopolitanism as the ability to stand outside of having one's life written and scripted by any one community, whether that is a faith or tradition or religion or culture, and to draw selectively on a variety of discursive meanings. In contrast, Kahn (2006, pp. 167-68) suggested that cosmopolitanisms also govern the practices of localized individuals and institutions. This could occur in everyday social interactions between individuals and groups or forms of religious worship in different parts of the world. Anderson (1992, p. 11) coined the term '*long-distance nationalism*' to describe continued allegiance to a country or region where one either no longer lives or indeed has never lived. Kahn's (1992) review in his existing work, titled 'Malaysians are images of diversity', pointed out that Malays are identifying themselves differently in different contexts, just as Australians would.

I found this dichotomy of Malays identifying themselves differently in different contexts useful in comprehending Malay students' idea of ethnic and religious identity when they are overseas. Early exposure living overseas facilitates regarding experiences differently. The group of Malay students with previous experience living overseas has a tendency to make some comparisons with their current situation in Western Australia, especially in relation to their ethnic and religious identity. However, a different view of cosmopolitan identity was highlighted by students who had never been overseas in relation to their exposure to the new environment and culture. This includes their efforts to be 'accepted' within the local culture whilst at the same time maintaining their Malay values and cultures/*adat* and being guided by Islamic practice.

Upon conducting interviews with the informants, I have categorized them into two main groups, one of which has never had experience of living overseas and the other of which has had previous experience living or visiting overseas, pursuing study, work or leisure. The idea of fresh cosmopolitan emerged as through the usage of the term by my Malay informants as they see themselves as being a first-timer being outside Malaysia (fresh) or as having experience staying, studying of visiting other countries beyond Malaysia. In this context, I used the term fresh cosmopolitan referred to someone removed from where they are closely associated within their own culture and economy. So, they will be interconnected to their 'new sense of place and culture' (Manzini 2007, p. 236). Experience cosmopolitan is referred to as someone who has some previous experience and the possibility of being influenced by the events they had encounterd in other parts of the world. In the case of Malay cosmopolitans, either first-timers or those with previous overseas experience, reciprocity is considered a way for Malay students to attempt to break the ice or overcome barriers in their interpersonal interactions overseas.

According to Kahn (2004), Malay-ness has the potential to be a cosmopolitan i.e. non-exclusionary identity, one that implies religious and cultural interaction, and commercial exchange. However, in this process reciprocity is highly idealised, since it is a vital principle of society (Hobhouse, 1951). Reciprocity is treating other people as other people treat you, voluntarily and not as a result of a binding exchange agreement (Kolm 2008). It is a form of mutual or cooperative exchange of privileges or favours that is anticipated between two or more individuals or groups. The idea of reciprocity is common to every culture and there is a universal norm of reciprocity that obligates people to reciprocate each other in an appropriate or sufficient manner so that giving and returning something may be compared (Gouldner 1960). Gouldner (1960, p. 176) pointed out that reciprocity can also be called a 'starting mechanism', which helps to initiate social interaction and is functional in the early phases of certain groups before they have developed a different customary set of status duties. Furthermore, Gouldner also suggests that the idea of reciprocity can also be analyzed as a moral norm, that is, as one of the principal components of moral codes.

The idea of reciprocity and moral reciprocity is found in a Malay proverb, 'Orang Berbudi Kita Berbahasa, Orang Memberi Kita Merasa' (Every person who is rewarded with a gift, must be thankful). This proverb cannot be translated literally into the English language, but essentially it refers to the idea that if somebody does us a good turn, we must at least show our appreciation by being courteous to them (moral reciprocity). The second part refers to the idea that if someone gives you something (food or other things), you should enjoy it. This idea is pervasive in Malay culture and is related to how the Malay students' face their challenges and adjust their identities. As revealed by one informant, Wani, whom I referred to as an 'experienced cosmopolite' because of her previous experience living overseas, her Muslim identity has always come first. Wani stressed the importance of mixing with others besides the Malays and in a reciprocal manner. According to Wani:

[I] did not mix much with Malays because there are few of them [in the US], but there are so many of them here [in Australia]. However, I do advise my friends that, if they want to get to know other cultures, it is better to mix around, not only with the Malays. For example, mix around with your class-mates and also supervisors. If you mix around only with Malay[s], you would not gain a lot of experience. Last time I always mix with the Americans, Chinese, and Indians. That is why I have many non-Muslim friends.

So if you are talking about their custom, I knew that they have practice like 'Baby Shower'[2], and I have experienced attending them. My American friends have 'Baby Showers', and I joined them, because it is just part of their custom, not religion, so it does not matter to me. However, if it is held in church, I might reconsider attending them because as a Muslim, there are principles I need to adhere to. (Interview excerpts with Wani)

---

[2]   'Baby Shower' refers to parties held in honour of women who are about to become mothers, thus accompanying one of the major role transitions that most women undergo during their lives. Traditional baby showers are characterized by exclusively female guest lists. Usually the recipient's mother is included, as well as her sisters and possibly some aunts, nieces or female cousins. Typically friends are present, particularly friends who have had babies. While mothers of all ages are therefore included, unmarried girls (sisters, cousins, or nieces) are likely included only if they have reached adolescence. This helps to consolidate the atmosphere which is suggestive of an initiation into the mysteries of motherhood. The atmosphere of initiation and mystery is further heightened because traditional showers are always held prior to the birth of the first baby, unless nature accidentally intervenes. The atmosphere is also characteristic of a child's party. At a traditional shower the gifts are from individuals or from groups, and cover an enormous range of values. One central purpose which the traditional baby shower serves, then, is to equip the new mother with the clothes, toys, and furnishings she is going to need for the new baby. The gifts serve an economic purpose, but at the same time serve to reinforce the new mother's dependence on a community of other women. And this dependence is not only based on financial and even emotional support (Fischer & Gainer 1993, pp. 320-324).

Wani's cosmopolitan status is an asset to her since her previous experience had made her more prepared when she came here. She also elucidates her survival experience and how she was fine without any assistance when she first arrived here. According to Wani, she had a Palestinian student, an international student who voluntarily[3] came to see her on the day she arrived. She got to know other Malays once she had settled down. Her declaration characterises her new Malayness or cosmopolitan identity in terms of vocalness and openness compared to the traditional Malay society. According to Wani, her earlier exposure in living overseas and dealing with new culture has contributed to the way she acts and sees things beyond the local context.

> [G]enerally when I am in Malaysia, I realized that the fact that I have been away before. I was an undergraduate there [in the US] and after coming back from the US, I started working again. I realized that previously [before going to the US], I was not that outspoken in school or in high school. But, after coming back from the US, I realized that I have been more vocal in my views. If I want something to be done or if I see something [in her opinion] that is not right, I would speak up and suggest that it is not right and try to correct them. (Interview excerpts with Wani)

For the inexperienced or the first-timer, arrival in Australia was met with a lot of expectations, as explained by Mas.

> At least when we have friends, we have hope. When we are in need, we can hang on to the people of the same group, who understand our *adat*, our needs and the way we think. There was one time—in fact, two times—I had to take my child to a hospital Emergency Department. My friends here helped me willingly and supported me spiritually.

---

3   The Palestinian student was requested by the International Centre office to assist Wani on the day she arrived, since she was the only Muslim student around at that time. She agreed to assist Wani by showing where to get *halal* food, the location of the prayer room etc.

> Then, we became close friends and eventually we became like family. If they were in need, we helped. If we were in need, they helped. Twice I had to take one of my kids to the Emergency and leave the others with my friends, and they looked after them and had them sleep over at their house. (Translated interview excerpts with Mas)

The importance of communication emerged when Mas needed to take one of her children to hospital. Mas felt that her friends were like family and that she could trust them to look after her children. On the other hand, her friends could not have refused to help her they were like family, and as such she believed they felt obliged to assist and support her. Fascinatingly, most of the informants and other Malay students here seemed to know other Malays in advance, either friends, colleagues, relatives or even an on-line friend they had never met face-to-face. This eventually creates a small interconnected Malay community that is of importance to one another. Therefore it became their initial step in familiarizing themselves to the new environment, and provides assistance in their adaptation process. This includes the informal e-mail group for Malay postgraduate students known as MAWAR (Malaysian Western Australia Ring). This e-mail group provides general information to new students before or after arrival. Anyone from Malaysia who is coming to Western Australia to pursue study can request for their name to be added to the group e-mail list regardless of their ethnic group. One issue of concern for new inexperienced academic cosmopolitans is how to deal with the idea of coming out of their comfort zone. This is shown in Figure 7.1.

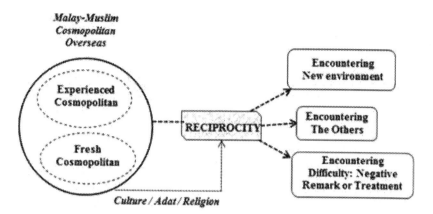

Figure 7.1 Between Adat and Religion: Tradition in Consideration

According to Syed Hussein Alatas (1954, pp. 1-2), in Islam, religion is considered not only as an individual and personal affair, but also as a social system. Islam is not only a religion in the Western sense, but also a social order. It is a way of life, and it has to control every single aspect of our lives. In other words, Syed Hussein Alatas has demonstrated that it is possible to be a person of one's own time and place, rooted in one's own culture, yet also a cosmopolitan, a citizen of the world (Kessler 2008). This also refers back to discussion on identity theory by Fenton (2010) whom distinguishes between culture and religion where the Malay postgraduates has elaborate the idea of a community they founded upon these attributes when they are in Australia. Malay-Muslims overseas negotiate their lives and identities in relation to their perpception of Malay culture/*adat* and/or religion. Rafi, one of my informants, felt that *adat* (traditional custom) is not important now and did not see how Malay *adat* applies in Western Australia. However, somewhat contradicting that assertion, he also believed that some Malay *adat* is still implemented by other Malay students (and sometimes even by him). Therefore, *adat* is like a residue (remaining or surviving (Nagata 1986, p. 42)). Nagata used the term residue to refer to customs that are considered Malay, but not Islamic. In this context, Islam has risen above the *adat*. When pursued further on the matter, Rafi recalled attending a '*Cukur Jambul*' (shaving or tonsure of hair) ritual of one of his Malay friends who just had had a baby. He felt the ritual was in one way considered a part of the Malay *adat* but in another way is merely what Islam encourages us to do. According to Rafi:

> [H]ere there are two situations. If it is *'Cukur jambul'* alone, then I feel that it is the *adat*. However, carry out the *kenduri* [communal feast] to welcome the newborn is considered *sunat* [something that is gladdened by religion], then I feel it is a necessity [an obligation]. (Translated interview excerpts with Rafi)

Rafi had the tendency to perceive Malay *adat* and Islam as dual yet complementary forces in some situations. This complementarity makes it difficult to differentiate the two since Islam has become an essential part of Malay *adat* and vice versa in some situations. The *'Cukur Jambul'*[4] ritual is held in conjuction with the birth of a new baby in a family. According to Islamic *syariat* (law), the term *'cukur jambul'* does not exist in accordance with the teaching of the Prophet Muhammad (p.u.h.), but generally is believed to originate from Hinduism. As a part of Malay *adat* practice, this ritual is conducted on the seventh day after the baby is born. In order to proceed with the ritual, a few things need to be prepared like a tub filled with three bowls or saucers that are filled with *'air tepung tawar'* (fragrant rice water used to brush on the baby's head), *'beras kunyit'* (yellow rice, literally turmeric rice), and *'bertih'* (popped rice). After the baby's hair has been cut off or shaved, the hair is put into a young coconut shell and buried outside the house.

However, this is traditionally how the ritual of *'Cukur Jambul'* was conducted. In relation to Islamic practice, the ritual is now viewed as part of Islamic *sunat* practice in accordance with the dictates of Prophet Muhammad (s.a.w.). To explain, on the seventh day after the birth of his two grandsons, the Prophet Muhammad (s.a.w.) performed the *'aqiqah'*[5], shaved their heads and gave them names.

---

4 Zuraidah Zainon 2006, 'Cukur Jambul Amalan Bidaah Orang Melayu', *Utusan Malaysia* newspaper, Malaysia,11/09/2006. <http://www.utusan.com.my/utusan/info.asp?y=2006&dt=0911&pub=utusan_malaysia&sec=bicara_agama&pg=ba_02.htm&arc=hive>

5 *'Aqiqah'* in Islamic terminology refers to sacrificing an animal on the

124

The hair that was shaved from the babies was then weighed and the equivalent value paid out by the father in gold or silver. The monetary value of this gold or silver is to be divided among the poor. During the *aqiqah* ritual, the baby will be given a taste of something sweet, like dates (crushed in a small pinch put in the baby's mouth). Islam encourages the baby's hair to be shaved off so that strong healthy hair will grow.

What is stated by Rafi can be referred to these two situations, situated between Malay *adat* and religious practice. In the case of Malay postgraduate students who have given birth while in Western Australia, the ritual of *'Cukur Jambul'* is still widely practiced in accordance with Islamic practice. At both, the practice is in accordance with the Islamic way, with guests and the ritual was followed by a *kenduri* (feast) to serve the people who came on that day. One slight alteration to the ritual involved in one of the rituals I attended was the use of dried dates and *'ZamZam'*[6] water instead of the traditional fragrant rice water. According to Abu Hassan Din Al-Hafiz (2006), a prominent Islamic Scholar in Malaysia, Islamic society should understand that traditional *(adat)* or common practice rituals should be enacted not in accordance with *'nass'* or *'dalil'* (a known, clear legal injunction, or the text of the percept of the law that is written or unwritten (Houtsma 1993, p. 881)), which should be rejected, especially if these are associated with other religious beliefs and practices.

---

occasion of a child's birth. The ritual of Aqiqah is highly encouraged among Muslim Malays on the seventh day after birth. *Aqiqah* is performed to announce the birth of the baby and invite family members, neighbours, and friends to celebrate the blessed occasion. The poor are often included in the celebrations and offered food. Two sheep are to be sacrificed for a boy, and one sheep for a girl. Cows and camels may also be sacrificed and slaughtered in an appropriate and humane *(halal)* way< http://www.hidaya.org/>.

[6] *ZamZam* water came from the Well of ZamZam in Mecca, Saudi Arabia. According to Islamic belief, it was a miraculously-generated source of water from God which began thousands of years ago when Prophet Ibrahim a.s (Abraham) infant son Ismail (Ishmael), was thirsty and kept crying and was kicking at the ground when where suddenly water sprang out. This water is the ZamZam water. <http://www.answers.com/topic/zem-zem >

For the Malay-Muslim postgraduate students, in some contexts Islam, when considered on its own, plays a much clearer role in their everyday lives, especially when compared to their cultural practices. Even with exposure to other peoples and cultures, the tendency to hold on to their religious beliefs and practices was also revealed in Raha's experience. Raha recalled a situation where she had a debate with her housemate, a Chinese girl of Christian and Buddhist background who considered herself a 'free-thinker' (as stated by Raha). In general understanding among the Malays, a freethinker refers to a person who forms their own opinions about religion on the basis of reason. Freethinkers include atheists, secular humanists and rationalists. Campus Freethought Alliance (CFA), for example, defined freethinker or free thought as 'the application of critical thinking and logic to all areas of human experience, and the rejection of supernatural and authoritatian beliefs'.[7] According to Raha:

> [T]hat which is considered *wajib* (obligatory) [in Islam], we do not have to question. We have to practise it, and it is not a choice. This includes thinking whether we should continue eating *halal* food or whether we should perform our prayer. This is not a choice. That is why I am scared because a lot of people have been forgetting this. Even back in Malaysia, we forget to practise the things that we should, and as humans we forget a lot. Just imagine we are here, overseas; nobody is going to remind us on these matters. That is why I said, for me, I need to explore and experience the situations. I felt it was good for me to be here, and living with Josie, a person who is a *free thinker*. Her mother is a Christian, and her father is a Buddhist. Being a friend with her actually strengthened my faith in Islam. This is because she always attacks [debates with] and questions me. For example, one day a dog touched [brushed past] me, so, I went straight to my office and performed *'samak*[8]. She somehow got annoyed and we debated [as recalled by Raha]:

---

7   Please refer to Campus Freethought Alliance, 'Identity & Purpose: Basics' at: <http://www.campusfreethought.org/identity/basic.html >

8   *'Samak'* or *'taharah'* is the Islamic way of cleansing that is the purification

Josie: Raha, the dog is not even bad. Why do you have to wash with earth? Isn't earth much dirtier than the dog?

Raha: But this is how we do it.

Josie: Who taught you that?

Raha: My mother.

Josie: Why does your mother have to interfere with your religion?

Raha: Josie, you were born in a family of two religions. Your mother criticized your father's religion. Your father criticized your mother's religion. But, in my family, Islam is the only sacred religion. However, I never said other religions are not good. For me, every religion is meant to lead people to good deeds.

(Translated interview excerpts with Raha)

Raha considered living with Josie, a freethinker, demanding, especially in that it challenged her religious knowledge, practice and faith. Her exposure made her put extra effort into gaining further knowledge of Islamic belief and practice, and she became more sensitive to the purpose of these practices in her everyday life. Raha explained that the continuous queries and criticisms from Josie challenged her to be more knowledgeable of Islam and at the same time strengthened her faith in Islam. She felt this situation might not have taken place if she was back in Malaysia. Raha felt that these religious practices and knowledge are often taken for granted without any effort to really understanding the purpose of the practices according to Islam.

Raha's statement on the purpose of specific practices in Islam occurs to me in relating Malay interpretations of practice as culture/ *adat*, but not religion. However, in a recent occurrence involving

---

procedures in cleaning and cleansing all kinds of dirt according to Islamic law *(syara')* especially when dealing with filth related to dogs or pigs. It is done by washing the affected area 7 times, the first with water mixed with earth (soil or sand), and six times with clean running water to ensure purification takes place. <http://www.ehalal.org/samak.html>

a female postgraduate student, an obvious conflicting of views between Malay culture and religious orientations is portrayed by Nora, a female postgraduate student, who gave birth recently (March 2011) to her second daughter. Her mother-in-law came to Western Australia a week before her due-date with a *tukang urut* (masseuse). Often, Malay women will seek the services of a *tukang urut* soon after childbirth to help tone up their abdominal muscles by massaging them back to health. The *tukang urut* went back to Malaysia a week after Nora gave birth. A fortnight later, Nora's husband sent an sms to friends (which was passed on to other Malay students) informing them that there will be a *solat hajat*[9] at Curtin *Musollah* to pray for Nora. The reason was that Nora was believed to be experiencing postnatal *depression*[10]. In Malaysia a term used to describe this situation is *gila meroyan*[11]. Nora's husband had consulted a Malay *ustaz* (religious teacher) and also the local *Imam*[12] in Perth. They attempted to help control her by reciting verses from the Quran and conducted the *solat hajat*. However, there were also claims from a few Malay students that she was possessed. They even implied that the *tukang urut* left something behind. The next day, after performing the *solat hajat*, we were informed that Nora had been diagnosed with postnatal depression and admitted to hospital. After nearly a month in hospital, Nora was discharged and has gone back to Malaysia.

---

9   'Solat hajat'(wish prayer or supererogatory prayer) is usually carried out alone in isolation or sometimes is carried out with larger numbers in attendance when faced with problems or to fulfil one's intention.

10   *Postnatal depression* refers to a prolonged period of depression, flattened affect, fatigue, irritability, and insomnia which begins within a few weeks of delivery and may last for months. It is viewed as a stress reaction. Some of the other symptoms identified include sadness, changes in sleeping and eating patterns, crying episodes, increased anxiety and panic attacks. <http://medicaldictionary.thefreedictionary.com/Postnatal+depression>.

11   'Gila meroyan' is also known a postpartum *pyschosis* which is related to *postnatal depression, maternity blues* or *puerperal psychosis*. <http://keluarga.noorjannah.com/2008/04/gila-meroyan.html>

12   'Imam' usually refers to an Islamic leader such as one who heads a mosque. However, an 'Imam' on a higher order of contrast, can mean a leader of many aspects of Islamic life. As in Nora's case, he is considered among the most knowledgeable, the wisest, and the most gallant of all Muslim people.

She was told by her doctor to rest for at least two months before continuing her studies here.

Nora's experience is frightening for pregnant Malay postgraduate students. Reviewing Nora's situation in relation to religion requires consideration of the request for assistance from religious teachers and imam, conducting *solat hajat* and also statements of her being possessed. The participation of the *Ustaz* and *Imam* reveals how religion is an important element of consideration in Malay-Muslim students' everyday lives. *Solat hajat*, on the other hand, consists of both elements of religion and Malay *adat*/culture, as it is widely practised for many reasons, either personal or group purposes. Most *solat hajat* would be followed by a small feast prepared by an organizing committee or on a potluck basis.

Malay postgraduate students preserve and maintain their religious beliefs and practices where matters of one soul are concerned. Even though *gila meroyan* also existed in the Malay traditional society, there is also a tendency for a few Malays to conclude that its occurrence has something to do with the *tukang urut*. This relates back to a similar point highlighted in the poem in Chapter one on the idea of being Malay: *'Do not be scared to violate the forbidden, if the forbidden prevents development/progress'*. In this matter, I myself am not suggesting or denying the existence of the unseen elements in life. However, in the context of being a Malay and a Muslim, there are some contrasting views that remain and are not viewed as a religious issue among the Malays, but are instead seen as conventional beliefs most commonly found in traditional Malay society. In Malaysia, since the government improved modern health care facilities, the demand for *tukang urut* has declined. However, there are still a few *tukang urut* who service new mothers and the elderly.

This idea of reciprocity applied by the Malay postgraduate students is further explained in relation to how they initiate their student identities in the new context, for example when dealing with supervisors, colleagues or others. In the process, the Malay postgraduate students are bound to face positive and negative experiences in their process of adjustment, such as in finding suitable accommodation, identifying where to get *halal* foods, in dealing with the weather and in exploring ways to spend their leisure time.

However, in the process of engaging in their life experience with reciprocity in mind, they are also constantly remembering and applying their Malay culture/*adat* and religion in their life. This could be related to my earlier statement that Malay culture is bulwarked by Islamic religious values. As long as the prevailing Malay cultural/ *adat* practices are not against their religious practice, Islamic and community-oriented rituals like *cukur jambul* (shaving or tonsure of hair), *kenduri* (feast) and *solat hajat* (supererogatory prayer expressing an intention or vow) continue to be practised by the Malay postgraduate students

Conclusion

When Malays cross the Malaysian border as students and leave Malaysia, they will undeniably become part of a new system of values (Donnan & Wilson, 1999). To what extent are they able or do they want to secure the new value systems in their daily lives? How do they judge their Malay cosmopolitanness identity, and how are they judged in terms of *adat* and religion? I have attempted to answer these questions through the experiences faced by Malay-Muslim postgraduates in relation to their interpersonal communications with others. The most important symbolic system uniting Malays combines their language with their religious belief and practice. While Malay-Muslim students encounter a range of new circumstances in Australia, their needs and learned cultural practices assist them in maintaining, adjusting and, very occasionally transforming their social identities. Barth (1981, p. 207) argued that because identities are signaled as well as embraced, one would expect role constraints. A person would be reluctant to act in a new way for fear that such behaviour might be inappropriate for his/her identity, and the person would be quick to classify forms of activity in terms of one cluster or another of ethnic characteristics. Border crossing among Malay-Muslim postgraduate students, therefore, does not result in Malay-Muslim students changing their existing identity to any great extent. However, the extent to which they hold on to their ethnic and religious identity differs across individuals before returning to Malaysia.

Upon their return to Malaysia, the new Malay cosmopolitan identity constructed in Western Australia, was not presumed to lead to any sort of stressful situation in the future, although there are exceptions to it. When arriving in Western Australia, the Malay-Muslim postgraduate students anticipated changes in relation to their survival and adaptation to their new environment. These changes were not expected to be permanent, unless the student was applying to become a permanent resident or to obtain citizenship overseas. The fact that Malay-Muslim identity is strengthened by continuous practice of Malay culture and Islam religion supports the idea that the best way to be Malay is to be with Malays. The communication of shared systems of symbolic verbal and nonverbal behaviour is meaningful to group members who have a shared sense of belonging and who share traditions, heritage, language, and similar norms and behaviours (Fong & Chuang 2004, p. 6).

This article also highlighted that even though all Malay-Muslim postgraduate students are distinct in their own ways, most of the experiences they face refer back to their Malay culture/adat and Islamic values. Therefore, these features are considered more compelling than other cultures for Malay-Muslims living temporarily beyond Malaysian borders. In comparison with other similar findings across other scholarly studies, this study is important particularly in emphasizing the role of religion and/or adat, specifically how they become more 'self-consciously' religious, as fundamentally underlying identity adjustment by the Malay-Muslim postgraduate students overseas.

References

Abu Hassan Din Al-Hafiz 2006, in article 'Cukur jambul amalan bidaah orang Melayu' by Zunaidah Zainon, Archive : 11/09/2006 Utusan Malaysia Online: http://www.utusan. com.my/utusan/info.asp?y=2006&dt=0911&pub=utusan_ m a l a y s i a & s e c = b i c a r a _ a g a m a & p g = b a _ 0 2 . htm&arc=hive&arc=hive

Anderson, Benedict 1992, *Long Distance Nationalism: World Capitalism and the Rise of Identity Politics*, CASA, Amsterdam.

Barth, Fredrik, 1981, *Process and Form in Social Life: Selected essays of Fredrik Barth: Volume1*, Routledge & Kegan Paul, London.

Donnan, Hastings & Wilson Thomas M. 1999, *Borders: Frontiers of Identity, Nation and State*, Berg, Oxford, New York.

Eagleton, Terry 1991, *Ideology: An Introduction*, Verso, London, UK.

Fenton, S. 2010, *Ethnicity*, 2nd edn, Polity Press, Cambridge, UK.

Fischer, Eileen & Gainer, Brenda 1993, 'Baby Showers: A Rite of Passage in Transition', *Advances in Consumer Research*, vol. 20, pp. 320-324.

Fong, Mary & Chuang, Rueyling, 2004, *Communicating Ethnic & Cultural Identity*, Rowman & Littlefield Pub, USA.

Goffman, Erving 1989, 'On Fieldwork', *Journal of Contemporary Ethnography*, vol. 18, no. 2, pp. 123-32.

Gouldner, A.W. 1960, 'The Norm of Reciprocity: A Preliminary Statement', *American Sociological Review*, vol. 25, no. 2, pp. 161-179.

Hall, Stuart 2002, 'Political Belonging in a World of Multiple Identities", in *Conceiving Cosmopolitanism: Theory, Context and Practice*, eds Steven Vertovec & Robin Cohen, Oxford University Press, Oxford, pp. 25-31.

Hannerz, Ulf 1990, 'Cosmopolitan and Locals in World Culture', in *Global Culture: Nationalim, Globalization and Modernity*, ed M. Featherstone, Sage, London.

_____ 2004, 'Cosmopolitanism' in *A Companion to the Anthropology of Politics*, eds David Nugent and Joan Vincent, Blackwell, Oxford, pp. 69-85.

Hisashi Endo 1999, 'Adat in Transition' in *Political Culture and Ethnicity: An Anthropological Study in Southeast Asia*, ed Toh Goda, New Day Publisher, Quezon City, Phillippines.

Hobhouse, L.T. 1951, *Morals in Evolution: A Tudy in Comparative Ethics*, Chapman & Hall, London.

Hooker, M.B. 1970, *Adat Laws in Modern Malaya*, Oxford University Press, Kuala Lumpur, pp. 71-90.

Houtsma M. Th. 1993, *Brill's E.J.: First Encyclopaedia of Islam, 1913-1936*, Leiden, Netherlands.

Kahn, Joel S. 1992, 'Class, Ethnicity and Diversity: Some Remarks on Malay Culture in Malaysia' in *Fragmented Vision: Culture and Politics in Contemporary Malaysia*, eds Joel S. Kahn & Francis

Loh Kok Wah, ASAA with ALLEN & UNWIN, Australia, pp. 158-178.

_____ 2004, 'The Premise of Difference: Race, culture, nation and cosmopolitan practice in (pen)insular Southeast Asia', Revised text of lecture delivered at *Ateneo de Manila University*, 9 February 2004.

_____ 2006, *Other Malays: Nationalism and Cosmopolitanism in the Modern Malay World*, Southeast Asia Publication Series, Singapore.

Kendall, Gavin P., Woodward, Ian & Skrbis, Zlatko 2009, *The Sociology of Cosmopolitanism: Globalization, Identity, Culture and Government*, Palgrave MacMillan, United Kingdom.

Kessler, Clive S. 2008, 'Syed Hussein Alatas (1928-2007): Wise Muslim Rationalist, Culturally Grounded Cosmopolitan' in *Profiles in Courage: Political Actors & Ideas in Contemporary Asia*, eds Gloria Davies, J.V. D'Cruz & Nathan Hollier, Australian Scholarly Publishing, Melbourne, pp. 169-183.

Kolm, Serge-Christophe 2008, *Reciprocity: An Economics of Social Relations*, Cambridge University Press, Cambridge.

Kristeva J. 1991, *Strangers to Ourselves*, Harvester Wheatsheaf, New York.

Manzini E. 2007, 'Design Research for Sustainable Social Innovation', in *Design Research Now*, ed R Michel, Birkhäuser Basel, pp. 233-45.

Nagata, Judith A. 1986, 'The Impact of Islamic Revival (Dakwah) on the Religious Culture of Malaysia' in *Religion, Values, and Development in Southeast Asia*, eds Bruce Matthews and Judith Nagata, Institute of Southeast Asian Studies, Singapore, pp. 37-50.

Peletz, Michael 1987, 'The Exchange of Men in 19th Century Negeri Sembilan (Malaya)', *American Ethnologist*, vol 14, no. 3, pp. 449-469.

Provencher, Ronald 1971, *Two Malay Worlds: Interaction in Urban and Rural Settings*, Center for South and Southeast Asia Studies, University of California, Berkeley.

Syed Hussein Alatas 1954, 'The Islamic State', *Progressive Islam*, vol. 1, no. 3, pp. 1-2.

_____ 1996, *The New Malay: His Role and Future*, Association of Muslim Proffessionals, Singapore, pp. 6-7.

Szerszynski, B. & Urry, J. 2006, 'Visuality, Mobility and the Cosmopolitan: Inhabiting the World from Afar', British Journal of Sociology, vol. 57, no. 1, pp. 113-131.

Wilder, William D. 1982, *Communication, Social Structure and Development in Rural Malaysia: A Study of Kampung Kuala Bera*, Athlone Press, London.

Zainal Kling, 1989/1990, 'The Socio-cultural Unity of the Malay World', in *Melayu Sri Lanka*, ed Abdul Latiff, pp. 97-117.

_____ 1997, '*Adat: Collective Self-Image, in Images of Malay-Indonesian Identity*', in *Images of Malay-Indonesian Identity*, eds Michael Hitchcock and Victor T. King, Oxford University Press, Oxford, pp. 45-51.

Maintenance and (Co-)Creation of Tradition in JapaneseTransnational Corporations/Organisations in Indonesia

Dr. Yukimi Shimoda

Abstract

This study considers a boundary between tradition and modernity. Transnational corporations and organisations are often associated with the image of providing 'the essence of modernity' through business activities across geographical boundaries. In turn, close observation in everyday activities in the workplace reveals that individual employees are maintaining and (co-)creating tradition. This makes a sharp contrast with the image of 'modernity'.

This study based upon ethnographic field work in Indonesia explores the daily activities of both Japanese expatriate and Indonesian employees, who worked for Japanese transnational corporations and organisations. In transnational office spaces, Japanese expatriate and Indonesian employees encounter and engage in maintaining and (co-) creating each other's traditions as obligation and/or in a positive manner. They cross geo-spatial boundary of the two countries, and time, which they spent for fostering their traditions in home countries. These changes occur subtly and slowly in everyday life among employees. It depends on the point of view whether changes brought by their interactions are considered as detraditionalisation or modernisation. In conclusion, this study highlights the ambiguity of the boundary between tradition and modernity.

Introduction

> People, events, organizations, and whole societies are no longer simply tied to single places or particular times. Instead, the essence of modernity is its ability, indeed necessity, to connect local times, spaces, and people with global agendas, standardized time horizons and constantly shifting spatial arrangements (Friedland & Boden 1994, pp. 3-4).

The existence of transnational corporations/organisations can be considered as one of those who have been providing 'the essence of modernity' in terms of their participation in global flows of information, goods and people through business activities beyond geographical boundaries. However, observation within modern transnational corporations/organisations tends to reveal the maintenance and (co-)creation of tradition among employees. By exploring the everyday activities of both Japanese expatriate and Indonesian employees, who worked for Japanese transnational corporations/organisations, this ethnographic study investigates the extent to which tradition and modernity play their roles in transnational office spaces. In conclusion, this study highlights the ambiguity of the boundary between tradition and modernity.

Co-Existence of Tradition and Modernity

Tradition and modernity are certainly different. We often use these terms in different situations and contexts. Tradition is, for instance, 'a description of a general process of handing down', while modernity is that of 'something existing now, just now' (Williams 1985 [1976], pp. 208, 319). Scholars explain that:

[t]radition—that which is handed down—includes material objects, beliefs about all sorts of things, images of persons and events, practices and institutions. It includes buildings, monuments, landscapes, sculptures, painting, books, tools, machines. It includes all that a society of a given time possesses and which already existed when its present possessors came upon it and which is not solely the product of physical processes in the external world or exclusively the result of ecological and physiological necessity (Shils 1981, p. 12).

On the other hand, modernity is 'the intertwined emergence of capitalism, the bureaucratic nation-states, and industrialism' (Friedland & Boden, 1994, p. 2) and 'modes of social life or organisation which emerged in Europe' in about the seventeenth century and has spread in the world, which results in its association with the specific time and geographical space (Giddens, 1990, p. 1). There claims suggest that tradition is somehow bounded with the past, while modernity is with the present.

Nevertheless, tradition and modernity are not either-or concepts, but can exist in the same time and space. They are on a single line in process of time. Responding to discussions of modernity and post-modernity, which tend to be considered to cut off from each other, some argue that '[d]etraditionalization [. . .] cannot occur when people think of themselves as belonging to the whole' (Heelas 1996, p. 4). This, in turn, means that traditionalisation can 'occur when people think of themselves as belonging to the whole'. However, such shift from belonging and not-belonging is very individual process and complex. In everyday lives, it is an unclearly overlapping phenomenon. Traditionlisation and detraditionalisation coexist in practice, together with 'tradition-maintenance and the construction—or reconstruction—of traditional forms of life' (Heelas, 1996, pp. 7-11).

In office spaces of transnational corporations/organisations, new (or unfamiliar) goods, people, and information brought about modernisation (particularly in the sense of technological development) are converged. Taking into account Foucault's view that the feature of modernity is 'the adaption of new disciplinary mechanisms' (Friedland & Boden, 1994, pp. 24-25), transnational corporations/organisations provide such 'new disciplinary mechanisms'. Their offices are, in a sense, the centre of modernity in host societies, especially in developing countries. In Malaysia, for instance, Smith's studies (2002, 1999, 1994) demonstrate that Japanese foreign direct investment brought modernisation by introducing 'capital, technology and management expertise' in its post-independent period, together with middle-class lifestyle. Under modernisation, host national employees were making efforts to keep a balance between new cultures and theirs, such as deities and religious practices.

Within a society, the transformation from tradition to modern is in general seamless and often overlapped, and the process is less visible. In contrast, by connecting different space and time, transnational corporations/organisations present the process more visibly due to the noticeable contrast between two, or multiple, societies. The examination of Japanese transnational corporations/ organisations in Indonesia will demonstrate the way in which Japanese expatriate and host national employees participated in maintaining and (co-)creating each tradition in an imposed society, which reveal the process of traditionalisation and detraditionalisation—or modernisation—and its complexity.

Methodology

I conducted my fieldwork in the latter half of the 2000s in Indonesia. There were about11,000 Japanese long-term residents, who had been in Indonesia more than three months (MOFA 2010, p. 38). My main field site was an office of a non-profit Japanese organisation (JO), which was located on a floor of a high-rise office building in the centre of Jakarta.[1] The Jakarta Office of the JO (JOI) was providing services for Indonesia in cooperation with both the Japanese and Indonesian governments. Over a hundred staff members worked in the JOI. The Japanese expatriate staff comprised one third of the total number. The rest were Indonesian national staff members,

---

[1]   In the interests of confidentiality, the details of the organisation and the respondents that appear in this paper are undisclosed.

including drivers, and several locally employed Japanese staff. A majority of the Indonesian white-collar staff was female, while most of the Japanese expatriate staff were males. This is a common feature of transnational organisations/corporations in the world (see Caligiuri & Lazarova 2002, p. 761).

In the JOI, I conducted participant observation and formal and informal interviews, working as an unpaid intern every day for one year. The semi-structured formal interviews lasted approximately one to three hours and were conducted once or twice with about 30 Japanese staff members and about 40 Indonesian staff members. They included both regular and contract-base employees. The age range of the respondents covered late-20s to late-50s: the majority of Japanese respondents were in their 30s and the Indonesian respondents were concentrated in their late 20s and the early 30s. I also approached more than 10 Japanese expatriate employees and about 10 host national employees, who worked for other organisations/corporations. When I had an opportunity to visit their offices, I tried to observe their working environments. Several Japanese expatriate wives were also interviewed. I transcribed the recorded in-depth interviews and analysed them, together with the field notes.

Maintenance of Tradition

The numerous interviews with Japanese expatriate employees and participant observation revealed similar exclusive life styles identified by existing expatriate literatures (e.g. Fechter, 2007; Cohen, 1977; Glebe, 2003), although there were rich spaces for interpersonal interactions with host nationals (Shimoda, 2011). In Western style flats in high-rising apartments in the heart of Jakarta, many Japanese expatriate families maintained some flavours of Japan: cooking Japanese dishes, decollating walls with seasonal ornaments, and using *tatami* mattress in living rooms.

Similarly, in offices of Japanese corporations/organisations which were equipped with modern technology, such as computers, the Internet, and the TV meting system, as well as the telephone, some traits of Japan could be observed. As such overseas branches were, as a matter of course, part of the organisational system of Japanese corporations/organisations, employees were required to work, by following Japanese organisational procedures and ethics.

Apart from work styles, there were other Japanese influences in offices. *Ocha*[2] (Japanese green tea) is one of them. When I visited Japanese expatriate employees in their offices for interviews, without being asked, I was sometimes served *ocha* in a traditional Japanese tea cup and wooden (or plastic) saucer, or alternatively English and Indonesian tea without sugar, rather than tea with sugar and coffee with condensed milk, which were very common in Indonesia. Such corporations/organisations requested or trained their staff members to serve tea to suit the taste of Japanese guests.

In the JOI, tea ladies served tea to the staff every morning. Not only the Japanese staff were but also Indonesian staff members, who wished, served *ocha*. Both Japanese and Indonesia guests were served *ocha* most of the time. One day, in a meeting with staff members of an Indonesia's domestic advertising company, a tea lady served them *ocha* as usual. One of them clearly showed her excitement. The staff member who was curiously looking at a green tea in a traditional Japanese tea cup said, 'this is Japanese tea!', and drank it. In response to my question, she confirmed that it was her first time to drink Japanese tea. In another meeting, one Indonesian counterpart told me that he was looking forward to drinking *ocha* whenever he visited the JOI.

On the other hand, typical characteristics of Indonesian offices also could be seen in Japanese corporations/organisations. In reception areas of particularly Japanese factories where hundreds, or thousands, of Indonesian workers were employed, there were often the national symbol mark of Garuda and the framed pictures of the President and the Vice-President on the wall. There were also *musalla* (room for Muslim people to conduct daily prayer). Although there was no symbolic decollation of Indonesia in the JOI, *musolla* was located within the modern open office space in a high-rising office building. The JOI also followed the Indonesian public holidays, for instance as *Idul Fitri* (a Muslim holiday), *Imlek* (Chinese New Year),

---

[2]   In a strict sense, the word of *ocha* consist of 'o' as a prefix and *cha* (green tea). The prefix of 'o' is often used as an honorific indicator for selected nouns. Some nouns, like *cha*, are almost always used with the 'o' prefix.

Nyepi (a Hindu holiday), *Waisak* (a Buddhist holiday), and Christmas, set on the careful concern of Indonesia's various cultures. Due to the differences of holiday systems, it sometimes happened that when the JOI closed, the headquarters opened, and vice versa. There were some staff members who wore *batik* (an Indonesian wax-resist textile) clothes particularly on Friday. In the time of my fieldwork, *batik* was reappraised as tradition, since Indonesian *batik* had been included in the Representative List of the Intangible Cultural Heritage of Humanity published by the United Nations Educational, Scientific and Cultural Organization (UNESCO) in 2009 (UNESCO n.d.). The popularity of *batik* clothes were growing more than before. Even those who had avoided batik as out of fashion became willing to wear them.

Thus, Japanese transnational corporations/organisations maintained both Japanese and Indonesian traditions. Nevertheless, as the following section explains traditions were in fact (co-) created among their employees.

(Co-)Creation of Tradition

In the JOI, some traditions mentioned above were not only maintained, but creating—or in a sense co-created—among Japanese and Indonesian staff members. *Ocha* was usually prepared and served by tea ladies to almost all Japanese staff members, several Indonesian staff members, and guests. The taste made by the tea ladies was the same as what people could drink in Japan. One day, I was having a late lunch in a pantry located in the office, during which I was talking to one of the tea ladies. Suddenly, a receptionist came and requested the tea lady *ocha* for a few guests. She immediately set Japanese tea cups on a table and started making *ocha* skilfully. When people make tea in Japan, they usually pour tea into cups little by little several times in order make its density equal. She was exactly doing so. I asked her from whom she had learnt how to make *ocha*. She shyly smiled and said that her Indonesian predecessor had taught her how to make it. She placed the cups with plastic saucers on a tray and carried them to a meeting room.

In another time, also in the pantry, one Indonesian staff member was making *ocha* for herself. She told me that she liked *ocha*, which was, she felt, healthier than ordinary Indonesian teas with sugar. Not only her, but also did other Indonesian staff members drink *ocha* during working. There were also those who preferred to use sugar for *ocha*. Drinking *ocha* had been becoming a common culture among Japanese and Indonesian staff members. Considering some modification of the traditional way of drinking *ocha*, they were co-creating a new 'tradition' of drinking *ocha* at least within the JOI in the host society.

In a similar vein, to wear *batik* clothes was shared by Japanese staff members. Not all, but several Japanese staff members enjoyed wearing *batik* clothes occasionally: casual *batik* shirts (with short sleeves and cotton) on Friday for pleasure and formal *batik* (with long sleeves and sometimes silk) on work-related official ceremonies and wedding receptions. One day, I saw that one male Japanese staff member wore a formal silk *batik* shirt with long sleeves. I had never seen him wearing *batik*. In response to my query, he explained that he had bought it in consultation with a senior Indonesia staff member. On the day, as he had to attend a very formal ceremony, he thought that it would be appropriate to wear batik.

There were those who really enjoyed wearing batik. One male Japanese staff member wearing batik shirt said, 'I would not be able to wear this kind of clothes in the office in Japan'. More than male staff members, female Japanese members seemingly took pleasure in wearing *batik* clothes, such as blouse, skirts, and dresses, which were fashionable for them. If not clothes, they wore a scarf with *batik* patterns around their necks. *Batik* clothes were easy to purchase every shopping mall. Although these clothes used *batik*, the designs of clothes were often adapt the trend of these days in order to attract young Indonesians who started enjoying wearing batik that was in fashion. Some female Japanese staff members even asked local tailors to make blouses and skirts with batik, which they had bought in a local market, modelling on clothes they had brought from Japan. There were also those who wore *batik* clothes even after retuning Japan. They probably enjoyed 'playful experimentation' in which they 'articulate[d] a new way of life and multiple belongings' temporarily, as Nowicka (2010, pp. 21-22) finds among Polish migrants in Scotland who wear Polish tartan. Together with Indonesians who wore *batik* clothes as a trend, Japanese staff members, as well as other Japanese expatriates, were participating in creating traditions.

In addition, by adopting Indonesia's public holidays and introducing part of Japanese ones, the JOI modified the calendar systems of both Indonesia and Japan, and created a new calendar system. In so doing, the staff were constructing an alternative organisational culture, which was different from the headquarters in Japan, although they were forced to follow the system as a regulation.

In addition, the Japanese and Indonesian staff were creating a unique mixture of three languages (English, Japanese, and Indonesian) in their everyday lives in the office where English was a working language. Several Japanese words were commonly blended into English sentences spoken by the Indonesian staff: *hai* (yes), *iie* (no), *arigatō* (thank you), *sumimasen* (excuse me), *tantō* (person in charge), XX-*san* (Mr. XX or Ms. XX), *anō* (ah, uh, excuse me), and *giri giri* (almost to the limit). In turn, common Indonesian words, such as *tolong* (please), *silahkan* (go ahead, please), *bisa* (can), *boleh* (permissible), *saya* (I), and *anda* (you), were also used by the Japanese staff within English sentences. Among the staff, the three languages were skilfully combined, as in 'Minta tiga ocha ne (three Japanese teas please) and 'Please *tiga ocha*' [*minta* (Indonesian) = please, *tiga* (Indonesian) = three, *ocha* (Japanese) = Japanese tea, *ne* (Japanese) = a Japanese ending word]. These were simply a combination of the three languages' vocabularies, not the creation of a new language. Some mixed the three languages, since they wished to learn and use the other's languages according to their own ability, which was also a 'playful experimentation'. Some used them in order to avoid misunderstanding by repeating the same (or similar) sentences in both Japanese and Indonesian. No matter what intensions the staff had, however, this mixture of the three languages became a kind of culture, or tradition, among the staff in the JOI.

Part of the above activities was supported by the staff partly because of their sense of 'entailing respect and duty', which tends to perpetuate tradition (Williams 1985 [1976], p. 319). For instance, the staff member, who bought a *batik* shirt for a formal ceremony, perhaps felt his obligation to wear *batik*, which was a formal Indonesian cloth, and present his respect to Indonesian counterparts. The tea ladies made *ocha*, which was their duty ordered by the office in the earliest days of the JOI. The mixture of the three languages was the efforts of some staff members who wished to show their respect to the other by demonstrating their ability of using the other's language. They were creating each other's traditions cooperatively and occasionally a new form of tradition through the modification of each other's traditions, although their reasons were vary (or no particular reason).

Detraditionalisation, and Modernisation

As shown above, traditions existed in the modern office of the JOI. The maintenance and (co-) creation of tradition occurred in the transnational office space of the JOI which became a place of connecting individual employees, who lived and have lived in different sense of time and socio-cultural spaces in home and host countries. The traditions brought by the Japanese staff which could be historically traced back to Japan were not that of the Indonesian staff, and vice versa. The circumstances of maintaining and (co-)creating traditions among the Japanese and Indonesian staff did not naturally emerged, since each group had their rooted common past and was partly force to be cut off from it in the office. Hobsbawm (1983, p. 1) points out that '"[t]raditions" which appear or claim to be old and are often quite recent in origin and sometimes invented'. He introduces the concept of 'invented tradition', which are 'both "traditions" actually invented, constructed and formally instituted and those emerging in a less easily traceable manner within a brief and dateable period' (Hobsbawm 1983, p. 1). The traditions of the JOI were partly created in formal ways due to the organisational regulations (e.g. holiday system) and partly fostered among the staff voluntarily for their convenience and pleasures (e.g. *batick* cloths, mixed languages). Activities of maintaining and (co-)creating tradition in the JOI, therefore, could be seen as a kind of the process of conducting to 'invent' traditions in its new environment.

The traditions invented by the JOI staff were not exactly the same as the ones, which the Japanese and Indonesian staff could find in their own societies. For instance, there were staff members who added sugar in *ocha*. By taking part in maintaining and (co-) creating each other's traditions, the modification of specific traditions occurred. Japanese and Indonesian cultures were changed in accordance with the appropriateness of situations and individual capacities. In this sense, the process of maintaining and (co-)creating traditions become as that of detraditionalisation.

Furthermore, it could be said that the maintenance and (co-) creation of traditions were also the process of modernisation. In the sense that Japanese and Indonesian traditions were 'new' to the Indonesian and Japanese staff respectively. Traditions, such as *ocha*, *batik*, and unfamiliar languages, became modern to them. They encountered each other's traditions—the continuance of the past— as the present. In the discussion about the organisational system of American transnational corporations, Leggett (2003, p. 44) points out the connection of the Western imagination of Jakarta and the Indonesian with a colonial history, and states that '[t]he flexible processes of capital accumulation are thus experienced by the agents of capital [expatriate and host national employees] from a position at "the interstices of the old and the new, confronting the past as the present" (Pollok, *et al.*, 2002: 4)'. Leggett' persuasive analysis focuses on the colonial connections from the historical viewpoints. Nevertheless, the case of the JOI suggests that the encounter between the past and the present could be understood in alternative viewpoints. It was also occurring in the both ways, from the Japanese staff to the Indonesian staff, and from the latter to the former, and its meaning could be read in different contexts. The JOI provided 'transnational social spaces', which are 'preconditions for and, at the same time, sedimented outcomes of, the globalization process' and which formed socio-cultural practices by crossing spatial boundaries of two or more nation-states (Pries 2001, pp. 5, 17-18). In the space of the JOI, the staff learnt each other's traditional socio-cultural practices and were adapted them as modern ones.

It is arguable if the Indonesians think Japanese, or Asian, cultures as modern, which is often associated with the West. 'At the heart of Indonesia's felt attraction for things Western has been the sense that the West provides the avenue, the direction, to "becoming modern"' (Elson, 2006, p. 262). However, in Malaysia, for instance, the 'Look East' policy lead its industrialisation through the introduction of Japanese work ethics and management system in the 1980s, by emphasising the superiority of Japanese society supported by the high economic growth rate of those days (Smith, 1994). The Japan's economic strength was certainly competitive with that of the West. Under this policy, simultaneously, Malaysia learnt about Japanese consumption activities, or the 'Japanized' version of the West (Smith 1994, p. 336). The similar situation was observed in Indonesia where the number of Japanese transnational corporations/ organisations also significantly had increased in the 1980s. During my field work, it was not rare that *sushi* restaurants and *karaoke* boxes[3] were found in newly opened huge, modern shopping malls, where middle class Indonesians were enjoying their leisure times. In sushi restaurants, *ocha* is served to customers and became familiarised in the Indonesian society.

In the similar vein, some might argue if Indonesian cultures were modern to the Japanese people. As mentioned above, female Japanese staff members used batik clothes and accessories. Not only these staff members, but also Japanese wives who accompanied their husband introduced *batik* into their everyday lives from clothes to tablecloths and coasters. Analysing the consumption of Hong Kong popular culture in Japan since the mid-1990s, Iwabuchi (2002) claims that the Japanese fans of Hong Kong popular culture admire 'Asianism' as Japanese media representations of 'Asia' not because of the nostalgia of 'Asia' before encountering the West, but because of Hong Kong's maintenance of 'Asia', which Japan is losing, in a sensitive balance of 'Western-induced capitalist modernity'. He points out that '[a] certain degree of economic development is thus a minimum condition for other Asian cultures to enter "our" realm of modernity' (Iwabuchi, 2002, pp. 568-569). Living in Jakarta, the capital city of Indonesia, who was a middle income country (OECD

---

3 A *karaoke* box is a place where customers can rent one of small and medium-sized rooms with equipment for singing by the hour. It is popular to go there with friends and families. Although *karaoke* was originally invented in Japan, it is arguable if Indonesian people, particularly young Indonesians, recognise the fact (Shimoda 2011, pp. 176-177).

2009), most of the Japanese expatriates were amazed by the size of the city and the degree of its development, which was seemingly comparable even with Tokyo. Jakarta could provide such 'a minimum condition' for Japanese expatriates to see Indonesian cultures, such as batik clothes with modified design, as part of modernity.

Thus, tradition and modernity are intricately interwoven. The interpretation of tradition and modernity depends on individuals' viewpoints and/or contexts.

Conclusion

The modern office space of the JOI is one of the places where the development of modern transportation and communication technology brought information, goods, and people together. One of the senior Indonesian staff members told me that it had been a very special activity for her to use e-mail and the Internet when she had entered the JOI more than ten years ago. For the staff member, the current office also provided the similar environments in the host society. In such space, the Japanese and Indonesian staff were encountering each other's traditions and participating in maintaining them as obligation and/or in a positive manner. The maintenance of each other's cultures was simultaneously (co-)creation activities. However, the activities of maintaining and (co-)creating traditions among the staff were not supported by their continual past. The geo-spatial mobility of the Japanese and Indonesian staff from Japan to Indonesia and from local houses to the JOI respectively cut them off from their traditions. In so doing, they crossed geo-spatial boundary of the two countries, and time, which they had spent for forming their traditions. Accordingly, traditions were detraditionalised and modernised.

Transnational corporations/organisations certainly bring 'the essence of modernity' in the host society in various forms: not only technology and information, but also detraditionalisation and modernisation of traditions. Such changes are occurring subtly and slowly in everyday life among employees. Participants' activities can be seen in different ways, which depend on the point of standing. The boundary between tradition and modernity blurs and hard to be distinguished. In his discussion on modernity, Schmidt (2009, p. 30) concludes that the questions of its convergence and divergence 'should better be treated as methodological artifacts' based upon either countries and regions or upon the long-term historical social formation of a society: the former tends to highlight differences and the latter similarities. In a similar vein, tradition and modernity could be considered as 'methodological artifacts', in which focuses shift from the continuation of the past or the creation of the present.

References

Caligiuri, P & Lazarova, M 2002, 'A Model for the Influence of Social Interaction and Social Support on Female Expatriates' Cross-cultural Adjustment', *The International Journal of Human Resource Management*, vol. 13, no. 5, pp. 761-772.

Cohen, E 1977, 'Expatriate Communities', *Current Sociology*, vol. 24, no. 3, pp. 5-133.

Elson, RE 2006, 'Indonesia and the West: an Ambivalent, Misunderstood Engagement', *Australian Journal of Politics & History*, vol. 52, no. 2, pp. 261-271.

Fechter, A-M 2007, *Transnational Lives: Expatriates in Indonesia*, Ashgate, Hampshire and Burlington.

Friedland, R & Boden, D 1994, 'NowHere: An Introduction to Space, Time and Modernity', in *NowHere: Space, Time and Modernity*, eds R Friedland & D Boden, University of California Press, Berkeley, Los Angeles, and London, pp. 1-60.

Giddens, A 1990, *The Consequences of Modernity*, Polity Press, Cambridge.

Glebe, G 2003, 'Segregation and the Ethnoscape: The Japanese Business Community in Düsseldorf', in *Global Japan: The Experience of Japan's New Immigrant and Overseas Communities*, eds R Goodman, C Peach, A Takenaka & P White, RoutledgeCurzon, London and New York, pp. 98-115.

Heelas, P 1996, 'Introduction: Detraditionalization and its Rivals', in *Detraditionalization: Critical Reflections on Authority and Identity*, eds P Heelas, S Lash & P Morris, Blackwell, Massachusette and Oxford, pp. 1-20.

Hobsbawm, E 1983, 'Introductin: Inventing Traditions', in *The Invention of Tradition*, eds E Hobsbawm & T Ranger, Cambridge University Press, Cambridge, London, New York, New Rochelle, Melbourne, and Sydney, pp. 1-14.

Iwabuchi, K 2002, 'Nostalgia for a (Different) Asian Modernity: Media Consumption of "Asia" in Japan', *positions: east asia cultures critique*, vol. 10, no. 3, pp. 547-573.

Leggett, WH 2003, Culture, Power, Difference: Managing Ambivalence and Producing Identity in the Transnational Corporate Offices of Jakarta, Indonesia, Ph.D. Thesis, University of Illinois.

MOFA, 2010, *Kaigai Zairyu Hojin Su Chosa Tokei: 2009 (Annual Report of Statistics on Japanese Nationals Overseas: 2009 (as of 1st October 2008))*, CAB Consular and Migration Policy Division, the Ministry of Foreign Affairs, Japan.

Nowicka, M 2010, 'Transcultural Encounters of Diversity—Towards a Research Agenda. The Case of Polish Presence in the UK', MMG Working Paper 10-04, Max Planck Institute for the Study of Religious and Ethnic Diversity, Göttingen.

OECD 2009, *DAC List of ODA Recipients*. Available from: http://www.oecd.org/dac/aidstatistics/43540882.pdf [17/10/2012].

Pries, L 2001, 'The Approach of Transnational Social Spaces: Responding to New Configurations of the Social and the Spatial', in *New Transnational Social Spaces: International Migration and Transnational Companies in the Early Twenty-First Century*, ed. L Pries, Routledge, London and New York, pp. 3-33.

Schmidt, VH 2009, 'Convergence and Divergence in Societal Modernization: Global Trends, Regional Variations, and Some Implications for Sustainability', in *The New Middle Classes: Globalizing Lifestyles, Consumerism and Environmental Concern*, eds H Lange & L Meier, Springer, Dordrecht, Heidelberg, London, and New York, pp. 29-49.

Shils, E 1981, *Tradition*, University of Chicago Press, Chicago.

Shimoda, Y 2011, *From the Porous Spaces on the Bubble: The Life and Work of Japanese Expatriate Employees in Indonesia and their Relations with the Host Society*, Unpublished, The University of Western Australia.

Smith, WA 1994, 'Japanese Cultural Image in Malaysia: Implications of the 'Look East' Policy', in *Japan and Malaysian Development: In the sShadow of the Rising Sun*, ed. J K. S., Routledge, London and New York, pp. 335-363.

Smith, WA 1999, 'The Contribution of a Japanese Firm to the Cultural Construction of the New Rich in Malaysia', in *Culture and Privilege in Capitalist Asia*, ed. M Pinches, Routledge, London and New York, pp. 111-136.

Smith, WA 2002, 'Managing Ethnic Diversity in a Japanese Joint Venture in Malaysia', in *Japan, Canada, and the Pacific Rim: Trade, Investment, and Security Issues (UBC Year of Japan: 2002-2003)*, Canada.

UNESCO n.d., 'Indonesian Batik', the Intangible Cultural Heritage. Available from: http://www.unesco.org/culture/ich/index.php?pg=00011&RL=00170 [26/10/2010].

Williams, R 1985 [1976], *Keywords: A Vocabulary of Culture and Society*, Revised Edition edn, Oxford University Press, New York.

SOCIAL CAPITAL NETWORKS AND MORAL ASPECTS: HOUSEWIVES' PETTY TRADING AND CONSUMPTION OF LIFESTYLE COMMODITIES

Dr. Siti Zanariah Ahmad Ishak

Abstract

The housewives' involvement in petty trading in a Malay community of Sarawak has allowed them to consume lifestyle commodities. Petty trading is conducted with an objective in mind, this being the accumulation of capital for the consumption of lifestyle commodities. They traded among themselves in social networks existed in the village. This chapter does not regard trading and consuming from the perspective of common capitalist activity. Therefore, its aim is to investigate the activities of trading and consumption as an act of social action which includes fostering moral obligation. The moral aspect is then argued from the concepts of modernity and cosmopolitanism. Free to-air Malaysian television which broadcast an array of foreign and locally produced dramas becomes the model of city lifestyles and thus influence specific lifestyles goods consumed by the housewives. This study is based on the ethnographic method of data collection in a marginalised worker community of a Malay village located near Kuching City, Sarawak, Malaysia.

Introduction

The following analysis of the housewives' petty trading in a Malay community of Sarawak reveals their endeavour on consumption of lifestyle commodities. There are different ways and degree of involvement in petty trading. Their trading includes selling-buying activity in social capital networks, which is more mobile, compare to permanent (often home-based) trading. Petty trading is conducted with an objective in mind, this being the accumulation of capital for the consumption of lifestyle commodities. Miller (1998) argues that consuming goods has allowed women to create a particular sense of self and to structure their relationships with others. The activity of trading and consuming relates to modernity as a self-reflexive project that creates self-identity. According to Gauntlett (2008) the self-reflexive project of self-identity is 'an endeavour that we continuously work and reflect on' (p. 107).

In the case of the housewives in this study, the money they posses and the role of trader they perform has allowed them to consume, if not as much as middle class women but not as little as what Gerke's (2000) terms as 'lifestyling' (p. 137) which he defines, 'the display of a standard of living that one is in fact unable to afford' (p. 137). An ethnographic study in 2006-2007 was conducted among housewives of Kampung Tabuan Melayu, a marginalised worker community in urban neighbourhood of Tabuan in the city of Kuching, Sarawak. Many of them married at a young age (16, 17, or 18 years old) and therefore lack the academic or vocational qualifications necessary to enter the formal work force. However, they are actively involved in petty trading activities to supplement their husbands' earnings and increase their consumption of lifestyle commodities.

Following from Habermas's concept on modernity, Miller (1995b) contends that consumption is an integral aspect of modernity. He further points out that in consuming goods one is 'living *through* objects and images not of one's own creation' (1995b, p. 1, emphasis added). Consumption is viewed as an act of social action, moral obligation and active political participant (Sassatelli 2007). In the globalisation era, foreign commodities are easily accessible in the local sphere. In relation to cosmopolitanism the consumption of goods connects consumers with images that transcend national boundaries. The commodities from foreign countries mediate consumers with cultural diversity. However, the consumption of commodities from other countries do not necessarily make a person a cosmopolitan just like a tourist who visits different countries, he or she do not necessarily embrace cultural diversity. On the one hand, Gerke (2000), for instance, found that lower-middle class Indonesians consume global food, drink, and branded fashion from North America to demonstrate their preference for commodities that merely symbolises modern, urban lifestyles. On the other hand, a cosmopolitan displays an attitude of 'a willingness to engage with the Other' (Hannerz 1996, p. 103). According to Delanty (2006) 'the cosmopolitan imagination occurs when and wherever new relations between self, other and world develop in moments of openness' (p. 27). Consumers, who are cosmopolitans, are commonly associated with expatriate professionals (Thompson & Tambyah, 1999) or wealthy citizens. However, an ethnographic research in the second-hand marketplace in Nuku'alofa, Tonga unearths a process whereby ordinary traders display the cosmopolitan outlook in the market that sell overseas goods from their diasporic relatives who reside in North America and New Zealand (Besnier's, 2004).

In addition, this chapter illustrates the response of the housewives to television's depiction of modernity, which is part of the cosmopolitan project of free-to-air Malaysian television (Ahmad Ishak, 2012). The substantial imported television programs including Hindi movies from India, telenovelas from Latin America, drama serials from Indonesia, the Philippines, South Korea, Hong Kong and Japan are broadcast on Malaysian television stations. Md Syed (2012) finds that Malay women use Asian dramas as 'a site for negotiating modernity' (p.1). Moreover, Tabuan housewives recognise and embrace different cultural images and identity of middle class and wealthy women depicted on television. The aspect of morality practices in their social capital networks is well suited with the positive values ascribed to female protagonists in dramas and movies.

Dr. A.H.M Zehadul Karim

Overview of Housewives, Petty Trading and the Consumption of Lifestyle Commodities

In interviews with the housewives of Kampung Tabuan it was clear that most characterised themselves primarily as *diam rumah ajak* (staying at home only) or *surirumah* (a housewife). They accept their primary status as housewives. Nonetheless, the term 'housewife' in Malaysia, and in other parts of Southeast Asia (see for example Illo 1995 in the Philippines), has a broader application than what it suggests in the West. In the Malay context, the notion of a *surirumah* has been inherited from peasant society. It refers to both full-time housewives, and housewives who are to some degree or another involved in food production or income-producing activities. As in times past, their involvement in petty trading is today not conceptualised as being a part of the formal economy, because their business ventures are not subject to regulation by the government, such as the requirements to obtain licences and to pay taxes.

Manderson (1983) provides historical evidence from the local chronicler, Mohamed Ibrahim in 1871, who noted that Malay women were involved in food production for the family. A number of more contemporary studies have since provided evidence which demonstrates the involvement of Malay women in activities that generate additional income, or in producing rice for the family in Kelantan (Rudie, 1994); Terengganu (Strange, 1981; Firth, 1966) and Kedah (Carsten, 1998). According to Li (1989), Singaporean Malay women who contribute financially to the household through their involvement in the formal economy primarily provide a supplementary income to that of their husband. Her earnings rarely contribute to core household expenses.

Furthermore, Malay women are often responsible for managing the money earned by their husband (Firth, 1966). Although the management of household finance includes budgeting and spending, studies undertaken on the spending habits of low income Malay housewives has only focused on that of essential commodities for family consumption and not the consumption of lifestyle commodities, for instance in an urban community in Singapore (Li, 1989); Malaysia (Ghazali, 2003) and in rural community in Malaysia (Ong, 1987). One of the reasons is because feminist studies of gender and consumerism neglect women's participation in consumption (Casey & Martens, 2007; Schroeder, 2003). In the Malaysian context, and more particularly in relation to the rise of the middle class in the 1990s, Talib (2000) has highlighted the increased consumption of luxury goods and services; and spending pattern of husbands and wives (Yusof & Duasa, 2010).

In the 1960s, the consumption of commercially manufactured goods was beginning to influence patterns of family consumption among south-west Sarawak Malays in Kuching Division (Harrisson, 1970). The conspicuous consumption of luxury items commonly occurred during the Muslim religious festival of *Hari Raya*, but in fact that was in the interests of the family (Harrisson, 1970). He further notes that purchase of personal lifestyle commodities, such as American-style sports shirts and jewellery, were undertaken by young men and women, but not housewives. Ong (1987) observed that in a rural area in Selangor, West Malaysia, money was spent on television sets and expensive furniture by young men and women who, because of their jobs in multinational factories, could afford them. However, the mothers of these young workers or housewives diligently pool money from their husbands' earnings, their own earnings, and their children's cash remittances, to spend on essentials and if at all possible luxury goods for their families, rather than for themselves.

The following section investigates the specific nature of petty trading and consumption among the housewives of Kampung Tabuan. I explain how moral aspects such as mutual obligation, compassion and trust are the foundation of petty trading and the consumption of lifestyle commodities that leads to Tabuan housewives' attempted engagement with modernity.

Petty Trading and Consumption of Tabuan Housewives

Petty trading refers to those activities that are conducted by the women within the village that lead to the accumulation of financial resources. Tabuan housewives demonstrate differing degrees of involvement in petty trading. Most are involved periodically or part-time, for instance during the evenings, on weekends, or during festival seasons. For the permanent trading, more time is required to be devoted to business activities such as in grocery selling or sewing from home. The items traded are typically seasonal fruits, vegetables, and home-cooked foods; as well as lifestyle commodities, such as ready-made dresses, garments, personal beauty products, expensive handbags, jewellery (gold, crystal, and silver) and furniture. Another form of consumption desired by housewives which differs from commodities consumption is travel by airplane to Kuala Lumpur and pilgrimage to holy land of Mecca and Medina.

Here, I shall illustrate an example of the interplay of Tabuan household earning and spending on a lifestyle commodity. Fasha[1], a Tabuan housewife and trader provides an example of buying hair care treatments.[2] Fasha desires Indian feminine beauty modelled on Bollywood movies. Even though Fasha is not an Indian, she prefers to associate her dark skin with Indian ethnicity. Her nickname, 'Tambi,' is a Sarawak Malay word that refers collectively to South Asians who have darker skin. In fact, Fasha is more comfortable being called Tambi than being called by her real name. The word Tambi has a positive connotation because she said 'Tambi are good looking, they wear beautiful fashion and kind-hearted'. These descriptions are well-suited with female protagonists in Bollywood movies. She also associates her husband with Indian courageous attitude. In one of my conversations with Fasha, she used the word Tambi to explain to me how Aaron ran to chase the lorry that accidently hit his taxi-van which was parked in front of their house. Fasha said, 'the way Aaron ran was just like a Tambi in a Bollywood movie!' By this, she meant that in the act of pursuing the lorry driver, Aaron looked to her to be athletic, handsome and heroic.

Fasha was not happy with her natural hair, which she claimed was *jaek* (ugly) because it is full of body and wavy. She insisted she

---

[1]   These informants were given pseudonyms in order to protect their privacy. The pseudonyms chosen for informants were mostly names of actors or characters from foreign and locally produced popular culture as well as local names.

[2]   Although the spending of housewives on hair care is not as common as their spending on clothing items and gold jewellery, I chose Fasha's case because of her focus on one type of lifestyle commodity. Moreover, Fasha's revelation on her family's earnings and her consumption are reliable and consistent with my observations.

would rather have long and straight hair. Although she is happy with the look of her newly acquired straight hair, she complained that it is expensive to maintain. She goes to a hair salon twice a year to straighten and sometimes colour her hair. She also buys relatively expensive hair care products. Every six months, she spends RM 250 on straightening, hair care products, and hair colouring. Altogether she spends 37% of her total net RM132 monthly income (RM41) on her hair.

Fasha's husband, Aaron, a taxi-van driver has a take-home income of RM1000. Aaron's major expenses are the van instalments and petrol, which leaves him with only RM300 per month for household spending. Fasha's take-home income is RM220. The income came from selling weekend breakfasts and snacks on the school bus. After spending on the food ingredients, her net earnings are RM132.

Table 9.1 Aaron's and Fasha's Approximate Monthly Household Earnings and Fasha's Lifestyle Commodity Consumption

Summary	
Aaron's take-home income	RM 1000.00
Aaron's net earnings	RM 300.00
Fasha's net earnings	RM 132.00
Total net household earnings	RM 432.00
Fasha's hair care per month	RM 41.00
Fasha's hair care spending as a percentage of her earnings	37.1%
Fasha's hair care spending as a percentage of total household earnings	9.4%

A husband's earnings are spent appropriately on household essentials and his children's needs, not, unless the money is a gift from the husband, on his wife's (Li 1989). Tabuan housewives too are not obliged to be responsible for the provision of household essentials. They commonly say that, in relation to the money they reserve for their personal spending, *bagus agik pakei duit sendiri* (it is good to spend with our own money). Even if a Malay husband spends money on his wife's personal non-essential wants, she will not feel comfortable in taking the money from his earnings. According to Li (1989), this feeling emerges from a 'sense of debt and dependence' (p. 22). Li explains that Singaporean Malay women feel that way because 'the wife fears she could be criticized for demanding, and then spending, money that someone else has laboured to earn' (p. 22).

Hence, gendered norms in relation to economic responsibility in the Malay family influences the way Tabuan housewives use their money for two competing requirements: supplementing the household budget and consuming lifestyle commodities. The amount that Tabuan housewives spend on household essentials depends on individual circumstances and preferences. For instance, Balkish (nickname Bibi who is also associated with positive image of Bollywood actress) is a home seamstress who has saved almost all her income for over ten years to assist her husband in building their own house. In contrast, Sofea Jane and Zulaikha prioritise the money they earn for their personal consumption. They earn money but it is spent on themselves rather than on the household. In contrast to Balkish's commitment to her husband, Sofea Jane, saves most of her earnings to go for *haj*. Although she desperately needs to renovate her old kitchen, rather than spending all her personal savings, she pooled money from her own savings, her children's savings, and her husband's savings to pay for the renovations. In addition, the spending decisions of Tabuan housewives are also influenced by the amount of their husbands' incomes, and, if applicable, their children's remittances.

Malaysia's National Economic Policy has encouraged women from rural and underprivileged backgrounds to become involved in the economy through the provision of micro-credit schemes (Masud & Paim 1999). The involvement of Tabuan housewives in petty trading, however, differs somewhat from other Malay women's involvement in small-scale marketplace entrepreneurship. Malay housewives in Kelantan state,[3] for instance, dominate trading at the Kota Bharu market (Rudie 1994). Kelantan Malay women have also been successful in the formal business sector through their common involvement in wholesaling, retailing, and manufacturing (Idris & Shahdan 1991). The authors also show that the objectives of Kelantan Malay businesswomen are to create wealth and reinvest it in order to generate even more profit. In comparison to Kelantan

---

[3]   Kelantan is one of the Malaysian states located in eastern Peninsular Malaysia.

Malay businesswomen, the petty trading of housewives in Kampung Tabuan is generally motivated by the desire to earn extra money to spend on personal lifestyle goods. Moreover, unlike Kelantan Malay businesswomen, Tabuan housewives have yet to extend their trading to the busy marketplace in Kuching city.

In this regard, Tabuan women explain their involvement in petty trading as either *cari duit lebih* (to earn additional income) or *pakei isi masa lapang* (to fill in free time). This suggests that the housewives see themselves as supplementary rather than primary income earners for their families. The first of these responses was typically given by Tabuan housewives who were endeavouring to supplement their husband's inadequate earnings. The second answer was typically given by Tabuan housewives whose husband's earnings were sufficient to meet the basic needs of the household. This implies that such women have more liberty to spend on personal lifestyle commodities.

The term 'socio-trading network' refers to the activities of buying and selling that utilise social networks among Tabuan housewives. They encourage their friends, neighbours, and relatives to buy from them rather than from anonymous others. In fact the aim of many Tabuan traders is to maintain cash flow, favours and mutual obligation among their social network with sometimes little concern for profit. The first is through Informal Rotating Credit Schemes (IRCS). In these schemes, members accumulate money to buy more expensive goods. It is a process that will be explained in the following section. The second type of social network trading occurs when Tabuan housewives both buy and sell goods from each other both for daily essentials and lifestyle commodities. They are simultaneously consumers and sellers for certain types of goods that are traded in the village. For example, Aleza is one of Yatimah's regular customers. She buys her home-cooked food. In turn, Yatimah buys garment from Aleza. Regardless of the value of the items being traded, the selling and buying activities are often the basis for the development of long-term relationship between members of the network.

In order for Tabuan housewives to be able to maximise their chances of selling goods, they depend on cultivating a sense of mutual obligation among those in their social capital networks. This has been a recognised practice in rural Malay society when organising social and religious activities in a spirit of 'co-operation' (*gotong-royong*) among neighbours and close friends. The concept of *gotong-royong* is, for example, commonly demonstrated in the organisation of wedding functions. However, the concept of *gotong-royong* has evolved in the urban setting of Kampung Tabuan. Through IRCSs, Tabuan housewives utilise social networks as much for economic reasons as social ones.

Mutual obligation is facilitated through housewives' discipline in controlling the price of certain goods. For instance, Tabuan traders commonly set a relatively low price for the food that they produce and sell. As such, the products that are sold in the village are kept at a minimum so that members of their networks can afford to buy them. Another way to enable their members to afford more expensive goods is to offer payment through instalments. In setting a lower price sellers are demonstrating compassion for their customers. In the Sarawak Malay dialect, they talk about *sik kempang ati* (not having the heart) to sell the food at the standard retail price. This is an important characteristic of trading in Kampung Tabuan; through the recognition of a common or shared economic status a sense of unity prevails. The traders who do not follow this convention are said to display behaviour that is *sik patut* (inappropriate). In daily conversation, the phrase *sik kempang ati* is used to empathise with a person who is facing hardship.

IRCSs are another type of social network trading that allows Tabuan housewives' to participate in the consumption of lifestyle commodities. IRCSs are well known and still practised in many communities in developing countries, such as the Philippines and Indonesia. It is the collective action of a group of people who agree to meet for a defined period in order to save and borrow money together.

IRCS acts in much the same way a bank does: people deposit money for a certain period. The underlying features of such payment arrangements are mutual obligation, trust, and co-dependence by both members and the leader (who acts as an organiser and seller). IRCSs draw on the community's cultural disposition toward mutual aid.

In Kampung Tabuan, an IRCS is known as *main hoi*, literally *main* means 'play' and *hoi* means 'a cycle of time.' Thus, *main hoi* translates to the doing of an activity which has to be completed in one cycle of time. Other places in Malaysia have different names for the activity such as *Kut* in Pulau Pinang (Ghazali, 2003). In women's groups *main hoi* is managed by a so called trustworthy leader. Success in *main hoi* depends on the trust between its leader and the group's members. Some members are involved in *main hoi* on an ongoing basis, whilst some members' participation is sporadic. Because of this it is crucial for a leader to continually recruit new and trustworthy members. This activity fosters trust among women within the community, and permits the consumption of goods which might normally be too expensive to acquire through cash. The practice of *arisan*, which occurs among the the Modjokuto community in Java, shares similarities with *main hoi* in Kampung Tabuan in that it has both consumption and a communal motives rather than just a communal motive. Geertz (1962) has argued that the motive behind *arisan* 'is not the money you receive, but the creation of *rukun* (communal harmony) . . .' (Geertz, 1962, p. 243).

Technically, there are two types of *main hoi: hoi duit* and *hoi barang. Hoi duit* means 'doing an activity for a certain period to save money.' Similarly, *hoi barang* means 'doing an activity for a certain period to save money to buy goods.' In Kampung Tabuan, Rita is one of the women who has, since 2002, been successfully organising both types of *main hoi.*

For *hoi barang* Rita collects money from the network's members each month. Each month, a member of the network takes her turn to purchase goods of her own choice from the pot of money. The most common goods purchased through *hoi barang* are gold, crystal jewellery or furniture; such as beds, wardrobes, sofas, and display cabinets. However, most of these goods, except jewellery, are for family consumption. Rita's role is to collect the monthly payments and identify the jewellery or furniture, the cost of which equals the value of that contributed by the network members. She also provides other forms of support to her close network members, including providing interest free loans and how to pawn gold in the bank. The typical amounts that the members receive for yearly *main hoi* are RM300 or RM500.

When I ask why they participate in *main hoi duit*, Tabuan housewives have a common answer; monetary gain. As Maya Karin said to me, 'I will never have the chance to hold such a large sum of money if I do not participate in *main hoi duit*.' Thus, *main hoi duit* is a way to possess a large sum of money at one time to spend how they wish. The spending can be for daily use for their family, or for non-essential lifestyle goods. For instance, Maya Karin told me that she spent the pot of the money for the *Hari Raya* celebration, buying new dresses for herself and her children, and preparing special food for her family. Without the money from *main hoi duit* she believes that she would not have been able to celebrate in such style. Rita, on the other hand, saves money from *main hoi duit* to spend on travel to Kuala Lumpur.

There are two consequences associated with the social-trading networks, *main hoi duit* and *main hoi barang*. Firstly, consumption becomes a significant way to establish and consolidate social relationships among housewives in Kampung Tabuan. Secondly, Tabuan housewives perpetuate the village's communal values by choosing to buy from local community networks. This form of trading allows for the creation of relationships with others (Grumpert & Drucker, 1992). Miller (1987; 1998) sees the desire for goods as a way for people to escape poverty and to express love for one another. This notion, as demonstrated by Tabuan housewives, contradicts the long-held view that materialism is problematic. This view holds that the more people become concerned with acquiring material possessions, the less concerned they become with each other.

Most Tabuan housewives are typically locked out of accessing loans because they have no guarantors or permanent jobs. The social networks provide them with economic purchasing power that they would not otherwise have if they were dependent on conventional financial institutions. Tabuan women's social-trading network is an example of the process of modernity being able to operate in a marginal community.

Consumption: the Connection With, and Imagination of, Other City Lifestyles, and the Meaning of Consumption

In this section I explore the meaning of Kuala Lumpur to Tabuan housewives and their desire for the urban lifestyle(s) of the Other.

They want to be connected with the people and goods of Kuala Lumpur but each individual has unique desire that suit her preference image. This desire reflects Tabuan women's imagined connection with modern and cosmopolitan lives. I also outline briefly the way in which television depicts images of Kuala Lumpur. One of the more significant lifestyle commodities for Tabuan housewives is clothing items. Tabuan traders acquire clothing from various places outside Sarawak, including Kuala Lumpur. I illustrate the meaning of the lifestyle commodities, particularly clothing items, sought by Tabuan housewives.

As well as being the capital city of Malaysia, Kuala Lumpur (popularly known as 'KL') symbolises for Malaysians development and modernity.[4] For economic reasons, including the presence of foreign labour and goods, Kuala Lumpur is a place that can be considered a cosmopolitan city parallel to neighbouring Singapore. For the population it encompasses multi-ethnic populations where the majority of Chinese and Indian are allowed to practice their own culture alongside with the practice of Malay culture as the official national identity of Malaysia.

Besides foreign programs, there are drama and film broadcast on televisions. Most Malay popular culture genres, including TV dramas, films, and musicals are produced in Kuala Lumpur. Tabuan housewives enjoy watching TV3 for depictions of wealthy, middle-class lifestyles of Malays in Kuala Lumpur. One such drama series is *Sembilu Kasih*, (Thorny Love), a story about a wealthy Malay family who own a luxury home replete with swimming pools, expensive cars and chauffeurs. This type of subject matter is in fact common in Malay dramas aired on TV3. They also feature scenes depicting corporate work places where 'professionals' appear in smart Western dress, as well as contemporary city shopping complexes, hotels, and luxury restaurants. The majority of the characters in these Malay dramas reflect cosmopolitan, middle-class people who are mobile, wealthy and highly educated; and as such do not represent the ordinary Malay.

---

[4] In conversation, Tabuan housewives refer Kuala Lumpur to any place of urban lifestyles at Klang Valley in Peninsular Malaysia if the specific name of the place is unknown.

Images of this sought are immensely attractive to Tabuan housewives. They enjoy watching representations of cosmopolitan lifestyles on TV3 more than other programs on the government channels (TV1 and TV2). The government channels tend to present a more balanced portrayal of Malays, depicting both urban and rural lifestyles in their dramas. This contention finds support in the answers provided to my interview questions. For instance, when I asked 'what is your favourite television channel?' 23of a total 30 respondents (or 76.7%) responded with TV3 (see Table 9.2). When pressed further during more informal conversations the typical answer was 'cerita/ rancangan ya kacak' (the dramas/programs are good). Priyanka explains that in saying the dramas are *kacak* she means that the situations and people depicted on TV3 drama serials are 'real.' In contrast to the popularity of TV3, only one respondent chose the longest established government television channel, TV1. TV2, another government channel, was chosen by 5 respondents because, according to those housewives, the channel offered dramas as good as those aired on TV3. As it shows, NTV7 and Astro were the least watched stations.[5]

Table 9.2 Favourite Television Stations among Tabuan Housewives

Favourite TV Stations	TV3	TV2	TV7	Astro	Total
No. of Informants	23	5	1	1	30
	76.7	16.7	3.3	3.3	100

The lifestyle aspects of the other that Tabuan housewives desire are affluence attractive people, a choice of modern commodities and affordable shopping destinations. When I asked what the housewives thought about the people and places in Peninsular Malaysia, Hasliah who has never been to Kuala Lumpur thought that Malays living there are 'wealthier and own good houses than people here (Kuching)'. A young woman named Neelofa curious on the appearance of men in KL:

Neelofa: What do guys in KL look like?
Zana: Well?

---

[5]   There is a reception problem for NTV7 in Kampung Tabuan, and Astro is the paid satellite station that rarely owned by the villagers.

Neelofa: Hmm . . . They're tall, lean, and fair-skinned, aren't they?

Zana: Not really. Some do have the features you mentioned.

Neelofa: (disappointed and lowered her tone of voice) Oh . . . I thought they are good-looking.

I assume that Neelofa's assumption about men's appearance in Kuala Lumpur is what she imagines from the characters in Malay drama serials and movies. There are many instances that Tabuan women see their family members in Malay drama serials and movie characters. Amor sees her mother in-law who owned many gold jewelleries in a well-off woman character in *Mami Jarum*, whilst Meilan sees Zed, Rita's son in a handsome and well-off male character in *Sembilu Kasih*, meanwhile Kareena adored Kajol, the female protagonist in a Bollywood movie, *Dushman*.

Kuala Lumpur is only accessible to Sarawakians by plane travel. There are several domestic airports connecting Kuching with other cities in Sarawak, however Kuala Lumpur and other destinations in Peninsular Malaysia, together with direct flights to foreign countries, are classified as 'international departures' and thus leave from the international airport. First time visitors from Peninsular Malaysia to Kuching who want to return to Kuala Lumpur, for instance, often become confused when ushered to the international departures gate. Whilst the nomenclature has been applied for technical purposes, it perhaps reinforces the symbolism of Kuala Lumpur as a foreign or international destination.

Tabuan people often use travel to Kuala Lumpur to visit family to show that they are connected to modern and cosmopolitan people. If they do not have that connection, some visit their 'adopted' relatives. For example, Yatimah told me that her visit to Kuala Lumpur always starts with sightseeing and then visiting her 'adopted relatives.' Another reason, however, was to buy wholesale garments to be sold in Kampung Tabuan. A visit to Kuala Lumpur demonstrates Tabuan women's social status, in that they have connections with Kuala Lumpur. Many Tabuan housewives prioritise visiting Kuala Lumpur if they have the opportunity, the money, and the ability to access the knowledge necessary to travel there. In the case of Meilan and her daughter Diana the opportunity to visit Kuala Lumpur came when Rita invited them to join with her family's trip. Meilan was willing to pawn her only precious asset, her gold necklace, to purchase the air ticket. Meilan's aim, firstly, was to visit her daughter who works in a factory near Kuala Lumpur; and secondly, to go shopping and sightseeing.

Although social-trading networks are critical in enabling the purchase of lifestyle commodities, Tabuan housewives also ask relatives with connections in Kuala Lumpur to purchase goods. Anita, for example, asked her sister-in-law to buy a stylish fabric for her called *kain brokat*. Anita told me that her sister-in-law is a singer in a nightclub in Kuala Lumpur. She proudly told me her sister-in-law's occupation, feeling that the job represented an affluent and glamorous city lifestyle (and therefore her sister-in law would know the most fashionable fabric design). Other lifestyle commodities from Kuala Lumpur are also sought after by Tabuan housewives. Bella Dally, motivated by a television advertisement, wanted me to purchase for her a CD player in KL so that she and her five-year-old daughter could listen to recorded verses of the Quran. Although Bella Dally is not overtly religious, she talked a lot about raising her daughter with Islamic values. Here is the conversation in response to my failure to purchase the CD player in Kuala Lumpur:

> Bella Dally: I saw it in the ad on television. It must be sold in Kuala Lumpur.
> Zana: Kuala Lumpur is a big city. If you had told me where to find it, I might have been able to buy it for you.
> Bella Dally: It must be there because I saw it on television.

I was often asked by Tabuan housewives who have never been to Kuala Lumpur whether goods are cheaper in KL than Kuching. In fact, since they incur extra transport costs when shipped from Peninsular Malaysia, goods are generally more expensive in Sarawak. Their concern with price is further evidenced in day-to-day conversations between Tabuan housewives who exchange information about where to find the cheapest necessities. The concern regarding price assists the women in maximising their spending on personal, non-essential items.

Despite *Jalan Masjid India* (Indian Mosque Street) in Kuala Lumpur being a famous and affordable shopping destination for Tabuan people, they also regularly visit popular shopping destinations at the border towns of Tebedu (about 35 km south of Kuching) and later Serikin (about 40 km south-west of Kuching) on the Sarawak and West Kalimantan (Indonesian) border. These two destinations have, since the late 1990s, been developed by the Sarawak state government. Indonesian traders sell cheap products to Sarawakian consumers, including garments, batik sarongs, textiles, wooden furniture, household items, and food items. Although not well known to Tabuan people, Amor and her husband, Julaihi, told me about *Bukit Kayu Hitam*, a town on the border of Malaysia and Thailand although they have never been to the place. Both of them talked about opening a second-hand clothing store in Kuching to sell jeans and shirts from Thailand.

Conclusion

The social-trading networks are particularly important in this regard as they provide a means for affording expensive lifestyle goods, and create a marketplace for those selling goods bought often in Kuala Lumpur or in Sarawak. The moral aspects of mutual obligation, compassion and trust underscore the housewives' economic participation as traders and consumers. Their consumption includes clothing items, jewellery, personal care items, furniture, and electronic devices which some of the commodities have allowed them to have the good image of television and movies characters from other culture. Kuala Lumpur is imagined as a foreign place that is different from Kuching. The city is regarded as a model for the affluent lifestyles that Tabuan housewives aspire to. Television has contributed to the construction of cosmopolitan images of Kuala Lumpur as a prosperous place, a shopping haven, an Islamic centre, cultural diversity and a travel destination. Some Tabuan housewives and men talk about lifestyle commodities from the border towns with Indonesia and Thailand to consume outside goods. The comfortable feeling to have an image's association with people from other culture shows the recognition of cultural diversity beyond the national boundary.

References

Ahmad Ishak, SZ 2012, 'Imagined cosmopolitanism: imported programs on the free-to-air Malaysian Television (1963-2006) paper presented at the *Conference on Media and Society [C-MAS 2012]*, Universiti Malaysia Sarawak, 24-26 September 2012.

Besnier, N 2004, 'Consumption and cosmopolitanism: Practicing modernity at the second-hand marketplace in Nuku'alofa, Tonga', *Anthropological Quarterly*, vol. 77, no. 1, pp. 7-45.

Carsten, J 1997, *The heat of the hearth: the process of Kinship in a Malay fishing community*, Oxford University Press, Oxford, New York.

Casey, E & Martens, L 2007, 'Introduction', in E Casey & L Martens (eds.) *Gender and consumption: domestic cultures and the commercialisation of everyday life*, Ashgate Publishing Ltd, Farnham, pp. 1-11.

Delanty, G 2006, 'The cosmopolitan imagination: critical cosmopolitanism and social theory', *The British Journal of Sociology*, vol. 57, no. 1, pp. 25-47.

Firth, R 1966, *Housekeeping among Malay peasants*, The Athlone Press, University of London, London.

Gauntlett, D 2008, *Media, gender and identity: an introduction*, 2nd edn, Routledge (Taylor & Francis e-Library), London.

Geertz, C 1962 'The rotating credit association: a "middle rung" in development', *Economic Development and Cultural Change*, vol. 10, no. 3, pp. 241-263.

Gerke, S 2000, 'Global lifestyles under local conditions: the new Indonesian middle class', in BH Chua (ed.), *Consumption in Asia: lifestyle and identities*, Routledge, London, pp. 135-158.

Ghazali, S (2003) '*Kut* (informal rotating credit) in the livelihood strategies of urban households in Penang, Malaysia' *Area*, vol. 35, no 2, pp. 183-194.

Gumpert, G & Drucker, S.J 1992, 'From the agora to the electronic shopping mall', *Critical Studies in Mass Communication*, vol. 9, pp.186-200.

Hannerz, U 1996, *Transnational connections: culture, people, places*, Routledge, London.

Harrisson, T 1970, *The Malays of south-west Sarawak before Malaysia*, Macmillan, London.

Illo, JF 1995, 'Redefining the *maybahay* or housewife: reflections on the nature of women's work in the Philippines', in WJ Karim (ed.), *'Male' and 'female' in developing Southeast Asia*, Berg Publishers, Oxford/Washington.

Idris, NA & Sahadan, F 1991, 'The role of Muslim women traders in Kelantan', in M Ariff (ed.), *The Muslim private sector in Southeast Asia: Islam and the economic development*, Institute of Southeast Asian Studies, Singapore.

Li, T 1989, *Malays in Singapore: culture, economy, and Ideology*, Oxford University Press, Singapore.

Manderson, L 1983, 'Introduction', in L Manderson (ed.), *Women's work and women's role*, The Australian National University, Canberra, pp. 1-14.

Md Syed MA, 2012, 'Malay women as discerning viewers: Asian soap operas, consumer culture and negotiating modernity, *Gender, Place & Culture: A Journal of Feminist Geography*, First article pp. 1-17

Masud, J & Paim, L 1999, 'The economic empowerment of rural women through involvement in micro-enterprise', in M Ismail & A Ahmad (eds.), *Women & work challenges in industrializing nations*, Asean acedemic press, London, pp. 133-152.

Miller, D 1998, *A theory of shopping*, Polity, Cambridge.

Miller, D 1995b, 'Introduction: anthropology, modernity and consumption', in D Miller (ed.), *Worlds apart: modernity through the prism of the local*, Routledge, London, New York pp. 1-22.

Miller, D 1987, *Material culture and mass consumption*, Basil Blackwell, Oxford.

Ong, A 1987, *Spirit of resistance and capitalist discipline: factory women in Malaysia*, State University of New York Press, Albany.

Rudie, I 1994, *Visible women in east coast Malay society: on the reproduction of gender, in ceremonial, school, and market*, Oxford University Press, Oslo.

Sassatelli, R 2007, *Consumer Culture. History, Theory, Politics*, Sage, London.

Schroeder, JE 2003, 'Guest's editor's introduction: consumption, gender and identity', *Consumption, markets and culture*, vol. 6, no. 1, pp. 1-4.

Slater, D 1997, *Consumer culture and modernity*, Polity Press, Oxford, UK.

Strange, H 1981, *Rural Malay women in tradition and transition*, Praeger, New York.

Talib, R 2000, 'Malaysia: power shifts and the matrix of consumption', in BH Chua (ed.), *Consumption in Asia: lifestyle and identities*, Routledge, London, pp. 35-60.

Thompson, CJ & Tambyah, SK 1999, 'Trying to Be Cosmopolitan' *The Journal of Consumer Research*, vol. 26, no. 3, pp. 214-241.

Yusof, A & Duasa, J 2010, 'Household desicion-making and expenditure patterns of married men and women in Malaysia', *Journal of Family and Economic Issues*, vol. 31, no. 3, pp. 371-381.

Traditional Catechu Production and Survival Strategies of the Producers in Bangladesh: A Study on Forest Resource Management

Dr. M. Zulfiquar Ali Islam

Abstract

The present paper is devoted to mirror the traditional catechu production techniques and survival strategies of the producers in Bangladesh. It explores their native ways and strategies of forest resource management which they formulate and undertake to confront with the economic adversity faced by them. The paper attempts to detail their everyday experiences and traditional knowledge about the hidden values and utilization of this unique forest resource first, and then it attempts to estimate its loss and degradation caused by man and nature as well. The paper also endeavors to locate the responses to its management at the community and organizational levels in Bangladesh. The productive catechu resource utilization befitting in their traditional fashion and sustainable livelihood strategies for its producers are pinpointed in this paper. The paper employs the method of social survey, case studies, and focus group discussions for gathering empirical data and other secondary data are also consulted for the same purpose. The collaborative entrepreneurship taken by natural scientists, social scientists, lawmakers, and policy planners may guide the catechu producers to make it sustainable for their living in economic adversity. The paper concludes with some policy recommendations, which may be adopted by the policy planners and implementers for their future development content of catechu production and its producers.

Introduction

The catechu plant (*Acacia catechu.*) is a unique forest resource and it is found extremely valuable and productive for the livelihood of human population. This ecological and/or cultivated resource plays a ubiquitous role in contributing to the economic subsistence of respondents of the present study. The respondents usually use this forest resource in producing catechu used in chewing betel-leaf. Also, the people of Bangladesh use the heartwood product of catechu locally called *khayer* to heal the diseases of their cattle and in small-scale textile production as natural-dye matter.

The hidden value and usefulness of its enormous resources is not always apparent; and in most cases, it is not even known to our people. The catechu plants are often slashed out, or eradicated to make way for cultivation and housing as well. The plight of catechu plants in Bangladesh is alarming as their protection laws and regulations are not yet made by the national law and policy makers till now. It is however, disappointing to know that the catechu plantation and catechu production management in Bangladesh has not, to date, received any attention either by government and/or non-government organizations or by the natural and/or social scientists. This alarming situation claims that social mobilization and effective national catechu plantation and catechu production management should be introduced for conservation and restoration of this unique ecological resource. In this context, the present paper devotes itself to explore the hidden values and ecological utilities of catechu and survival strategies of catechu producers in Bangladesh. It is wedded to finalize its job with prescribing a number of suggestive policy recommendations for the catechu management with special focus on the sustainable livelihood of its producers in Bangladesh.

Conceptual Clarification

The present research finds two categories of people working for producing catechu as 'catechu producers'. One category comprises of those who own the means of catechu production and a few of them disburse their manual labor for its production. Another category has no ownership but sell their manual labor for producing catechu. Both categories are considered here as catechu producers due to their direct and indirect involvement in the catechu production. The term is used in this paper on the basis of their involvement in the catechu producing activities.

Data Sources and Research Methodology

Gopalpur village is selected here as study locale in the present research. It is located in Charghat Upazila (sub-district) of Rajshahi District in northwestern Bangladesh and its distance from the upazila is about four kilometers.

The ecological features of the study area indicate that Charghat Upazila and adjoining regions are enriched with catechu plant and also it is suitable for its forestry. A considerable number of populations of different villages of this *upazila*[1] traditionally continue their subsistence on the catechu production activities from the period of British India. A sizeable number of catechu producing households are found as inhabitants of Gopalpur who are impelled to confront with various adversities in continuing their subsistence on catechu production. And thus the choice of this village as study area is rationalized.

A household level interview was conducted in the study area to gather empirical data on the catechu production. The present study has randomly chosen 100 catechu producing households from Gopalpur. All the catechu producing households are judged as the appropriate primary sampling units here. The household heads were directly interviewed and in this way respective household head represents each sampling unit. In addition to survey, the research collected data through conducting 6 focus group discussions (FGDs), oral histories and case studies in the study village. A total of 4 informal interviews with the *samaj*[2] and local leaders are incorporated in this research for gathering additional empirical data. The data collection activities was started in March 2006 and ended in August 2006. The sample size of Gopalpur is 100 catechu producing households and its population is 579 (Table 10.1).

Table 10.1 Sample Catechu Producing Households and Their Population at a Glance

	Gopalpur		
	Total	Male	Female
Total Households	325		
Sample Households	100		
Household Size	5.79		
Population — Total	579	257	322
Population — %		44.39	55.61
Sex Ratio	100:125		

The sample population of this study village comprises 257 (44.39% of the total) males and 322 (55.61% of the total) females. The sex ratio of its population is 125 females per 100 males. The household size of the study population is 5.79.

Usefulness of Catechu Plants in the Study Area

The habitat of this plant in Bangladesh is rich in Rajshahi, Chapai Nawabganj, Natore and Pabna districts of northwestern part of the country (Hye, 2002, p.14). It is a spiny tree. It comprises over 5000 species. It is found in tropic zones of the globe, chiefly Australia, Africa, and Indo-Pak-Bangladesh Sub-continent. About 22 Traditional species of catechu are found in this Sub-continent (Bhatnagar, 1948). Catechu is a medium sized tree spanned from 70 to 80 ft in height and from 8 to 9 ft in girth (Watt, 1972). It is observed that this plant has dark brown outermost bark, inner bark, yellow sapwood, and dark red heartwood.

The respondents mentioned that the plantation of catechu is not yet known by them. It is ecologically planted in the forest and/ or in the bushes around the cultivable land and/or homestead plot. They rather think that the plantation of catechu is obviously natural; human intervention in this regard seems to be infertile.

The prickled branches of catechu plants are used by the respondents in fencing their cropping field. It is also used as fire fuel in their various domestic activities. During the winter, they slash its branches and/or boughs excepting for its top one for these purposes. Traditionally, the rural people of Bangladesh utilize the timber of its trunk for doors and windows, and other rural furniture, and its trunk as pillars of non-concrete house, button for holding roof materials, and the like. They admitted that the longevity of its timber continues from one generation to the next. The respondents of Gopalpur chiefly utilize this unique ecological resource for producing semi-solid catechu.

Traditional Catechu Production Activities

The catechu producers have to visit neighboring villages for buying catechu trees. They contract with the owners of trees earlier in some cases and/or buy directly during their visit. They have to collect trunks and branches of catechu tree from *hat* (local market). They owners of the catechu trees carry its logs to this local market for sale. They are originated from different adjoining villages and areas of Charghat. For collection, they chiefly depend on this *hat* held twice a week at Charghat Upazila Head-quarters. The reference rate of catechu logs that produce 1 kg semi-liquid catechu is Taka 120. They carry trunks and branches of catechu tree from *hat* to their house by locally made rickshaw van.

Chopping Catechu Logs

The producers themselves have to uncover the heart-wood of catechu logs. They employ their male family members and/or hired laborers to do same. They remove its bark from catechu log, and hard solid substance below its bark and above its heart-wood with an ax as well. After the removal, they chop the heartwood into small pieces those are suitable extracting for its juice. In chopping these logs, they require to build a triangular small hut with a roof. The wall and roof materials are made of bamboo. This hut prevents the dispersion of small piece of heart-wood during its chopping.

Juice Extraction and Solidification

The catechu producers have to build special type of hearth for extracting catechu juice first and then boiling it as well. The hearth has usually 8 faces. They set 1 earthen jar on each face to extract juice from small chip s of catechu heartwood. They also use square and/or long rectangle hearth and set a long and flat *korhai* (made of CI sheet) on it to thicken the extracted juice.

The respondents chop the catechu log into small chips and put it into the earthen jars. They pour water into these containers and start to boil it on their Traditional earthen hearth. After its first boiling, they separate the extracted juice and put it into another container and then they boil those chips once again and a small amount of juice has been extracted in this attempt. They boil extracted catechu juice for solidifying its substance on another square shaped earthen hearth.

They reported that usually it is thickened into semi-solid state. Then they put it into a large metal jar and move this liquid with a stick for making it normal. They mix one kind of whitish powder locally called as "*khayer* powder" during this period. It is used here to prepare lower quality of catechu for low income group consumers in some parts of rural Bangladesh. They preserve it into earthen jars for sale to local traders of Charghat Bazar.

The price of about 35 kg quality *lali kayer* (semi-liquid catechu) is Taka 7000 (US $ 100). The processing of *guti kayer* (catechu bar) require more than 3 months that has to be processed under eclectic fans in a house. The local traders reported that 2.5kg semi-liquid catechu is required to produce 1 kg catechu bar. The reference rate of about 35kg catechu bar is Taka 2100.

Other Use of Catechu Wood Materials

They dry catechu chips, barks, soft wood, and branches in the sun. They are used to use all these wood materials to boil juice and other domestic cooking activities. In fact, they need no additional fire fuel for catechu boiling and thickening activities. All these catechu wood materials are found adequate as fire fuel at this level of catechu production. The respondents reported that they sell one full earthen jar remnant of firewood (*koila*) to the blacksmiths and goldsmiths. The price of 1 jar of 15kg is Taka 12. They sell its ashes to the traders who supply it to the local tooth powder industries. The reference rate of ashes is Taka 70.

Labor Involvement

The male and female members of catechu producing households are involved in the production activities. In some cases, the children also pay their physical labor in assisting their parents. Some of producers who have good economic standing employ hired labors. Usually, the female are engaged in fuelling the traditional hearth, placing chips in the sun from the hearth premises to the yard, cleaning and repairing hearth, and other light works. The hired female labor is paid Taka 30-35 for daylong works. On the other hand, the males are engaged in building chopping and hearth sheds, cutting catechu trees, carrying logs from local market to house, chopping logs into chips, estimate the final product as semi-solid catechu, carrying semi-solid catechu and ashes it to the local market for sale, and the like. The hired male labors are paid Taka 40 for 6 am to 1 pm works.

Survival Strategies of the Catechu Producers

Most of them reported that they have no training and education for catechu production. They are continuing this job traditionally from one generation to the next. They land owners and/or peasants slashed out catechu plants as its hidden value is unknown to them and they find it as non-productive prickle plants. Thus, nowadays the catechu producers have been suffering from sheer lack of technical education and training for catechu production and of adequate supply of catechu logs in the market. Additionally, the imported catechu is hugely used by the people in chewing betel nuts and betel leaves. In this alarming situation, the catechu producing households of Gopalpur formulate and undertake other than usual initiatives in their own ways to supplement their irregular and contemptible familial income from catechu production.

Female, Child and Elderly Members' Involvement in Economic Activities

The inadequate income of the catechu producing households of study village pushed them (88.00%) to engage their female, child and elderly members in various economic activities to supplement their familial income (cf. Arens and van Beurden 1977; Islam 2004). Although the operation of economic activities outside the homestead premises by female members is culturally restricted and treated as humiliating one for the familial status in social arena, their prodigious needs compelled them to do the same.

Handicrafts Production

It is evident that more than 31 percent of the total respondents have Traditional technical and artistic skills for producing handicrafts. The perusal of quantitative data indicates that they produce various handicrafts within their household premises. They have artistic skills of needlework, bamboo work, and work of mat made of date-leaf. The *kantha* is one kind of bed-cover specially designed with Traditional needlework. It is operated by a few numbers of the women. While they usually produce *pati* (rough mat made of date-leaf) for their own household consumption, some of them made *sheetal pati* (fine mat made of date-leaf) and sell it for earning cash money. The male members also produce winnowing fan, baskets, *khalpa* (used as wall-material and material of fencing the homestead), *khalsun* (means of trapping fish), etc. They use the ecological resource of bamboo in producing these handicrafts.

Other Small Business

It is observed that 34 percent catechu producing households run some sort of small business for maintaining their familial subsistence. Most of them mobilize an amount of money in business at the homestead level. It is reported that some of them buy paddy during the harvesting period at a low-price. They parboil and dry paddy in the sun at their homestead yard. And finally they husk paddy and sell rice in the market and in their neighborhood as well. Another proportion of them keep shop of daily necessaries at their homestead.

Homestead Forestry

One-third of total respondents engage themselves in homestead forestry. They cover their homestead area with trees and bushes. They plant catechu, fruit trees, and trees for timber and fire fuel. The homestead forestry contributes to keeping their homestead environmentally sound and provides economic support for familial subsistence as well.

Homestead Agriculture

All the homestead agricultural activities are traditionally done by women while the farm activities are operated by men. Accordingly, the homestead agriculture is considered by the female members of catechu producing households as more feasible means to continue their subsistence as their low income from catechu production does not provide them with adequate support for survival. They are culturally encouraged to perform agricultural activities at their homestead plot rather than farm activities. Hence, they have not to face any unpleasant situation in doing such activities. They perform these works easily at their own homestead. It is reported that the field level wage labor usually denigrates their social and familial status while the homestead agriculture is culturally befitting for catechu producing women.

It is reported that almost all respondent households engage their female members in homestead agriculture. They grow beans, pumpkin, cucumber, basil, and other ivy vegetables, which climb up their roofs and trees. They also garden chili, lady's finger, horseradish, brinjal, coconut trees, etc. The activities of digging the soil, sowing, planting, watering, caring and finally harvesting of homestead garden crops are traditionally operated by the women.

Cattle Raising

Almost all the responding households are engaged in cattle raising activities for supplementing their familial survival. They nourish their cattle within their homestead. Their cattle are mainly cows and goats. They feed green grass, straw, oil cake, wheat-bran, rice-bran, and also serve water to their cows and goats. Some of them rear cows and goats on the sharecropping basis. They keep cows and goats for breeding. They share the price of young cows and goats at a certain age. The sharecroppers have to give no share of its milk to the owners. They earn money by selling milk at a rate of Taka 18-20 per liter. They also use dung as green fertilizer and sometimes they sell this fertilizer to the neighbor farmers. Some of them reported that they dry it in the sun for their own fire fuel consumption and sell the fuel stick of dried dung in the market. The price of one stick is Taka 3.

Poultry Raising

Another popular economic activities done by the catechu producers of Gopalpur (29.00%) is poultry raising. They raise poultry in order to supplement their family income. They feed food scraps, broken paddy rice, bran of rice and wheat, pulse seeds, crushed snails, etc. to their chicken and ducks. Some of them sharecrop in chicken and ducks from their neighbor and relatives. They do it on fifty-fifty share arrangement. They share the chicken and ducks. They sell their share of chicken and ducks. Sometimes they sell eggs of their own chicken and ducks for supplementing their family income.

Selling Manual Labor in Odd Jobs

The field data identify 14 percent of the total respondents who are impelled to be involved in odd jobs and to sell their manual labor for wage on irregular basis. It is found that they sell their labor for wage in cash or kind for their subsistence. They mostly obtain employment of agricultural activities at the homestead of the employers. They reported that some of them also sell their labor for gaining employment in the Food for Works Program and in any development project activities. In fact, these catechu producers have to be involved in these odd jobs when they lost capital as well in catechu production.

Haolat

Above all the multiple and diverse economic strategies for continuing their existence in the unsafe economic environment, the catechu producers are used to practice an economic loan system. It is locally called *haolat*. They loan rice, flour, oil, spice, chili, vegetables, fuel sticks and other daily necessaries from their neighbors and/or relatives. They have to pay equal amount of such things back to their neighbors and/or relatives. This loan is interest-free. It is nothing but a principle of reciprocity in the time of economic hardship practiced by them. In some cases, they have to loan cash based on the same principle from their neighbors and/or kin members. In the devoid of organizational support, they are very much supportive to each other in their neighborhood.

Concluding Remarks

The catechu producers are traditionally highly dependent on catechu—the unique ecological forest resource. They have been suffering from lack of technical education and skills for catechu production profitable. Additionally, the catechu forest resources are slashed out by the peasants unknowingly. The imported catechu grabs the local market of traditionally produced catechu. The producers have to face economic hardship on a regular basis as the low and irregular income from catechu production does not keep their familial subsistence up to mark. In this alarming situation, they have to formulate and adopt alternative economic survival strategies for subsistence. They usually tend to adopt multiple economic strategies, as none of those is adequate and effective for their familial and social survival. They are not provided with any financial assistance from any organizational sources—government and non-government— in formulating and undertaking their survival strategies in the precarious economic environment. While the catechu production claims adequate technical education and training, tools, and economic assistance, social mobilization, the traditional catechu producers are forced to confront with economic hardship in the sheer lack of organizational support. Because of the administrative and organizational failure in this regard, they formulated corrective economic strategies rather than preventive ones in continuing their familial survival within their Traditional fashion.

Policy Recommendations

The paper concludes with some policy recommendations, which may be adopted by the policy planners and implementers for their future development content of catechu production and its producers. The government and non-government organizations should respond to the enormous sufferings and needs of traditional catechu producers in Bangladesh.

i. The government should provide the catechu peasants with HYV technologies for catechu gardening. They should be properly mobilized to garden the catechu plants.
ii. The traditional catechu producers should be provided with technical education and skills for profitable catechu production. They should be provided with required suitable

tools and machines for such production in terms of low cost, time and labor.

iii. In the economic hardship, the traditional producers should be assisted by the Government and non-government organizations (GOs and NGOs) economically in continuing their catechu producing activities.

iv. They expect that the government and non-government organizations should mobilize the community people for being aware of the hidden value of catechu plants for sustainable livelihood.

v. The GOs and NGOs should facilitate the catechu producers for exporting their products in other countries that help procure foreign currency for the nation.

The collaborative entrepreneurship taken by natural scientists, social scientists, lawmakers, and policy planners may guide the catechu producers in such a way that would be sustainable for their subsistence in the confrontation with economic adversity.

Endnotes

[1] *Upazila* is a higher tier of the local government administration in Bangladesh which comprises two or more unions. It is estimated that the administrative area of a *upazila* is about 180 to 200 sq. km on an average, and an approximate number of persons living there is, around 175,000 to 200,000.

[2] *Samaj* is an informal social organization in which the rural people of Bangladesh organize themselves for having counseling, juridical support, and reciprocal assistance in observing rituals and festivals.

References

Arens, J., Beurden, J. v., 1977. *Jhagrapur: Poor Peasants and Woman in a Bangladesh.* Third World Publications, Birmingham.

Bhatngar, S.S., 1948. *The Wealth of India.* C.S.I.R., India.

Hye, M. A., 2002. "Studies on Catechu and Its Utilization for the Production of Derived Dyes", a PhD Dissertation, Department of Chemistry, University of Rajshahi< Bangladesh.

Islam, M. Z. A., 2004. "Riverbank Erosion and Survival Strategies of Female Displacees: A Case of Two Riparian Villages of the Lower Ganges River in Bangladesh", *Social Science Journal*, Vol. IX, July.

Watt, G., 1972. *A Dictionary of Economic Products of India*. International Book Distribution (India), Dehra Dun.

GLOBALIZATION TO MODERNIZATION: INTERROGATING LINEARITY IN THE STUDY OF SOCIAL CHANGE[1]

Dr. Habibul Haque Khondker

Abstract

This paper discusses different strands of theories of social change: development theories as measured in per capita income, well-being, and modernization theories critically. The paper presents both the mainstream and alternative versions of the modernization theories arguing that there has been a return to modernization discourse in the early decades of the twenty-first century. Building on Roland Robertson's thesis that globalization predates modernization as a social process. Criticizing the equation of globalization with westernization or capitalism leads to globalization, the paper draws upon Amartya Sen's arguments to suggest that the earlier globalization was centered around China and the Middle East. This view of a pre-Western globalization has been termed by Jan Nederveen Pieterse as oriental globalization. The thrust of the paper is: rather than viewing globalization as an outcome of modernization, the sequence needs to be reversed. Based on historical evidence a more plausible assessment would take the roots of globalization to

---

[1] The paper originated from the Keynote address to the Bangladesh Sociological Association Conference in Dhaka on December 21, 2012. I want to express my gratitude to Professors S. Aminul Islam and K.S. Saduddin for inviting me to the conference.

a pre-modern world and then modernization can be seen as late-comer. Both the discussions of societal modernization as well as the social processes of modernization are consequences of historical globalization. The linear thinking is sometimes antithetical to historical understanding of social change as a global process. Global modernization that cuts across the dichotomy of the East versus the West has now become a paradigm of social change.

Introduction

Studies of social change, broadly defined, as changes in the totality of human society whether at the global level or national local level contain various paradigms and perspectives. Paradigms are overarching meta-theoretical umbrellas or frameworks within which theories are housed. Perspectives are specific ways of analyzing or understanding the phenomena, i.e., social change. When we consider if a theory is Eurocentric or not we need to consider the source at the paradigmatic level. For example, if we want to examine if certain types of modernization theories are Eurocentric or not we need to go to meta-theoretic assumptions of the theory. I will return to this discussion below. The present paper dwells on various theories and perspectives of social change variously called, development, modernization, or globalization to tease out not only their contours and scopes but also to interrogate their meta-theoretical assumptions, inter alia, linearity. The challenge here is to problematize some of the simplistic assumptions of these perspectives and to interject a certain amount of reflexivity that has been lacking.

Development and Beyond

There are different perspectives in understanding social change. The perspectives come from various theoretical angles and disciplinary vantage points. Perspectival differences rooted in disciplinary differences, remain central. For example, take economics as an academic discipline; it looks at social change through the lenses of economic development. For the World Bank, a premier development institution of global reach, development equals to income calculated as per capita Gross National Income (GNI). The World Bank divides the countries of the world on a continuum from low to high income countries. Per capita income of US$1,035 or below is defined as low income countries. Lower middle income countries fall between US$1,036 to US$4,085. Upper Middle income countries fall between US$4,086 to US$12,615. Any country with a per capita income of US$12, 616 is counted as a high income country (The World Bank, 2013).

Such classificatory scheme has the advantage of simplicity and precision. Countries can be ranked with precision and the countries themselves accept these divisions. A low income country rarely rejects the classification and aspires to be a middle income country; and a middle income country aspires to change its position from lower to upper or from upper middle to high income country and so on. Under the new categorization, Chile with a per capita GNI of US$14,280, and the Russian Federation with US$12,700 GNI are now classified as high income countries. The Russian Federation barely made to the high income country list; that group is highly differentiated with countries such as Qatar with US$76,010 at the high end of the high income category or Singapore with a per capita GNI of US$47,210.

Most economists accept development as measured by per capita income, with a small number of dissenters who bring in ideas such as happiness or eudemonia, enhanced capabilities (Nussbaum & Sen, 1993; Nussbaum, 2001), well-being or flourishing of the people as indicators of development. Economics, despite a general consensus on what counts as development, is not completely free from controversies. For example, recent economic growth of India has been subjected to debates between renowned economists. While some economists such as Jean Dreze and Amartya Sen (2013) suggest that the development in India has not been inclusive and the social indicators of development as reflected in children's nutrition or female literacy or access to sanitary toilets, India scores low compared to Bangladesh, its poorer neighbor. Poverty remains endemic in India despite spectacular income growth (Kohli, 2012). Other economists such as Jagdish Bhagwati and Arvind Panagariya

(2013) disagree and accept Indian economic growth, unfazed by its exclusive nature. China's growth has been much more inclusive having lifted 600 million people out of poverty since economic reforms began in 1978. In this discussion economic development does not remain confined to the domain of economics and spills into the domains of politics and public policy.

Post-Eurocentrism

Political scientists examine how traditional polities give way to modern polities. Some political scientists see modern democratic state as the end point of political development. The disciplinary divisions are not as neat as one may think. Economic historians in discussing why some countries are rich and others are poor—some have wealth and others lack wealth—and how those countries without wealth can produce wealth, often draw upon Max Weber's ideas, especially the centrality of cultural values (Landes, 1998). Culture, social values and work ethics are taken into account by some economists as variables in explaining economic growth. One can immediately notice that in all these studies there is an apparent Eurocentric bias. I say apparently because at another time in history, say, in the seventeenth century or earlier when Europeans were drawing upon lessons of development or adopting certain crucial technology from China, they were also modernizing and that modernization or proto-modernization was unencumbered by an Eurocentric bias. No one called it Sinocentric modernization at that juncture of history. A pragmatic mind would not worry about the geography or source of origin. What was involved then as it is now in the modernization strategy of Deng Xiao Ping is that as long as it works, it should be used. It does not matter whether the cat is black or white, as long as it catches the mice, was the standard line of the late Deng, the author of new China.

Some of the key ideas of political change such as how to explain social and political revolutions, formation of states and the role of the states were offered by sociologists, notably Barrington Moore (1966), Charles Tilly (1984; 1990), Claus Offe (1984), James Scott (1985) or Theda Skocpol (1979). Their theories must be evaluated not by using the simple measure of whether they are Eurocentric or not but how useful these theories are in dealing with the issues at hand. Research based on evidence demonstrates a great deal of applicability of the theories based on concepts of class, power, social mobilization, nation and revolution, thus establishing the efficacy of the above theoretical frameworks. While it is important to identify the meta-theoretical assumptions of an intellectual product, one need not get overly concerned with such assumptions and focus on the theoretical soundness, empirical richness and logical viability of the work. Social scientists routinely accept and use works that contain seminal ideas about different social contexts without paying attention to their disciplinary roots. Since an analysis of social change through the prism of development studies calls for an examination of political conditions and institutions, studies of social change have to be interdisciplinary.

It would be useful at the very outset to separate modernization as a social process taking place wherever favourable factors are available which include leaders with a positive attitude to improve their society. This is to be separated from modernization theories, a set of theories that evolved in the American academic setting in the 1950s and 1960s and then spread its influence worldwide through globalization of social scientific knowledge. Much of that knowledge now seems dated and discredited in the face of new knowledge gained through the writings of historians and other social scientists. The discrediting or criticism of the theories should not be confused with the discrediting of the historical processes of modernization. In a globalized world, the vast majority of its over seven billion people have embraced modernization as revealed in the phenomenal increase in the use of popular technology such as the mobile phone and penetration of the internet.

Rise of Modernization Theories

Modernization theories dominated sociological discourses on social change in the post-World War II period. The proponents of modernization theories or the major modernization theorists were sociologists in terms of their disciplinary anchorage. The pivot on which modernization theories stood was the notion of progress, an unfolding and continuous improvement of society. The notion was embedded in Greek philosophy, which influenced the Enlightenment philosophy. The Eurocentric narrative which has been passed off as the mainstream narrative is linear and simple to state. First came the Renaissance from the fourteenth century through fifteenth and sixteenth centuries, a period of revival of art and literature, a period of remarkable creativity inspired by a rediscovery of ideas and inventions that went back to the classical Greeks. The Renaissance was a period of brilliance that dispelled the gloom of the Dark Ages. Then came the Age of Reformation in the sixteenth century which paved the way for the Age of Science and Reason that spanned from the fifteenth to the eighteenth centuries, culminating in the age of the Enlightenment. From the fifteenth century overlapping the tail end of the Renaissance since Copernicus (1472-1543), Kepler, (1571-1630), Galileo (1564-1642), Francis Bacon (156-1626), Rene Descartes (1596-1650), Newton (1642-1727), to Spinoza (1632-1677) and Leibniz (1646-1716) in the eighteenth century was the age of science and reason. The three great seventeenth century advocates of rational thinking, Descartes, Spinoza and Leibniz laid the foundation for the eighteenth century Enlightenment.

Sociology is a true heir of the Enlightenment. Sociology, as a discipline, was born in the context of the discourse over social progress when European society was exposed to changes induced by industrialization of the nineteenth century. In the writings of Saint-Simon, August Comte, and Herbert Spencer, the founding figures of Sociology, social change or social dynamics occupied a central concern. Classical sociologists such as Alexis de Tocqueville (1805-1859), Karl Marx (1818-1883), Max Weber (1864-1920) and Émile Durkheim (1858-1917) shared a common ground in their focus on social change though their interpretations had different emphases. The main difference can be summed up as a debate over social evolution or historical social change. In other words, does social change follow a pattern that is predictable and irreversible or not? Does social transformation follow paths evolving from a simple to a higher stage, from simple to complex? Or, is social transformation constituted by random, unpredictable events fraught with uncertainties? Historians of various eras have been engrossed in this debate. While some interpretations of Marxist view provided a predictable, mechanical view of social transformation, society evolving from primitive communism to slave society, to feudal and then to bourgeoisie society, advancing towards an end point, which would be socialism and its more developed stage, communism. Such a mechanical, historical materialist view, advanced by Stalinist academics has fallen into disrepute and historical determinism has now been rejected. Weber's hermeneutical and historical interpretations introduced a more rigorous basis of history linked to important world civilizations.

In developing the theories of social change and modernization, sociologists (and other social scientists) drew upon the contributions of classical sociologists such as the works of those who were grappling with the rise of the capitalist industrial society. Their focus was on different aspects of this social transformation. While Marx was preoccupied with the new social relations of exploitation and predicted a path towards an end to exploitation, Weber was concerned with the paradoxical consequences of Protestant transformations; Tocqueville was examining the social circumstances that gave rise to the democratic social order. Durkheim, who was the first systematic sociologist, examined the social and cultural consequences of the growing division of labour and specialization in society brought in by industrialization. These are, in their particular ways, the major intellectual figures of the mid-nineteenth and early twentieth centuries who were engaging with key aspects of modernity and the modern understanding of society which became a main concern of Sociology. The master trends of modernization were a move towards equality or equalization, administrative centralization reflected in the emergence of nation-state or state like organizations, industrialization, urbanization and the rise of "rationalized bureaucracy" in the sense of Max Weber. For the purpose of the discussions on modernization, one can see in these outlines of notions such as democratization, gender empowerment and issues of governance that rely on state capacity as well as rationalization that have both a as well as an individual dimension.

In the post-World War period, as sociologists turned their focus to social transformations often initiated by the state or a combination of market and state, they drew upon the legacies of the forebears.

Some social scientists examined the social consequences of economic development, others sought to explore the cultural and social institutional forces that stood in the way of economic development. By then, Sociology had embraced empiricism as a dominant methodological approach based on a positivistic epistemology. It is interesting to note here that at the formative phase of Sociology, founding figures such as Max Weber spent a considerable amount of intellectual energy on the epistemological and methodological debates in historical (social) sciences.

Some of the main problems of the post-World War II sociological studies of modernization were—as the critics pointed out later— that they were ethnocentric and used the West as the only modern society against which they measured the non-wWestern societies. The emptiness of the notion of a single modernity and the unilinearity of modernization was unraveled by Goran Therborn's contention of four routes to modernity in the world (Terborn, 1995). The accusation of Eurocentrism set aside, no theory has come under heavier attack than modernization theory. In the early stage of the discussion on modernization, many writers viewed it as a sign of the West's global dominance: modernity was seen as what the West had done and the way the West has done it. The rest of the world, viewed as "underdeveloped" would develop if they followed the Western model. Writers such as André Gunder Frank (1966), Samir Amin (1974), Fernando Cardoso (1977), Fernando Cardoso and E Faletto (1979) and Valenzuela and Valenzuela (1978), strongly criticized such unilinear and ethnocentric modernization theories. The Dependency Paradigm was born out of this critical engagement with modernization theories. The main criticisms of modernization theories were inter and multi-disciplinary. Some of the strongest criticisms came from sociologically oriented economists such as Andre Gunder Frank, who was trained as an economist under the watch of Milton Friedman at Chicago University, the petridish of free-market doctrine. Frank's criticisms were directed both at the discipline of economics, especially its narrowness of vision as well as ahistorical view of modernization writers. His heretical position inspired a generation of social scientists. Yet, it was too early for him to develop his critique of eurocentrism which flowered fully with his subsequent writings culminating in the publication of his *Re-Orient: The Global Economy in the Asian Age* (1998). His renewed attack against Eurocentric history helped us to rethink the linear narrative of the rise of the West and of modernization. Frank's work has to be situated in the context of critical theoretical works on orientalism by Bryan Turner (1978) or Edward Said (1978) and works produced by anthropologists such as Eric Wolf (1982), or Jack Goody (1996; 1998; 2006) and historians such as Janet Lughod (1991), or Kenneth Pomeranz (2000).

Of the criticisms of modernization theories, the critique of linearity was the strongest. The accusation of "eurocentrism" was not pushed to its logical conclusion. Even the critics of the modernization theories did not go so far as to argue the originality of western modernization. The synthetic quality of western modernization, industrialization and even enlightenment has been evolving with path breaking contributions of Marshall G.S. Hodgson (1974), Joseph Needham's multi-volume study of science and technology in China and Jack Goody's summative work. As far as the spread of scientific knowledge and technology was concerned, the world embraced new technology without questioning too much about its origin. In fact, the center of scientific creativity and technological innovation and manufacture shifted out of China and the Islamic world sometimes mediated by India to Europe and to the USA and later increasingly to Japan and now to back China. Although in the post-World War II period, the USA became the locus for innovation and invention, some of the European countries continued to remain the centers of innovation, but the locus of production and global marketing of new technological goods is now Asia. The rise of emerging economies in East Asia and South East Asia followed by the rise of the BRICS (Brazil, Russia, India, China and South Africa) weakened the arguments of the dependency paradigm. The suggestion that the only way out of dependence was de-linking was practiced only in a few places such as Albania, North Korea and China during the so-called Cultural Revolution with disastrous consequences. The rise of the emerging economies demolished the main argument of the dependency argument.

An alternative modernization perspective

It would be useful to provide an alternative narrative—a narrative that is not linear and more honest to the historical processes leading to global modernization. In this alternative narrative, we live in an Atlantic centric world in the first two decades of the twenty-first century. The Atlantic world began with the industrialization of the West and its spread world-wide. What some writers present as globalization began much earlier. So rather than modernization, a nation-centered process eventually gave way to globalization, a world-centric process that can be put on its head. It can be argued that globalization as a historical process that started connecting peoples, communities, civilizations and cultures began way before modernization. The history of globalization can hardly be dated systematically if we count the priests, traders and travelers roaming the world from the time of discovery of new routes and passages, new technology of building ships and so on. The main argument of this paper is that it would be useful to reverse the linearity in Contrast Giddens who states "modernity is inherently globalizaing" (in Held & McGrew, 2000: 92) and based on that Modelski et al., (2008: 3) summarize the position of Giddens—I would parenthetically, unfairly state—that modernization causes globalization. The equation of modernity with modernization is erroneous. In a similar vein, Modelski et al. paraphrase Immanuel Wallerstein's position in a nutshell, "Capitalism causes globalization" (Modelski, et al., 2008:3). Jan Nederveen Pieterse (2006; 2010; 2012) amongst others criticizes these positions as Eurocentric and posits the idea of a plausible oriental globalization.

An alternative narrative of modernization and its antecedents can be easily presented. The Enlightenment began in Central Asia in the years between 800 and 1200 that is from ninth and thirteenth centuries with the writings of Muslim philosophers, scientists and poets who raised a range of questions about the creation of the universe to functions of the human body (Starr, 2013). Unfortunately, that enlightenment was not sustained. The enlightened philosophers and scientists were lost to orthodoxy of religion. The so-called Dark Ages in Europe from the fall of the Roman empire in 410, i.e., the fifth to the thirteenth centuries, was the time span of an early phase of industrial revolution in China from the nineteenth century to the fifteenth century, and from the nineteenth to the fourteenth centuries in the Islamic world where the likes of Al-Khwarizmi (780-850), Al-Kindi (801-873), Al-Farabi (872-950), Al-Biruni (973-1048), Ibn Sina (980-1037) and Ibn Khaldun (1332-1406) shone the brilliance of knowledge and creativity that played an important part in the development of European Renaissance, albeit inadvertently. These scholars spanned a geographical region from North Africa to Central Asia.

During the Muslim rule of part of Europe, Al-Andalus (today's Spain) from 850 to 1492, the metropolitan centers of Cordova and Seville were centers of intellectual fermentation. In the words of Jones, "From the mid-tenth to the mid-thirteenth centuries, Muslim, Christian and Jewish scholars were used to working together in Spain, to their great mutual benefit . . . One of the great stimuli to co-operation was the desire of Christian Europeans to gain access to the knowledge of science contained in the Arabic versions of Greek books . . . In this way, Greek, Persian and Indian science, retranslated out of Arabic into Latin, reached Western Christendom. So did some of the technology of China, notably the ability to make paper, and perhaps the knowledge of gun powder" (Roberts, 1985: 140). By the early fifteenth century China was poised to dominate the world but to the bafflement of many historians today, China called off its mission. Braudel (1979) suggests that the relocation of the capital city from Nanking with access to seaports to the landlocked Beijing in 1421 could be one of the pieces of the puzzle to explain China's turning its back on world economy.

According to John Hobson (2004), from 1700 to 1780 a number of Enlightenment thinkers from Montaigne to Voltaire drew upon Chinese conceptions of politics, religion and philosophy. "Indeed, many of the major enlightenment thinkers derived their preferences for the 'rational method' from China" (Hobson, 2004:195).

Decline and Return of Modernization Discourse

In the 1970s, as a result of such critiques, modernization theories as such fell into disrepute. Sociologists moved to analyze new problems such as dependency theory and the world-systems theory of Immanuel Wallerstein (1974), providing detailed historical accounts of development and underdevelopment. The main contribution of this strand of studies was to bring historical studies on development back to the center stage. Drawing upon the Marxist-inspired historical debates over the transition from feudalism to capitalism, studies on colonial endeavors and empirical studies on the developing world produced a rich literature. Important historical works on underdevelopment such as Alexander Gerschenkron's classic study *Economic Backwardness in Historical Perspective: A Book of Essays* (1962) focused on late-starters of industrializing Europe. Using industrialization as the hallmark of economic progress, Gerschenkron examined the role of states in creating institutions (such as banks) and ideologies (i.e., ideas, dispositions, cultural values) as motors of economic growth. In works of literature, Social scientists such as Gunnar Myrdal's *Asian Drama* (1968) opened up new horizons in comparative development studies which placed a good deal of attention on culture and social values as impediments to economic growth. As sociologists of modernization turned their attention on various social trends at a macro-level, there were others who sought to examine changes at the individual level. The work of Alex Inkeles is representative of this new development. Inkeles and his associates embarked on a cross-national study of individual modernity in the mid-1960s for which they collected data from six countries. With the help of social psychologists, Inkeles developed an individual modernity scale, known as overall modernity index (OMI) that later attracted a fair amount of criticisms.

What is interesting is that no matter how radical the rhetoric of the development arguments, the leaders of the Third World were sometimes paying lip-service to the arguments, but when it came to adopting or implementing development policies, they were faithfully committed to the modernization paradigm. The modernizing elites in Asia and South America were successful in supervising the socio-economic development of their countries not by withdrawing from the dependent relations with the core economies but by playing to the same rules and beating the dominant economic power in their own game.

In the closing years of the twentieth century and the first decade of the present century, while some sociologists were lured by theories such as post-modernity in the wake of the collapse of the socialist system, theories such as neo-modernization and multiple modernities (Eisenstadt, 2000) or alternative modernities had emerged. These developments in sociological theories had answered some of the charges of ethnocentrism of the earlier modernization theories as the new frameworks allowed for examining societies that pursued modernity in their own terms, in view of their cultural and social specificities. Inglehart and Baker (2000) provided a reevaluation of modernization theories and defended a return of this framework in a modified form. The earlier model of modernization was one of a singular model that fits it all. The new approaches motivated by the rise of Japan and other modern societies that followed a different trajectory, gave impetus to sociological theorizations. The emergence of Japan as well as other East Asian economies not only provided impetus to the rise of the idea of alternative modernity, it also brought to the fore the issue of culture and social values in explaining economic developments. These developments also created possibilities to empirically examine the propositions of alternative modernities. It is worthwhile to look at the propositions of multiple modernities as well as a number of empirical surveys such as PEW surveys and international Gallup surveys where various social trends are monitored. Here the World Values Survey of Ronald Inglehart of the University of Michigan is worth mentioning (*World Values Survey of 2005*). Such cross-cultural surveys shed valuable light but they are no substitutes for more in-depth localized studies that combine both survey methods as well as qualitative studies.

No matter what the social scientists debate and propose as to the merits of modernization theory or if they are Eurocentric or not, those who are in charge of national development have a clear view of what they want to do. And they want more modernization. The leaders of the Third World were at best paying lip-service to join the chorus of anti-western, anti-modern rhetorics, but when it came to adopting or implementing development policies, they were faithfully committed to the modernization paradigm. The modernizing elites in Asia and South America were successful in supervising the socio-economic development of their countries not by withdrawing from the dependent relations with the core economies but by playing according to the same rules and beating the dominant economic power in their own game.

One has to take the example of China, the world's most populous society today (India following very closely and is likely to surpass China in 2050). For observers and social scientists, China changed its socialist model of development to embark on market-oriented capitalist development. This is looking inside from outside. From the points of view of Chinese leadership, China has been modernizing since 1949, first under Chairman Mao Tse Tung from 1949 to 1976, then under Deng Xiaoping from 1978 to 1998 and currently under Xie Jin Ping. Mao wanted to modernize China and propounded the theory of four-modernizations. China cannot grow on one leg; it had to develop its agriculture and industrialize at the same time. For agricultural development, it took the path of Stalinist collectivization which backfired. The goal was right but the means was not well-thought out. It was copied from Stalin's Russia with equally disastrous consequences. The so-called "Great Leap Forward" was an historic leap into backwardness. Deng's famous aphorism was that it does not matter whether the cat is black or white, as long as it catches the mice. In other words, to deal with the problems of poverty and backwardness, you choose socialism or capitalism or something else; it does not mater, you need to deploy the theory or strategy that works. Presently, as of 2013, China's goal has been to urbanize, an important aspect of modernization. It has chalked out a plan to create a mammoth 250 million urban residents by 2030. It is a reversal of back to the village movement during the Cultural Revolution.

However, one also has to take into account the fact that in today's world when we look at the high-income countries and/or countries with high HDI (Human Development Index), it is obvious that some of them are countries where early modernization sprang or are regions where people from early modernizing nations of Europe resettled. Japan remains an historical exception that mobilized its state capacity to launch its own development and modernization in the late nineteenth century following the Meiji restoration. Other Asian countries that made it to the high income and high HDI group were following the Japanese model in various degrees (e.g. Singapore and South Korea). The other high-income economies in the Gulf

States used their hydrocarbon resources (petroleum and gas) and generated wealth to transform their societies and to catch up with the modern world. In recent years, the rise of Brazil, Russia, China, India and South Africa (BRICS) presents another chapter in the history of modernization where highly populated countries have been able to catch up in important fields of their economies and societies with other G-20 countries.

In the field of economic development studies, as in many other domains of knowledge, various paradigms, theories and ideas have emerged at different points in history. Some ideas or propositions tend to assume dominant positions in certain contexts. One of the continuous debates in social science literature on economic development has been the relative emphasis on the social structural/institutional factors *vis-à-vis* cultural/psychological factors. Economists trained in rigorous positivistic frameworks were by and large insular to accepting such variables as cultural and psychological variables. Historical studies such as those by David Landes (1983, 1998) and anthropological and ethnological research have provided considerable evidence and arguments in favour of taking culture seriously. Recent developments in behavioral economics mark an important turning point in crossing disciplinary barriers. In the last couple of decades, there has also been a shift of focus from growth oriented to well-being oriented approaches to development. Amartya Sen's influence cannot be denied in this realm. There has also been a shift from comparative mega-projects to individual-focused studies. Within the segmented and individual-focused approach, it is now widely accepted that a women-focused approach yields many benefits to societies.

Women as a group have been identified as an important constituency in the discussion of social and cultural developments, spawning a sub-field of study within Development Studies, titled "Women in development" and "Women for development". Thus, the well-being of women has been identified as a goal of development with multiple beneficial effects for the individual household and society. The idea of microfinance has evolved through ground-level experiences in Bangladesh and elsewhere and is now recognized as a useful tool for uplifting poor women's socio-economic situation. In recent years, the approach of multiple modernities of S. Eisenstadt obtained some influence among sociologists. According to this paradigm, development options are not understood as a failure or lack of a general model, but as a singular manifestation of modernity. The idea of a non-universal, multiple modernity has bearing on gender and modernity in cross-cultural settings.

Discourse of Globalization and Glocalization

The discourses of globalization provided a new insight in to the processes of social change over a *longue duree*. In Roland Robertson's view, globalization predates modernization as ahistorical process, a point that receives wider support from historians. World system theorists too trace the pre-capitalist world-systems on Asia and the Middle East long before the rise of the capitalist world system that Marx and Wallerstein explored. Robertson has been a pioneer in the studies of globalization (Nettl & Robertson, 1968: Robertson, 1983, 1997, 2001a, 2001b; Robertson & White, 2003).

Some writers view globalization as the worldwide spread of "westernization". This view is either erroneous or contains only partial truth as shown by several writers (Tomlinson, 1999; Robertson, 1992; Robertson & White, 2003; Turner & Khondker, 2010). From a superficial point of view, various processes outwardly show that the world is, indeed, becoming westernized. One could see the popularity of western music, movies and fast-food chains such as McDonalds or Starbucks as examples of westernization or Americanization. More and more countries playing the top chart of pop songs of the USA and Hollywood movies and US-made television shows such as *American Idol* or serials (such a*Friends* and *The Simpsons*) are becoming ubiquitous to the extent that some writers even use the term "Americanization" to describe these processes of cultural transmission.

However, a closer look will reveal that these cultural goods have different meanings in different societal and cultural contexts with uneven impact on classes and age groups. Some rare products are consumed without any modification, most are modified and indigenized to suit the local contexts of understanding, and there are exceptional situations where the intentions are completely inverted. For example, McDonalds adapt its food to local eating habits such as in India or China; Dallas and Bollywood movies are understood according to the local perceptions of love and family that differ in North America, Israel, India, or Nigeria.

In the past, many writers found it necessary to distinguish modernization from westernization. Modernization was believed to be a set of cultural practices and social institutional features that historically evolved in Europe and North America, commonly referred to as the West. The need to separate Westernization from modernization was motivated more by nationalism than pure intellectual reasons, because historically speaking, most of the modern cultural traits began in the West, a historical fact that was difficult to accommodate in a nationalistic political culture. The Western scholars in the nineteenth century were also guilty of making exaggerated claims of western superiority. Max Weber, a German sociologist was correct to claim that the western rationality and science had become a universal characteristic element of modernity. However, he underestimated the achievements of Chinese science or technology or ignored the role of the East in creating the West. Rather than looking East and West as opposites, a more historically honest view would be to see East in the West as Jack Goody (1996; 1998) maintains.

Many Indian sociologists took pains to delineate the differences between modernization and westernization. Similar discussions exist with regard to the so-called Westernization of the Ottoman Empire, the modernization of Japan since the Meiji restoration of 1868, or the modernization of China in the early part of the twentieth century such as the May 4th Movement of 1919. In these late modernization processes, many societies were borrowing ideas, knowledge and technology most of which were generated in the early modernized societies in Western Europe. However, the geography of the West kept shifting. In the nineteenth century, when Germany was modernizing, the idea of the West was limited to Western Europe (mainly Britain and France). In some post-colonial situations, the demarcation was based more on political expedience (former colonies in Asia and Africa) than logical or intellectual merits. The distancing from westernization can also be understood as a reaction to centuries of domination and exploitation of the former colonies by the Western (mainly European) powers. However, over time a more objective consideration of history indicates that many of the traits that spread worldwide originated in certain geographical regions. Yet as these traits were transplanted elsewhere, they became mutated and assumed different forms in various contexts. For example, parliamentary democracy evolved in England, with roots that go back to the *Magna Carta* of 1215. But democracy did no evolve in a linear fashion. France leaped ahead of Britain in democratization after the French revolution of 1979. Britain lagged behind New Zealand and Australia in institutionalizing universal franchise. Many of the innovations in democracy came from the periphery and not the cores of European nations (Markoff, 1996). However, as Westminster-style parliamentary democracy was institutionalized in India, Malaysia and other former British colonies, they mutated in light of the local social and cultural milieu.

Westernization as a term is not equivalent to globalization. Nevertheless, westernization can be seen as an aspect of globalization. Certain institutional features and cultural traits that originated in the West were put in place in many other geographical regions lock, stock and barrel under the framework of global interconnections and diffusion or forced implantation under colonialism. Yet, over time these institutions and practices mutated and assumed new meanings. Therefore, westernization can be seen as the beginning of the process. The cultural features, borrowed or imitated themselves, mutated in the source countries. Thus, westernization as a category has limited conceptual value. One can associate certain literary forms, genres and traits as part of the cultural zone we vaguely call "the West", yet these are mere influences as one can see in artistic, literary and architectural styles.

Amartya Sen (2004) argues that the centers of earlier globalizations around 1000 AD were outside of the West in China and the Middle East, but the West did not shut its doors and instead learnt from the contributions of great Islamic philosophers, scientists and mathematicians. In the present phase of globalization, it is prudent for the non-Western societies to learn from the achievements of the West. Writers such as John Meyer (1980) have used the idea of isomorphism (a term borrowed from science, botany in particular) which means replication of the same form yet separated from the main source. His research has shown that modern education—not western education though it was perhaps modified and institutionalized in the West—has spread worldwide and a similar set of values and practices have emerged in diverse settings. Some institutions are increasingly becoming glocalized around the world, as people try to cope with a variety ofproblems and challenges from financial crisis to ecological crisis.

Industrialization, an important component of modernization, evolved in Europe from the later part of the eighteenth century to the end of the nineteenth century. Replacing animate source of power by inanimate source of power not only made the productive processes efficient, the surplus production and increased consumption led to a new lifestyle as it created the true working class as a class for itself. All these developments centering on the power of technology brought in by industrialization profoundly changed human society and led to a trans-national industrial society, a new phase of globalization.

Globalization, defined by Roland Robertson (1992) as the intensification of the relations of societies and a growing awareness of intensification need not be seen simply as compression of distance as steamship—and later airplanes—replaced sail-boats. Awareness was intensified thanks to telegraph, telephone, and now at the beginning of the twenty-first century, low-cost and costless telephony mediated by the Internet. However, Robertson and Inglis (2006) argue that "global consciousness" and "globality" had precursors in a global animus or spirit that they traced to Greek and later Roman thinkers.

Robertson, one of the pioneers in the study of globalization, did not view globalization as a recent phenomenon nor did he see it as a consequence of modernization. The theories of modernization came under serious attack in Sociology because of such assumptions as unilinearity and convergence. As our knowledge of the world increases, many writers point out that cultural differences are not all that superficial, and nonlinearity and multiliniearity are better descriptors of global modernity. Social sciences in order to claim scientific status cannot afford to forfeit its claim to universality and universal knowledge. However, social sciences must be context sensitive but not context dependent. It is in this sense that Robertson conceptualized globalization in the twentieth century as "*the interpenetration of the universalization of particularization and the particularization of universalism*" (Robertson 1992: 100 emphasis in the original). Khondker (1994), building on Robertson's framework, argues that globalization or/and glocalization should be seen as an interdependent process. The problem of simultaneous globalization of the local and the localization of globality can be expressed as the twin processes of *macro-localization* and *micro-globalization*. Macro-localization involves expanding the boundaries locality as well as making some local ideas, practices and institutions global. The rise of worldwide religious or ethnic revivalist movements can be seen as examples of macro-localization. Micro-globalization involves incorporating certain global processes into the local setting. Consider social movements such as the feminist movements or ecological movements or consider new production techniques or marketing strategies, which emerge in certain local contexts. Over a period, these practices spread far beyond that locality into a larger spatial and historical arena. Consider the print industry or computer industry with a specific location of its emergence that has now become a global phenomenon. Overcoming space is globalization. In this view of globalization, globalization is at the same time glocalization. This view is somewhat different from the way Giddens conceptualizes the relationship between the global and the local. Globalization, for Giddens, "is the reason for the revival of local cultural identities in different parts of the world" (Giddens, 2000: 31). In this view, local is the provider of the response to the forces that are global; we argue that local itself is constituted globally.

According to the dictionary meaning, the term "glocal" and the process noun "glocalization" are "formed by telescoping global and local to make a blend" (*The Oxford Dictionary of New Words*, 1991: 134 quoted in Robertson, 1995: 28). The term was modeled on the Japanese word *dochakuka*, which originally meant adapting farming techniques to one's own local condition. In the business world, the idea was adopted to refer to global localization. The word as well as the idea came from Japan (Robertson, 1995: 28). According to Wordspy, glocalization means "the creation of products or services intended for the global market, but customized to suit the local cultures" (http://www.wordspy.com/words). Although the term "glocalization" has come to frequent use since the late 1980s, there were several related terms that social scientists used and continue to use. One such related word, which has been in use in social sciences and related fields for quite some time is indigenization.

Transcending the East-West dichotomy

Some social scientists claim that social sciences such as Sociology and Political Science, even Psychology are products of western social experience, therefore when these fields of inquiry are transported and transplanted to non-European or non-western contexts such as Latin America, Asia, or Africa there is a need for indigenization of these subjects. The idea of indigenization has created quite a controversy among social scientists because it raises fundamental questions about the applicability of social scientific ideas and concepts. However, we suggest that indigenization can be seen as similar to localization. In both concepts, there is an assumption of an original or authentic "locality", or "indigenous system".

One of the consequences of globalization is that it opens up doubts about the originality and authenticity of cultures. If one takes a long-term view of globalization, "locality" or "local" itself is a consequence of globalization. Today, there are hardly any sites or cultures that can be seen as isolated or unconnected from global transnational processes.

The main propositions of glocalization are not too different from the main arguments of a sophisticated version of globalization: 1. Diversity is the essence of social life; 2. Globalization does not erase all differences; 3. Autonomy of history and culture gives a sense of uniqueness to the experiences of groups of people whether we define them as cultures, societies, or nations; and Glocalization is the notion that removes the fear from many that globalization is like a tidal wave, erasing all differences. A number of books and articles on the subject of globalization give the impression that it is a force that creates a uniform world, a world where barriers disappear and cultures become amalgamated into a global whole.

As we have entered the third millennium, many of the age-old problems of differences of cultures and religion remain. Glocalizaton does not promise a world free from conflicts and tensions but a more historically grounded understanding of the complicated yet, pragmatic view of the world. One of the key features of glocalization is interpenetration. The global is imprinted in the local as local mediates what is global. So what is global is not an objective, a thing out there, it is often mediated and interpreted in the local context.

Goody (1996) argues that the world is to be viewed not as the West versus the East but as the East in the West; it may be plausibly argued that today as we look at the centers of rapid modernization in China, Southeast Asia or India we see the West in the East. The globalization and the globalized modernization that is spreading across the world is a true composite of the East and the West.

References

Abu-Lughod, J (1991). *Before European Hegemony: The World System A.D. 1250-1350*. New York: Oxford University Press.

Amin, S. (1974). *Accumulation on a World Scale: A Critique of the Theories of Underdevelopment*, New York: Monthly Review Press.

Bhagwati, Jagdish and A. Panagariya (2013). *Why Growth Matters: How Economic Growth in India Reduced Poverty and the Lessons for Other Developing Countries*. New York: Public Affairs.

Braudel, F. (1979). *Civilizations and Capitalism: 15th-18th Century. Volume 3. The Perspective of the World*. New York: Harper and Row.

Cardoso, F. H. (1977). "The Consumption of Dependency Theory in the United States", *Latin American Research Review*. 12 (9) pp. 135-176.

Cardoso, F. H. and Faletto, E. (1979). *Dependency and Development in Latin America*. Berkeley: University of California Press.

Dreze, J and Amartya Sen, *An Uncertain Glory: India and Its Contradictions*. Princeton: Princeton University Press.

Eisenstadt, S. N. (2000). "Multiple Modernities" *Daedalus*. 129 (1).

Frank, A.G. (1966) "Development of Underdevelopment" *Monthly Review,* 18. pp. 17-30.

Frank, A, G. (1998). *Re-Orient: Global Economy in the Asian Age.* University of California Press.

Gerschenkron, A. (1962). *Economic Backwardness in Historical Perspective: A Book of Essays.* Cambridge, MA: Belknap Press of Harvard University Press.

Giddens, Anthony. (1990). *The Consequences of Modernity.* Stanford, CA: Stanford University Press.

Goody, J (1996). *The East in the West.* Cambridge: Cambridge University Press.

Goody, J (1998). *Food and Love.* Cambridge: Cambridge University Press.

Goody, J (2006). *The Theft of History.* Cambridge: Cambridge University Press.

Held, David and Anthony McGrew. (2002). *Globalization/Anti-Globalization.* Cambridge: Polity Press.

Hobson, J.M. (2004). *The Eastern Origins of Western Civilization.* Cambridge: Cambridge University Press.

Hodgson, M. (1974). *The Venture of Islam.* 3 volumes. Chicago: Chicago University Press.

Inglehart, R. and Baker, W.E. (2000). "Modernization, Cultural Change and the Persistence of Traditional Values", *American Sociological Review,* 65 (1), 19-51.

Inglehart, R. (2005). *World Values Survey of 2005.* Center for Social Research, University of Michigan.

Inglehart, R (1997). *Modernization and Postmodernization: Cultural, Economic and Political Change in 43 Societies.* Princeton, New Jersey: Princeton University Press

Inkeles, A. (1977). "Understanding and Misunderstanding Individual Modernity", *Journal of Cross Cultural Psychology.* 8 (2) pp. 135-176.

Inkeles. A and Smith, D. (1966). Becoming *Modern.* Cambridge, MA: Harvard University Press.

Inkeles, A, Broaded, C.M. and Z. Cao. (1997). "Causes and Consequences of Individual Modernity in China", *The China Journal,* No. 37, January pp. 31-59.

Khondker, Habibul (2004). "Glocalization as Globalization: Evolution of a Sociological concept". *Bangladesh E-Journal of Sociology.* 1(2).

Kohli, Atul (2012). *Poverty Amid Plenty in New India.* Cambridge: Cambridge University Press.

Landes, D. (1983). *Revolution in Time: Clocks and the Making of the Modern World.* Cambridge, MA: Harvard University Press.

Landes, D. (1998). *The Wealth and Poverty of the Nations.* Cambridge, MA: Harvard University Press.

Markoff, J (1996). *The Waves of Democracy.* Pine Forge Press.

Meyer, John W.; John Boli; George M. Thomas and Francisco O. Ramirez. (1997). "World Society and the Nation-State," *American Journal of Sociology* 103(1), pp. 144-181.

Modelski, G., T. Devezas, and William R. Thompson (eds) (2008). *Globalization as Evolutionary Process.* London and New York: Routledge.

Moore, B. (1966). *The Social Origins of Dictatorship and Democracy.* Boston: Beacon Press.

Myrdal, Gunner,. (1968). *Asian Drama: An Inquiry into the Poverty of Nations.* 3 volumes. New York: Harper Brothers.

Nederveen Pieterse, Jan (2006) "Oriental Globalization: Past and Present" in G. Delanty Ed.

Europe and Asia Beyond East and West. London: Routledge, 61-73.

Nederveen Pieterse, Jan (2010). "Views from Dubai: Oriental Globalization Revisited" in Nederveen, J and Habibul Khondker (eds) 21st *Century Globalization: Perspectives from the Gulf.* Dubai: Zayed University Press. 15-37.

Nederveen Pieterse, Jan (2012). "Periodizing Globalization: Histories of Globalization" in *New Global Studies.* 6(2) Article 1.

Needham, J (1954-1995) *Science and Civilization in China.* Seven volumes. Cambridge: Cambridge University Press.

Nettl, J.P. and Roland Robertson. 1968. *International Systems and the Modernization of Societies.* New York: Basic Books.

Nussbaum, M (2001). *Women and Human development: The Capabilities Approach.* New York: Cambridge University Press.

Nussbaum, M. and Sen, A. (1993) (Ed).*The Quality of Life.* New York: Oxford University Press

Offe, C. (1984). *Contradictions of the Welfare State.* Cambridge: MIT Press.

Pomeranz, K. (2000). *The Great Divergence: China, Europe, and the Making of the Modern World Economy.* Princeton: Princeton University Press.

Robertson, Roland. (1983). "Interpreting Globality," in *World Realities and International Studies Today,* pp. 7-20. Glenside, PA: Pennsylvania Council on International Education.

Robertson, Roland. (1992). *Globalization: Social Theory and Global Culture.* London: Sage.

Robertson, Roland. (1994). "Globalisation or Glocalisation?," *Journal of International Communication* 1 (1), pp. 33-52.

Robertson, Roland. (1995). "Glocalization: Time-Space and Homogeneity-Heterogeneity," in Mike Featherstone, Scott Lash and Roland Robertson (eds.), *Global Modernities,* pp. 25-44. London: Sage.

Robertson, Roland. (1997). "Values and Globalization: Communitarianism and Globality," in Luiz E. Scares (ed.), *Cultural Pluralism, Identity, and Globalization,* pp. 73-97. Rio de Janiero: UNESCO and Candido Mendes University.

Robertson, Roland. (2001a). "Globalization Theory 2000+: Major Problematics," in George Ritzer and Barry Smart (eds.), *Handbook of Social Theory,* pp. 458-471. London: Sage.

Robertson, Roland. (2001b). "The Globalization Paradigm," in Peter Beyer (ed.), *Religion in the Process of Globalization,* pp. 3-22. Wurzburg: Ergon Verlag.

Robertson, Roland and Kathleen E. White. (2003). "Globalization: An Overview," in Roland Robertson and Kathleen E. White (eds.), *Globalization: Critical Concepts in Sociology,* Vol. I, pp. 1-44. London: Routledge.

Robertson, R and D. Inglis (2006). "The Global Animus" in Barry K. Gills and William R. Thompson (eds) *Globalization and Global History.* London and New York: Routledge.

Roberts, J. M. (1985). *The Triumph of the West.* London: Guild Publishing.

Said, E (1978). *Orientalism.* New York: Knopf Doubleday

Scott, J.C. (1984). *The Weapons of the Weak.* New Haven: Yale University Press.

Sen, Amartya (2004). "How to Judge Globalism" in F. Lechner and Boli (eds) *The Globalization Reader*. Malden. MA: Blackwell.

Skocpol, T. (1979). *States and Social Revolutions*. New York: Cambridge University Press

Smith David and Inkeles, Alex and David H. Smith(1966). "The OM Scale: A Comparative Socio-Psychological Measure of Individual Modernity".*Sociometry*, 29 (4), pp. 353-371.

Starr, Frederick (2013). *Lost Enlightenment: Central Asia's Golden Age From the Arab Conquest to Tamerlane*. Princeton: Princeton University Press.

Therborn, G. (1995). "Routes To/Through Modernity" in M. Featherstone, S. Lash and R. Robertson (eds) *Global Modernities*. London: Sage.

Tilly, C. (1984). *Big Structures, Large Processes, Huge Comparisons.*

Tilly, C (1990). *Coercion, Capital and European States, AD 900-1990*

Tomlinson, John. (1999). *Globalization and Culture*. Chicago: The University of Chicago Press.

Turner, B.S. (1978). *Marx and the End of Orientalism*. London: George Allen and Unwin

Turner, B.S. (1994). *Orientalism, Postmodernism and Globalism*. New York: Routledge.

Turner, B.S. and Habibul H. Khondker (2010). *Globalization: East and West*. London: Sage

Valenzuela, J.S. and Valenzuela, A (1978). "Modernization and Dependency: Alternative Perspectives in the Study of Latin American Underdevelopment", *Comparative Politics*. 10(4) pp. 535-557.

Wallerstein, I (1974). *The Modern World-Systems*. New York: Academic Press.

The World Bank. (2013). http://web.worldbank.org/ WBSITE/EXTERNAL/EXTABOUTUS/EXTANNREP/ EXTANNREP2013/0, menuPK:9304895~pagePK:64168427~p iPK:64168435~theSitePK:9304888,00.html

About the Contributors

Dr. A.H.M Zehadul Karim has been teaching in the universities for more than thirty five years and presently he has been serving at the International Islamic University Malaysia. Prior to this, he was a Professor in the Department of Anthropology, Rajshahi University, Bangladesh since 1992. He received his MA and Ph.D. degrees in Anthropology from Syracuse University, USA, and also taught courses there at Syracuse University in the United States for two semesters in 1984-1985. Dr. Karim studied Sociology at Lakehead University for one year in Canada. He was also a faculty member at the University Science Malaysia for three years during 1995 to 1998. As of now, he has written about 120 articles, which includes published papers in professional international journals, research reports and contributions to international conferences abroad. Dr. Zehadul Karim has four published books and reports in his credential as writer; and presently, he has been involved in editing a few more. He has so far attended 40 international conferences as paper-presenter and as session-chair in around 18 countries of the world.

Dr. Aida Luz Lopez Gomez is an Associate Professor of Environmental Education Posgraduate Program at Mexico City's Autonomous University. She is candidate for Ph.D. in Sociology from the Autonomous University of Barcelona. She has been research manager and adviser on social policy oriented indigenous people, participatory planning and project design at the National Indigenous Institute, and the National Commission for Development of Indigenous Peoples in Mexico. She has been consultant for conducting several studies on Indigenous Population, Rural

Development, as well as Environment and Indigenous Peoples. She has been invited lecturer in various Mexican universities.

Prof. Dr. Ahmad A. Nasr earned his M.A. and Ph.D. from the University of Wisconsin-Madison, U.S.A. He taught sociological and anthropological courses at the International Islamic University, Malaysia. Works he has edited or written include: *Folklore and Development in the Sudan* , *History of the Abdallab as depicted in their Oral Traditions* (in Arabic) and *Eunuchs of the Two Holy Mosques*(in Arabic).He co-translated V. Propp's *Morphology of the Folktale* into Arabic and wrote its introduction.

Dr. See Hoon Peow is currently Executive Vice President at SEGI University. He holds a LLB (Hons), from University of Glamorgan, UK, M. Phil, from University of Malaya and PhD in Sociology and Anthropology from International Islamic University, Malaysia. He has many years of work experience in education both in academic and the administration. He has wide academic interest in humanities and social sciences and has published many books and papers on Folklore, Education, Islamization of Knowledge, Law, Comparative Religions and other topics, locally and internationally with reputable publishers and indexed journals.

Dr. Nor Azlin Tajuddin is currently a lecturer at the Department of Sociology and Anthropology, International Islamic University Malaysia. Azlin's interests are in quantitative and qualitative research methods and environmental anthropology and sociology. She has undertaken research on urban river pollution in Kuala Lumpur and Adelaide. While she was in Adelaide she became a member of Conservation Volunteer Australia and Friends of St Peters Billabong, engaging herself with on-the-ground environmental restoration activities.

Dr. Nurazzura Mohamad Diah is an Assistant Professor and Head of Department in Sociology and Anthropology at the International Islamic University Malaysia. She obtained her PhD in anthropology from the University of Western Australia, Perth. Her Ph.D research explored menopausal experiences among urban Malay women. She is a life member of the Malaysian Menopause Society and is currently doing research on topics relating to medical anthropology.

Dr. Ahmad Nizar Yaakub is currently a Programme Coordinator of International Studies at the Faculty of Social Sciences, Universiti Malaysia Sarawak. He was formerly a Deputy Dean of the same faculty before pursuing his PhD in International Relations at the University of Western Australia. His research interests include elections and democracy in Southeast Asia, Malaysian foreign policy, and negotiation and conflict resolution. His published works include a study of Malaysia's Foreign policy (2003), Dances with Garuda: Malaysia and Indonesia Bilateral Relations (2013), co-edited the books on Politics and Economic Development in Malaysia and East Asia (2004), and Coastal Community in the South West of Sarawak: The Roles of Market, State and Modernization (2006).

Dr. Rosila Bee Mohd Hussain is a Lecturer in Department of Anthropology and Sociology, University of Malaya. She obtained her PhD in Sociology from the University of Western Australia, Perth. Her research interests include issues of identity, inequality, youth and social change. To date, she has published numerous articles locally and internationally related to these topics and plan to conduct more in near future including cross-cultural studies in or outside Malaysia.

Dr. Yukimi Shimoda received a Ph.D. from the Discipline of Anthropology and Sociology, the University of Western Australia. She is currently working as a research fellow for the Japan International Cooperation Agency (JICA) Research Institute, where she is in charge of capacity development issues. Her research interests include migration, mobility, cross-cultural interaction, work relationships, and network. She is currently preparing a monograph based upon her Ph.D. research, which explores people's mobility and their interaction with local society

Dr. Siti Zanariah Ahmad Ishak is a senior Lecturer in the Department of Communication, Faculty of Social Sciences, Universiti Malaysia Sarawak. She received her PhD degree in Anthropology from The University of Western Australia. Her research interest is on the media audience, social change and women's studies. Currently, she is doing research on topic relating to portrayal of ethnicity in print media.

Dr. M. Zulfiquar Ali Islam is a Professor of Sociology at the University of Rajshahi, Bangladesh. He obtained his PhD in Sociology (Sociology of Disaster) from the Institute of Bangladesh Studies (IBS), University of Rajshahi, Bangladesh. He is currently doing research on indigenous ecological resource management, human population displacing disaster issues, child rights, and ethnic culture as well.

Dr. Habibul Haque Khondker has been a Professor at the Department of Humanities and Social Sciences of Zayed University, Abu Dhabi since 2006. Previously, he was an Associate Professor of Sociology at the National University of Singapore and a Research Associate at the Asia Research Institute. Dr. Khondker studied in University of Pittsburgh, Carleton University, Ottawa and University of Dhaka, Bangladesh. Dr. Khondker held visiting professorship at the United Nations University, Tokyo and was a visiting scholar at Cornell University, Columbia University, Institute of Social Studies, the Hague and University of Pittsburgh. He is currently conducting research on governance of labor migration in UAE and expatriates. Dr. Khondker has co-authored *Globalization: East and West* (Sage, 2010) with Bryan Turner; and co-edited *Asia and Europe in Globalization* (Brill, 2006) vwith Goran Therborn.